Return to the War on the Plaine des Jarres

RETURN TO THE WAR

ON THE PLAINE DES JARRES

FRED M. APGAR

Milan Book Publishing LLC

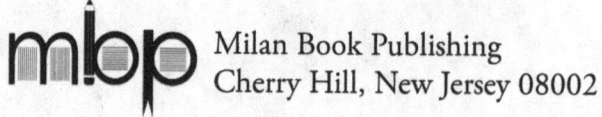

Milan Book Publishing
Cherry Hill, New Jersey 08002

Text design by Stefani-Ann Brousseau

First Printing, September 2024
ISBN: 978-1-964300-03-0

Categories
Memoir: Military

Printed through IngramSpark.

"In war, there are no unwounded soldiers."
Jose Narosky

More than 2.7 million men and women answered our nation's call and chose to wear its uniform while serving in Southeast Asia during the Second Indochina War. They did so with a sense of honor and duty, and each made significant sacrifices in their lives to bear our nation's cause. They served honorably and courageously. During their service to our nation, however, each was "wounded." **No one returned home unscathed.**

Every day of the war, our warriors displayed incredible acts of courage to save the lives of others. With little regard to their own well-being, they heroically stepped into the breach, lending assistance as needed and saving lives.

I grieve for the more than 58,000 service men and women whose names are on the Wall. They gave "their last full measure," sacrificing their lives and dying from injuries and illnesses they sustained during their service in Southeast Asia. Among the names on the Wall are those of nearly 2,000 fighting men who are still missing in action.

Regardless of rank or the role they assumed, the vast majority served with distinction, courage, and valor, and each, in their own way, contributed to the overall mission. This book is dedicated to the more than 2.7 million men and women who served in Southeast Asia during the Second Indochina War and to their strength of character that led them into battle. My thoughts and prayers are that you will find the eternal peace you so richly deserve.

A portion of the proceeds from the sale of each book will be donated to the Michael Reagan Portrait Foundation. Michael, a combat Marine veteran of the Second Indochina War, has drawn over 9,000 portraits for the families of Service men and women who have been killed while in service to our nation. It is called the Fallen Heroes Project. The portraits are provided free of charge and have brought untold comfort to our nation's Gold Star Families. To learn more about Michael's wonderful work, visit his website at *fallenheroesproject.org*.

Table of Contents

Part Three: The Incredible Journey, cont.

GLOSSARY OF TERMS

7ᵗʰ ACCS	7ᵗʰ Airborne Command and Control Squadron
ABCCC	Airborne Battlefield Command and Control Center (ABTripleC)
AAA	Anti-Aircraft Artillery (Triple A) – Soviet made guns ranging from 12.7mm to 85mm projectiles
ARC LIGHT	B-52 bombing missions
ARM	Anti-Radiation Missile – Weapons that homes in and are guided to enemy radio emissions
BDA	Bomb damage assessment – Determining the damage caused by stand-off weapons
BSOO	Battle Staff Operations Officer – Second in command of battle staff
CAS	Controlled American Sources – Covert military or para military operators
CAT	Civil Air Transport – CIA owned and operated by the CIA during the First Indochina War and morphed into Air America during the Second Indochina War
CBU	Cluster Bomb Units – An air delivered munition that ejects smaller munitions upon impact
CD	Classified Destruct – Classified material of no further use that must be destroyed either by burning or shredding
CIA	Central Intelligence Agency
CONUS	Continental United States
DABS	Director of the Air Battle Staff: the battle staff commander on ABCCC missions
DEROS	Date of Estimated Return from Overseas - The date of the end of a deployment on which one returns home
ELINT	Information obtained through the interception and interpretation of electronic signals

FAC	Forward Air Controller - A pilot who identifies and marks targets for strike aircraft and authorizes the release of munitions
FAG	Forward Air Guide
FLIR	Forward Looking Infrared Radar: A technique of obtaining images in the absence of light by capturing thermal signatures.
FRAG	Fragmentary Operations Orders: Listing of all scheduled flights that include call sign, targets, ordnance, and time on target.
IR	Infrared: Images obtained by cameras that capture infra red light.
KIA	Killed In Action
LOC	Line Of Communication
LS	Lima Site – Network of short, primitive landing sites located in rural areas of Laos
MIA	Missing In Action
MiG	Russian manufactured aircraft used by North Vietnam
MR	Military Region – Geographical areas established to designate military responsibilities
NBL	No Bomb Line – Areas designated by the Rules of Engagement in which the release of weapons is prohibited
NKP	Nakon Phanom Royal Thai Air Base
PACAF	Pacific Air Force – The controlling authority for all Air Force operations in the Pacific theater of operations during the Second Indochina War
PAVN	Peoples' Army of Vietnam (North Vietnam Army or NVA)
PDJ	Plaine des Jarres
PL	Pathet Lao – Officially, the Lao People's Liberation Army, a Communist political movement that seized control of Laos during the Second Indochina War
POW	Prisoner of War

RLA	Royal Laotian Army
RLAF	Royal Laotian Air Force
RLG	Royal Laotian Government
R & R	Rest and Recuperation
RTAB	Royal Thai Air Base
RTB	Return to base
RWT	Road Watch Team
SAC	Strategic Air Command – Major Air Force Command that directed and controlled all B-52 bombing missions during the Second Indochina War
SAM	Surface to Air Missile – Soviet made missile designed to shoot down aircraft. During the Second Indochina War, the SA-2, Guideline, was used extensively by the North Vietnamese
SAR	Search and Rescue operations for the safe return of downed air crewmen
SEA	Southeast Asia – For the purpose of this book, SEA refers to the countries of Laos, Cambodia, Thailand, North Vietnam, and South Vietnam
SERE	Survival – Evasion – Resistance – Escape A training program to provide downed aircrewmen with skills to survive
SGU	Special Guerilla Unit – A reference to Hmong soldiers who were members of the *L'Armee Clandestine*
SOG	Studies and Observations Group - Covert military or paramilitary operators
TAC	Tactical Air Command, Headquarters at Langley Air Force Base
TDY	Temporary Duty – Temporary assignment to another unit
TFA	Task Force Alpha – Located at Nakon Phanom Royal Thai Air Base, it interpreted the intelligence gathered by sensors inserted in Barrel Roll and Steel Tiger

TIC   Troops in Contact – Soldiers engaged in combat with enemy troops

UXO   Unexploded Ordnance – Live munitions that have remained since the war years and present a constant danger to the civilian population

ROE   Rules of Engagement – Restrictions placed on the use of Air Power

WIA   Wounded in Action

CHINA

NORTH
VIETNAM

Dien
Bien Phu

Hanoi

Luang
Prabang

Vientiane

Udorn

LAOS

MEKONG RIVER

HO CHI MINH TRAIL

THAILAND

Bangkok

CAMBODIA

Phnom
Penh

Saigon

SOUTH
VIETNAM

*Southeast Asia
of the Second Indochina War*

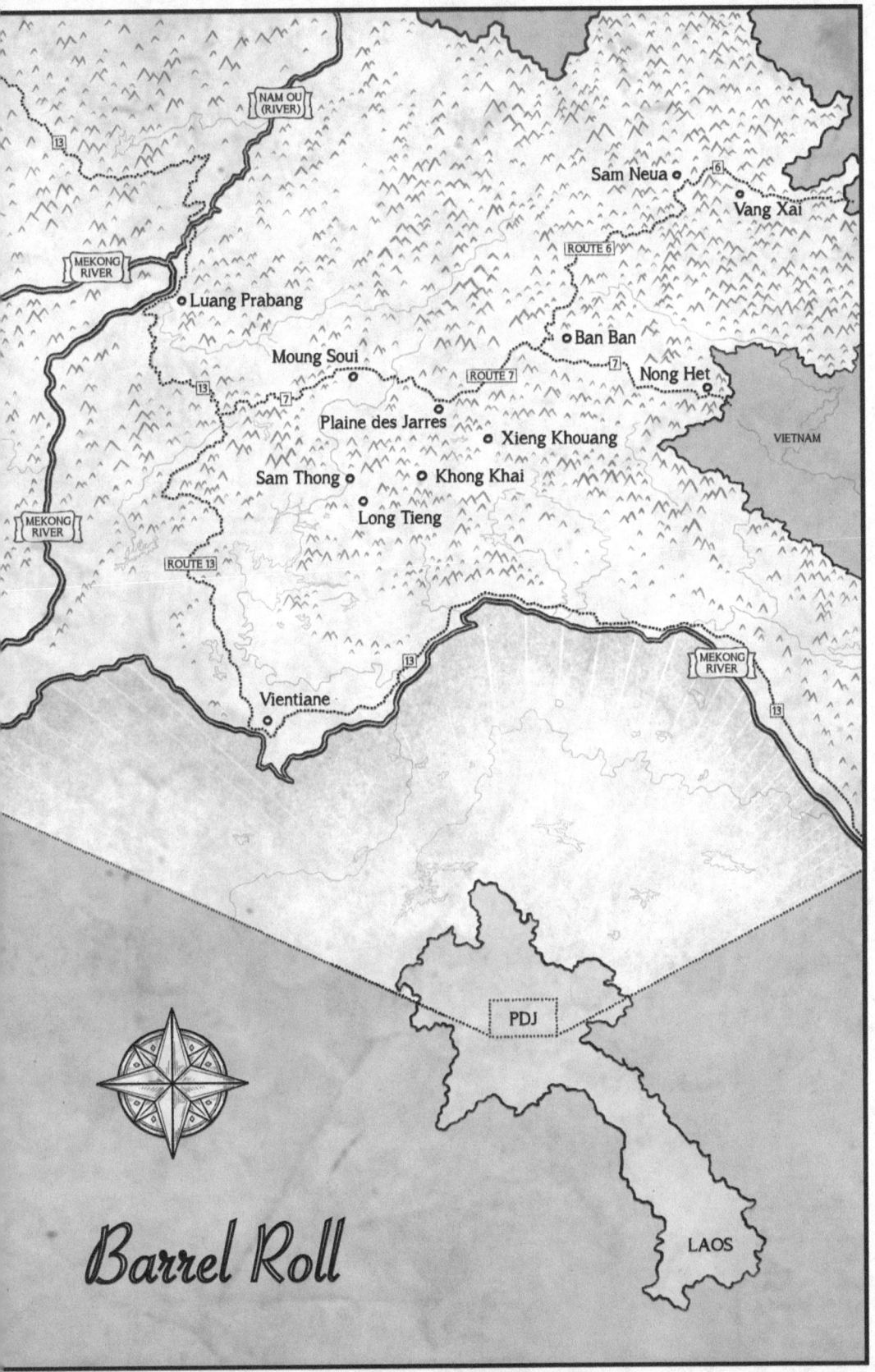

Introduction

As a kid, my friends and I spent countless hours playing in the nearby woods. We played Cops and Robbers and Cowboys and Indians. But our favorite game of all was War. We devoted hours to chasing one another, building hideouts, planning ambushes, and using fingers and sticks to shoot each other. Our stash of chestnuts we had accumulated on our way home from school became our weapon of choice. Once the supply of chestnuts was exhausted, they were replaced with stones and rocks. When we died, we did so quite dramatically, complete with sound effects as we dropped to the ground, just like in the movies we watched on TV and at the local movie theater. When we got older, BB guns replaced sticks and stones. I loved it.

My collection of Army soldiers also occupied a lot of our time. The soldiers were frozen in various poses: firing rifles while standing, kneeling, and in a prone position; firing machine guns; throwing grenades while holding a rifle in their other hand; aiming a pistol; thrusting bayonet-tipped rifles. A radio operator was kneeling while talking on a radio; Another soldier, obviously an officer, was leaning forward with a hand aloft, leading his troops into combat. Some were kneeling while aiming a bazooka that perched on their shoulder, and a few were standing while looking through binoculars. I have many fond memories of moving toy soldiers in mock battles with my friends' armies. With not knowing much about military strategy other than what we learned from watching movies on TV, we never tired of moving our soldiers into different formations, always trying to gain an advantage, and engaging in battle after battle. I have no doubt that young folks are still engaging in "War," but do so, now, through video gaming.

Our parents taught us that our nation's veterans were special people deserving of our respect and were to be held in high esteem. Those lessons were consistently reinforced by our teachers and our community.

Another powerful lesson we were taught was to always demonstrate respect for our nation's flag. I can clearly remember standing at attention whenever TV stations signed off with the playing of our National Anthem along with an image of a fluttering American flag. Unashamedly, patriotism was an important lesson we learned. Each school day began with everyone standing, placing our right hand over our hearts, and reciting the Pledge of Allegiance. For as long as I can remember, veterans, our flag, and our nation were always important to me. Veterans were my heroes who courageously defended our nation's freedom. I had an abiding love of our great nation, which remains with me today.

A Desire to Serve...

I always knew that one day, I would serve in the military. I had a burning desire to do so. And more definitively, I needed to serve in combat.

One major impact on my life was a movie I watched during my childhood years. It was titled, "A Walk in the Sun," and I recall watching it on our 13" Admiral television set, totally mesmerized by the soldiers' stories. The movie depicted the movement of a platoon of soldiers who had just landed on a beach near Salerno, Italy. Their mission was to move six miles through the countryside and take control of a farmhouse that was occupied by Nazi troops. I was fascinated by how the men in the platoon interacted with one another, prepared for battle, addressed their fears, and conducted themselves in combat. I was totally impressed by their courage and valor.

In addition, my parents had a collection of Life Magazine. I used to pore though the magazines and it was that assemblage of photographs that provided me with images of World War II; soldiers, aircraft, tanks, ships, jeeps, trucks, and huge guns. I was also introduced to the destructiveness of war. I recall pictures of city streets, filled with the debris of collapsed buildings, and roads filled with refugees, hauling carts and carrying huge bundles of their possessions. I was always haunted by painful expressions of sadness on their faces. There was never any expression of joy or happiness. I learned about the seriousness and destructive nature of war through pictures in Life Magazine.

Most importantly, I learned a powerful lesson regarding courage from the pastor of our church. From the pulpit, he shared with us his path to becoming a minister. He described, in great detail, his WWII experience. Two weeks after having participated in the Allied invasion of Sicily, our pastor participated in the Invasion of Italy. He landed at Salerno as a member of the 5th Army and was severely wounded during the landing. His wounds were life-threatening, and he laid on the beach, unattended, for several hours. In his agony, he prayed to God that if his life could be saved, he would dedicate his life to Christ, which he did. For me, it was another lesson learned, to honor and respect valor. The fact that Americans risked and sacrificed their lives for others, made a huge impression on me. And I knew that one day, I would risk my life to protect the people and country I loved most.

My Inspiration for this Book...

During my last two years of college in upstate New York, I was fortunate to have had a car to drive to and from school. During those trips, most times, I took a short detour through Wellsboro, Pennsylvania, to visit my Grandpa Apgar who was a resident at Broad Acres Nursing Home. I probably visited him on seven or eight occasions. I am so thankful I took the time to visit him, and I treasure the moments I was able to be alone with him. He was one of my heroes with whom I had spent countless hours on his farm, and I regret I didn't stop more often. The driveway leading to Broad Acres is a circular drive that is lined with huge oak trees, trees Grandpa told me he had planted.

Grandpa would usually be sitting in the same position that I remember from my childhood visits; his arms and legs would be crossed, and he always looked to be at peace and in great thought. Grandpa was always happy to see me. I could just tell. His eyes would widen when I walked up to him, and he would open his mouth in surprise. This was the man whom I had worshiped as a child. I loved the visits to the farm, and like him, I was up early, literally walking in his footsteps as he performed his daily chores. I was so intent on "being" him that, oftentimes, I stepped on his heels.

When the weather permitted, Grandpa and I would sit out on the front porch of the nursing home and talk. Mostly, we talked about what life was like as a farmer and the various jobs he had held as a young man. I was always fascinated by the stories he would tell about the years he worked for the Civil Conservation Corps (CCC). The nursing home in which he resided was the original building on the site called Broad Acres. Many years earlier, the facility had been the Tioga County farm. Grandma and Grandpa lived at the farm, and he farmed the land. They lived in a small cabin that stood for many years just across the road from the main building. I was saddened one day when I stopped for a visit to see that the cabin had been torn down, for my father had lived in that small home.

I know now that my visits were far too short. I have so many questions that I wish I had asked Grandpa. I would love to know more about his life experiences so that I could be closer to him. Did you have any girlfriends as a young man? Did you fight with your brothers and sisters? What were your grades in school? Did you have a subject in which you excelled and liked more than others? Did you ever get into trouble at school? What chores did you have to perform as a child? Did you ever want to pursue a career other than farming? What was the best gift you ever received? How did you meet Grandma? What did you and Grandma do for fun on weekend nights? Do you have any regrets in life? What advice do you have for me? The list of questions is endless; questions to which I will never know the answers.

While I could no longer ask my Grandfather those questions, I knew I could answer those questions about myself for my children. In 2005, I started work on a journal that would tell the story of a "small-town boy," his life and times. For some unknown reason, I started the project with Chapter 9, The Military Years.

With my brain stimulated, long-forgotten memories, or so I had thought, filled my mind. The recollections came roaring back, and as I began writing, they were replaced with new ones. Despite a sense of feeling overwhelmed by the recall of an abundance of events, I enjoyed the process immensely. It was a most gratifying and satisfying process. Of the five years of service in the Air Force, the most impactful was the year I had been deployed to Southeast Asia. It was there where I began my story of a "small-town boy," and it was there where this memoir begins.

The book is organized into three sections. The focus of Part One is on my arrival in Southeast Asia and the steep learning curve I faced to absorb all I could about the "secret war" in Laos prior to my first flight. Readers are provided insight into my year-long discharge of duties as an Air Intelligence Officer supporting the CIA's "secret army" in Northern Laos, codenamed Barrel Roll. Subsequent to my deployment to Southeast Asia, I was forced to follow the Second Indochina War from afar, and the second part of the book tracks the war to its ultimate conclusion and heartrending aftermath.

The third part of the book details the emotional and life-changing journey I embarked upon in 2014. I returned to the battlefields of the Plaine des Jarres, and in what was pure serendipity, I met total strangers who gave me the wonderful blessings of Brotherhood, Forgiveness, and Redemption.

I hope you enjoy this book,

Fred. M. Apgar

GOING HOME

Our "freedom flight" landed at Travis Air Force Base, the base from which I had departed exactly one year earlier. During our time in Southeast Asia, we were aware of student activism, and we read accounts of the growing anti-war sentiment back home. However, we were not prepared for the magnitude of that dissent and the violent nature of the opposition we met. The loathing for the returning veterans was etched on the faces of the demonstrators who greeted us as we passed through the main gate on the way to the rest of our lives.

Our thoughts, feelings, and needs were simple. We mourned the loss of our comrades who made the ultimate sacrifice in their service to one another and our great nation. We were grateful for having returned home safely. We were proud of our service and the sacrifices we had made. All we wanted to do was reconnect with the members of our families, re-assimilate into society, report to our next duty station, and get on with our lives. But for many, that was not to be. The emotional commitment they had made had taken a very deep hold on them, and, sadly for some, one from which they would never recover.

I felt a need to talk about the "world" from which I had just returned, but, to my surprise, no one in my family asked many questions about my year-long experience in Southeast Asia. It was confusing, and it didn't take long to realize and accept the fact I would be alone to process those thoughts and feelings. It was up to me, and me alone, to attach meaning to what I had witnessed and experienced during my year in Southeast Asia. While I am certain it was not the intended message of members of my family and friends, it seemed as if I was on my own.

I know now I pursued the only logical conclusion to the ambiguity of the war I was experiencing; I repressed those thoughts and feelings about the year of combat. That seemed to work, at least for a few years. No doubt, my ability to compartmentalize my life and repress any thoughts and feelings regarding my year of supporting the Hmong in Barrel Roll was aided by the necessity of focusing my energy, time, and resources on a marriage, graduate school, children, and a new career.

It took nearly 40 years for me to arrive at the realization and acknowledge the year of combat duty in the Second Indochina War had impacted my life more than I had ever thought possible. Events led me to the realization that the Southeast Asia experience had defined me as a person in many ways. I also realized something was missing from my life. A part of me had been left behind in Laos. I didn't know it at first, but I was being led on a journey, one in which I had to return to the war on the Plaine des Jarres and search for that part of me that had remained in Barrel Roll.

PART ONE

RETURN TO
THE PLAINE DES JARRES

MARCH
1969

§

"Blue Chip, Blue Chip, this is Alleycat..."

— 1 —

PACAF JUNGLE SURVIVAL SCHOOL

Broad-leaved, lush, tropical vegetation surrounded us, along with a buzzing and clicking from nearby wildlife and an oppressive humid air. Finally, I was experiencing a jungle environment, something I had only dreamed about in my childhood. It was with that child's enthusiasm I approached the entrance to the compound that would be my "home" for the next seven days. However, the hand-painted sign overhead replaced that childhood fervor with a seriousness of purpose for what I was about to experience. The sign read:

The College of Jungle Knowledge
Learn and Return

This was the first stop on my Southeast Asia deployment. Our flight from Travis Air Force Base had landed in Manila. An Air Force C-130 ferried us to Clark Air Force Base, a huge sprawling complex located on Luzon Island, a couple of hundred miles to the north. A small city, Angeles City, was located just outside of the main entrance to the base. I was in the Philippines to attend the week-long Pacific Air Force (PACAF) Jungle Survival School, a learning experience required of all air crewmen prior to their deployment to Vietnam.

I was assigned to serve as an Air Intelligence Officer for the 7th Airborne Command and Control Squadron (7ACCS). Flying in C-130 aircraft, the airborne command post controlled all air operations in Laos. The squadron was stationed at Udorn Royal Thai Air Base in northern Thailand, assigned to the 432nd Air Wing. We commonly referred to the squadron as the Airborne Battlefield Command and Control Center or ABCCC.

The instructors at the Jungle Survival School were all combat veterans of the Vietnam War, experienced in search and rescue (SAR) operations. They exuded a seriousness of purpose and a resoluteness to their mission, and very quickly that became my disposition as well. As soon as the orientation began, all romantic thoughts of experiencing jungle life disappeared, and I listened intently to the knowledge and wisdom that, perhaps, one day, might save my life.

The training experience was called SERE, an acronym referring to Survival-Evasion-Resistance-Escape. We were there to learn skills and techniques to use in the event an airborne emergency forced us to leave our aircraft. In the event of a shootdown, our initial efforts would be to SURVIVE in a hostile environment. We were instructed on how to use survival radios; how to change the battery, and techniques to conserve battery strength. We were taught radio communication protocols and used the radios to communicate with "rescue" helicopters, directing them to our location.

SAR (SEARCH AND RESCUE)

A reality of the war was that one or more American planes were shot down nearly every day. Whenever a pilot issued a "May Day" call, observed a shootdown, or heard an emergency beeper, the air war in the general vicinity of the shootdown immediately stopped. What followed was an impressive and well-orchestrated series of events, all planned and organized for the sole purpose of rescuing the downed airman/airmen. Whatever manpower and air assets were needed to effect the rescue were diverted to the scene. It was during SAR operations when incredible acts of bravery, courage, and self-sacrifice were on full display. I was humbled to have had the opportunity to "observe" firsthand and participate in numerous SAR operations.

Next, we were introduced to the survival vest. Other than a parachute, the survival vest was the most important piece of equipment we would wear during every flight. Our instructors consistently reinforced the importance of the survival equipment we carried. The survival vests contained a K-Bar survival knife, extra ammunition for a handgun that would be issued prior to each mission, a first aid kit, food rations, amphetamines, a tree-lowering device, water purification tablets, a signal mirror, a fire-starting system, a poncho, a string saw, white and orange plastic panels, and a pen gun with several different colored flares. We handled and inspected each piece of survival gear carried in the vests and learned about its proper use, a valuable hands-on experience. Then we used each piece of survival equipment. For instance, we practiced firing the flares from the pen guns because, during the final stage of a rescue, the pen gun was to be used to shoot a specifically requested colored flare into the air to denote an airman's location on the ground.

The instructors explained the use of the tree-lowering device, although we did not actually have any practical experience with its use. It was a simple tool, a strong parachute cord that was attached to the parachute harness. In the event a crewman had to leave his aircraft and his parachute got snagged in the tree canopy, he could release his parachute, and the tree-lowering device would safely lower him to the ground. It was simple and ingenious.

Our skilled teachers taught us about the fire-starting system, water purification tablets, and brightly colored rescue panels. At one point, we practiced using the survival mirror, attempting to reflect the sun's rays toward the nearby rescue helicopter. We even received a short course regarding the use of the supplies in the first aid kit. One of the enduring memories of that portion of our training pertained to skin lacerations. In the event maggots appeared at site of an injury, we were told to avoid disturbing them until all of the dead tissue had been consumed by the mass of wiggling larvae. Once the decayed flesh had been consumed, we were instructed to then eat the maggots taking advantage of its rich protein.

I carried two water bottles on all flights because we learned it was each crewman's responsibility to carry water. Most of us at ABCCC used one-pint plastic bottles; they were thin and rounded and fit nicely into the lower leg pockets of our flight suits.

The string saw was a roll of thick string that had tiny teeth. It was a classified equipment item that could saw through prison bars in the event of capture. I surmised that the plastic-like material was made from some sort of composite substance. In the event of impending capture, the string saw was to be hidden in a body cavity. However, it could also be used to process resources while evading enemy forces.

Another important survival item we learned about was the blood chit, a piece of white, plastic-like material. In bright colors, there was an American flag and words, written in 13 languages; English, Burmese, Laotian, Vietnamese, Cambodian, Old Chinese, New Chinese, Thai, Tagalog, Visayan, Malayan, French, and Dutch. The chit identified the downed airman as an American and encouraged the local population to provide assistance. The blood chit used during the Vietnam War read,

"I am a citizen of the United States of America. I do not speak your language. Misfortune forces me to seek your assistance in obtaining food, shelter, and protection. Please take me to someone who will provide for my safety and see that I am returned to my people. My government will reward you."

The reward, of course, was gold, which was carried on all Air Force rescue helicopters.

Outside, in a large clearing in the compound, we were introduced to the jungle penetrator. The penetrator, carried on all Air Force rescue helicopters, was a compact device that weighed about 20 pounds. Its weight and streamlined appearance enabled it to pass through jungle canopy to reach a downed airman on the ground. For visibility, the penetrator was painted bright yellow. Three seats (each 5" wide and 12" long) were spring-loaded in the upward position but could be lowered with ease by pushing down on them. Once seated, the aircrewman could be secured with a safety strap and then raised to the helicopter. We practiced securing ourselves to the jungle penetrator lowered from an Air Force Jolly Green Giant helicopter and hoisting ourselves on board.

JOLLY GREEN GIANTS

The 40th Aerospace Rescue and Recovery Squadron (40th ARRS) was activated at Udorn Royal Thai Air Base in September 1967. The helicopter they flew was the HH-53B, which was a variation of the Sikorsky CH-53 Sea Stallion, a family of heavy-lift transport helicopters developed for use by the Marine Corps. Affectionately referred to as Jolly Green Giants, the HH-53B's primary role was to rescue downed airmen. Almost immediately, the aircraft was upgraded with more powerful engines, added armor plating, retractable fuel probe, and improved electronics, counter-measures, and weapons systems. The new and improved version, HH-53C, was called Super Jolly Green Giants, or simply, Super Jolly Greens.

§

For our next part of our survival training, we hiked along jungle trails for the purpose of identifying edible vegetation and those plants that could provide a source of water. We spent an entire day building shelters, starting fires, making improvised tools, and learning the art of camouflage.

The EVASION portion of the training addressed proper methods of moving through the jungle so as to avoid contact with the enemy. We learned to avoid ridge lines because one's silhouette would be clearly visible from long distances. Our adept trainers also emphasized the danger of approaching lines of communication (LOC). Only after observing trails, roads, and waterways for an extended period were we to consider crossing LOCs, and then, only under the cover of darkness. We were advised to dodge villages altogether, taking wide detours to avoid contact with indigenous people. We practiced using a compass for land navigation and how to build a "hidey-hole" to avoid detection.

LOC (LINES OF COMMUNICATION)

An LOC is simply a "route" that connects military units with its supply depots. A focus of the war in Barrel Roll was on the interdiction of lines of communication (LOC) being used by the NVA and Pathet Lao to infiltrate and operate inside Laos. Success in any military operation is dependent on secure LOCs. The concept of LOC includes roads, trails, fuel pipelines, electronic communications, air routes, and so forth.

The major LOCs in Barrel Roll were Routes 6, 7, and 13 and the Nam (River) Ou. (See the map of Barrel Roll in this book for reference.) The Nam Ou, in particular, was of primary importance to North Vietnam since the river flowed from one of its primary supply depots, Dien Bien Phu, directly to Luang Prabang. In addition to those major LOCs, there were many other smaller roads, trails, and rivers that facilitated the movement of troops and supplies, however, since resources were limited, the major LOCs received the most surveillance and were subjected to attack. Routes 7 and 13 had improved surfaces, but Route 6 was unpaved and proved to be vulnerable to attack since it was narrow and wound through a series of mountainsides.

§

During the RESISTANCE portion of the training, we were subjected to simulated "hard" interrogations, placed in isolation boxes, deprived of sleep, and learned about a variety of interrogation techniques that were being used by the North Vietnamese, almost all of which involved torture. Once we learned about the severity of the torture and physical abuse to which American POWs had been subjected, I wondered if ever held captive, would I have the courage and strength to resist.

We devoted time to learning the Code of Conduct, a moral guide that set standards of behavior to which we were expected to abide. Our discussions focused on the meaning of each article of the Code and our obligation to abide by its tenets. The expectation of all who were held captive was to "return with honor."

We were all highly motivated and committed military personnel, and we accepted the Code of Conduct as it was written (without hesitation) to abide by it in the event of capture. In time, however, I came to realize how naïve we had been. As an Intelligence Officer, I had access to information regarding the abuse of Americans that was beginning to slowly trickle out of the prisons in the North. In time, I became aware of the unspeakable cruelty and torture our captured pilots and air crewmen were experiencing at the hands of the North Vietnamese. The prisoners, as we learned after their release in 1975, did share information with the North Vietnamese, and did so, considering the incredible physical torture and abuse to which they were routinely subjected. The Armed Forces quickly learned that, for some, it was impossible to fully adhere to all of the articles of the Code of Conduct. This consensus served to highlight the need to review and revise the Code.

THE CODE OF CONDUCT

Article I: I am an American, fighting in the armed forces which guard my country and our ways of life. I am prepared to give my life in their defense.

Article II: I will never surrender of my own free will. If in command I will never surrender the members of my command while they still have the means to resist.

Article III: If I am captured, I will continue to resist by all means available. I will make every effort to escape and aid others to escape. I will accept neither parole nor special favors from the enemy.

Article IV: If I become a prisoner of war, I will keep faith with my fellow prisoners. I will give no information nor take part in any action which might be harmful to my comrades. If I am senior, I will take command. If not, I will obey the lawful orders of those appointed over me and will back them up in every way.

Article V: When questioned, should I become a prisoner of war, I am required to give name, rank, service, service number, and date of birth. I will evade answering further questions to the utmost of my ability. I will make no oral or written statements disloyal to my country and its allies or harmful to their cause.

Article VI: I will never forget that I am an American, responsible for my actions, and dedicated to the principles which made my country free. I will trust in my God and in the United States of America.

I was looking forward to the final phase of training, the two-day jungle ESCAPE experience. Unfortunately, monsoon rains kept us inside. Trainees, equipped only with a survival vest, would be dropped off in the Luzon jungle for the purpose of traveling through the jungle to a "safe area" while evading local natives (Negritos). The Negritos simulated enemy forces, and their mission was to track and locate downed air crew members. While evading, trainees had to build a hidey-hole, spend a night in the jungle, and forage for food and water. We were told the Negritos almost always "captured" evading Americans. Once captured, trainees gave a token to the Negrito, who would then leave to "capture" other downed air crewmen. After being captured, the crewman pressed on to the "safe area," trying his best not to be captured again. The Negritos were compensated for their work and received incentive bonuses for each American they "captured."

— 2 —
ARRIVAL

We landed at Ton Son Nhut Air Base in Saigon, South Vietnam, around mid-day, on 25 March 1969. Depending on our branch of service, we were directed to different locations to drop off a copy of our travel orders and receive further travel instructions. Once we had checked in, we boarded a bus and were delivered to the Transient Officers Quarters. We weren't allowed to claim a bunk until 2000 hours. My night would be spent in a huge gymnasium that contained more than a hundred bunk beds. With nothing to do but seek some shade under a tin-roofed pavilion, a few of us enjoyed the air conditioning of the base theater to watch a matinee showing of "Herbie the Love Bug." After dinner at the Officer's Club, we finally got to claim a bunk, which proved to be a mad scramble. While some of the guys decided to experience downtown Saigon, I hopped up on a top bunk and immediately fell asleep.

After a fitful night's sleep thanks to the sounds of more than 200 snoring men, I was awake well before the 0700 wake up call, which enabled me to avoid another mad scramble to utilize the limited bathroom facilities. All personnel and belongings had to be out of the quarters by 0800. Evidently, it took all day to clean the barracks for that evening's guests.

I was fortunate and didn't have long to wait for my early-morning flight to Thailand. After a two-hour flight, we arrived at Don Muang Royal Thai Air Base in Bangkok where we waited under yet another tin-roof shelter.

After a little less than an hour under a blazing sun, our "Klong Hopper" arrived. Every day, a C-130 taxi service shuttled personnel to and from all air bases in Thailand. My destination, Udorn Royal Thai Air Base, was the next to last of the six Thai bases at which the Klong Hopper stopped. We sat in red web seats that lined each side of the fuselage. Pallets of cargo and our duffel bags ran down the center of the noisy, hot cargo hold. The load-master asked each of us the units to which we had been assigned, information he gave to the flight deck. In turn, the flight engineer contacted the Command Posts at each base with information about arriving personnel. Squadrons were advised accordingly so that representatives could meet the new arrivals at the base terminal when the Klong hopper arrived.

A thump announced our arrival, which was followed by a sudden blast of power from the reversed props. As the klong bird was taxiing to the terminal, the loadmaster was already lowering the cargo ramp. When the aircraft stopped, the ramp was fully lowered, and a pallet containing the personal bags and cargo for Udorn was quickly removed. It was late afternoon, and I arrived at what was going to be my new home for the next 12 months. Even before I stepped off the aircraft, I immediately felt the oppressive heat and humidity and smelled the odor of jet fuel and aircraft exhaust; sensations that would be a part of my daily life for the next year while deployed to Udorn Royal Thai Air Base.

UDORN

Udon Thani, or Udorn, is located in northern Thailand, about 50 miles south of the Mekong River, with Vientiane directly on the other side.[*] During the Second Indochina War, it was the sixth largest city in Thailand, and its economy was largely based on the presence of American forces stationed at Udon Thani Royal Thai Air Base.

The base was established in the 1950s out of fears that the Commu-nist-led Civil War in Laos would spread into Thailand. Beginning in 1961, the United States was granted permission to covertly use five Royal Thai Air Bases to fly air defense missions in Thailand and reconnaissance missions over Laos. Udorn's proximity to northern Laos made it a front-line facility during the Second Indochina War to attack targets in Laos and North Vietnam.

---

[*] See the map of Southeast Asia at the beginning of this book.

— 3 —
IN-PROCESSING

A representative from ABCCC greeted me at the terminal and drove me to the Central Base Personnel Office (CBPO) for in-processing. Before leaving, he indicated I should report to Squadron Headquarters at 0800 the next morning. I delivered a copy of my orders to the clerk at CBPO, but since it was late in the day, he said I could begin my in-processing the following day. For the night, and until I had obtained off-base housing, the Air Force had made provisions for me to stay at a hotel in downtown Udorn. An airman gave me a ride to town and told me to take a cab to the base in the morning. He said the cab fare would be five baht or 25 cents. What I did not know at the time, however, was how to instruct the cab driver to take me to the base.

In the morning, eager to begin my tour of duty in Southeast Asia, I donned a fresh uniform and left the hotel. There were plenty of cabs waiting at the hotel entrance. I got in and asked the driver to take me to the Air Force Base. He looked at me with a blank expression, apparently having no idea of what I had just said. I tried all kinds of words to get across my message. Using my best "pidgin English," I used words like "airplane" and "fly" to get my destination across, all without any positive results. He finally drove off, and I was sure that on my first day in Thailand, I was going to be abducted, mugged, robbed, and left for dead. But, happily, he drove to the main gate of the base. Later, I learned the correct word to use when referring to the Air Force Base was "camp." A lesson learned. Cabs were the preferred method of getting to and from town. They were plentiful and cheap. The cabs were also small and cars I had never seen before. Mostly, they were Toyota Corollas, an introduction to my first Japanese-made car.

As instructed, I reported to the ABCCC compound. I introduced myself to the Administrative Officer and delivered a copy of my orders. He indicated I would be assigned to Alleycat Orbit, which, at the time, meant little to me. After meeting the Squadron Commander, Colonel Jack, I was escorted to the Alleycat shack where I was introduced to the Intelligence Officer whom I would be replacing.

At the time, there were only two Intel Officers and two Enlisted Technicians assigned to the orbit. Both officers were short-timers, and in less than a month of my arrival, I became the senior Intel Officer, responsible for training officers and enlisted replacements. Fortunately, the two enlisted Intel technicians with whom I worked were in the middle of their tours, and both were highly knowledgeable and fulfilled their duties and responsibilities in an outstanding manner. For the first month or two of my deployment, I relied heavily on their expertise and experience to help me master my job responsibilities.

The senior Intel officer, Jim Stanitz, was my training officer, and his deployment would end just a couple of weeks after my arrival. The second Intel officer's deployment would end shortly after Jim's. Adequate staffing would continue to be a challenge throughout my year-long deployment with ABCCC.

Fortunately, Jim was on ground duty the day I arrived, and we agreed to meet in the afternoon after I finished my in-processing. After getting squared away with the squadron, I returned to CBPO to complete in-processing. I delivered my financial records to the Finance Office, and then I was off to the Base Hospital to drop off my medical and dental records. After lunch at the Officer's Club, I located the Equipment Management Office (BEMO) to pick up flight gear (i.e. combat boots, flight jackets and flight suits, sunglasses, ear plugs, and a pressure-resistant watch. The final in-processing stop was to have SERE photos taken and establish my pedigree (four personal questions). In the absence of SERE photos, the identity of a downed aircrewman could be confirmed by answering the pedigree questions correctly. I used my mother's maiden name, my dog's name, my college roommate's name, and the name of the college I attended. The confirmation of the downed crewman was needed since the NVA were known to have used survival radios to call for assistance and lure SAR aircraft into traps.

— 4 —
FIRST THING'S FIRST

Within a day or two of my arrival at Udorn, I found a place to live. I rented a room in a bungalow in town where three other ABCCC squadron members lived. It was about two miles from the base which was just a 25-cent cab ride away. The bungalow was also within walking distance of several local night spots, popular with the GIs. Each of us paid $50 in rent and $5 a month for the services of our very shy house girl, Som Kit. In addition to cleaning the bungalow, Som Kit washed our laundry and polished our flight boots every day. The four of us shared a bathroom that had hot running water. From time to time, we also shared that bathroom with a menacing-looking two-foot-long lizard.

The bungalow was located in a compound with several other buildings, one of which was the home of the owner. The compound was gated and armed guards stood watch at the gate 24 hours a day. During the year I lived in Udorn, I never encountered any problems, and there were a "few" occasions when I was on the streets late at night.

My morning routine was usually the same. I took a cab to the base and walked to the Officer's Club (OC) for breakfast. Officially, it was the Officer's Open Mess. Since flight operations were taking place around the clock, the Officer's Club was also open 24 hours a day. After breakfast, it was just a short drive in the base shuttle bus to the ABCCC compound. To get ahead of the steep learning curve I faced, I arrived at the Alleycat shack early and went to work.

I was assigned four days of ground duty, time in which I was expected to become fully knowledgeable about Alleycat's mission. Like all arriving members to ABCCC, I would be evaluated, first, on my knowledge of and ability to perform ground duties. Once those duties were mastered, I would then be assigned to two training flights and evaluated once more. Within the short period of time that Jim was with me, I had to learn as much as possible about the responsibilities of an Intelligence Officer at ABCCC.

§

*First Thing's First.** It made complete sense. One of my first tasks was to learn how to "tell time" and "spell." I was reminded of the old proverb "For Want of a Nail." The proverb, of course, tells the story of how a kingdom was lost merely because a nail could not be found to fix a horse-shoe on the horse of a messenger who was unable to deliver an important message during a battle. In other words, *the minute details are vitally import-ant in any venture, and that could not be more important than in warfare.*

The success of combat operations is dependent upon the concise exchange of information and the movement of resources to precise locations according to synchronized time schedules. Not surprisingly, the military had systems in place to ensure consistency and conformity.

Since combat operations necessitated the movement and coordina-tion of a variety of assets in an efficient and timely manner, operations needed to unfold according to precise time schedules. To avoid confu-sion, the military employed a standard time system in Southeast Asia.

> *"...the minute details are vitally important in any venture, and that could not be more important than in warfare."*

Technically, it was called Greenwich Mean Time, but it was referred

---

* A slogan with Biblical roots and used by Alcoholics Anonymous.

to as Zulu Time. Greenwich Mean Time (today it is called Universal Coordinated Time) represents the time at the prime meridian or longitudinal line that separates East from West. The prime meridian runs through Greenwich, England, hence the name. Zulu Time was expressed in terms of a 24-hour clock.

In Southeast Asia, we added 7 hours to the current time to determine Zulu Time. Zulu was the time we used during all operations, and it didn't take me long to get accustomed to it.

To avoid confusion and potentially fatal errors, letters were never spoken on the radio. Instead of saying A or D or N, and so forth, all personnel communicated letters by using the following new alphabet:

ALPHA	BRAVO	CHARLIE
DELTA	ECHO	FOXTROT
GOLF	HOTEL	IGLOO
JULIET	KILO	LIMA
MIKE	NOVEMBER	OSCAR
PAPA	QUEBEC	ROMEO
SIERRA	TANGO	UNIFORM
VICTOR	WHISKEY	X-RAY
YANKEE	ZULU	

One of the first topics Jim and I discussed was the handling of classified information. American presence and involvement in Laos during the Second Indochina War was probably one of the worst-kept secrets in the annals of American military history. Returning aircrews, who ferried ABCCC aircraft to and from Taiwan for routine maintenance overhauls, brought back international editions of news magazines. We enjoyed lots of laughs reading articles in which American officials denied a military presence and operations in Laos. Despite the repeated denials, it was common knowledge that Laos was, somehow, an integral part of America's involvement in the Second Indochina War. While the public was not fully aware of the extent of its operations, the CIA's "secret army" was not a secret.

Despite the public's knowledge of operations in Laos, the missions in which American and allied military personnel engaged were classified.

All materials regarding the operations were classified, and security and the handling of classified material was always paramount in our thinking. Pursuant to Air Force regulations, procedures were in place to ensure that all classified information was handled and protected in a secure manner. Current Executive Orders mandate that after 25 years, all classified documents are declassified unless compelling reasons dictate continued classification.

IT'S CLASSIFIED

Information is considered classified if it has been assigned one of three categories; Confidential, Secret, or Top Secret. The classification category Restricted refers to information pertaining to our nation's nuclear programs. Access to classified information is not just based on one's clearance status. Instead, access is permitted to only those individuals for whom it is determined they have a need to know the classified material in order to fulfill the requirements of their official duties.

A satisfactory Background Investigation, conducted by the FBI, is required for all government personnel whose official duties require access to classified information. An Expanded Background Investigation (EBI) is required for those whose responsibilities require access to information classified above Top Secret or pertain to Special Access Programs and/or Sensitive Compartmented Information.

At ABCCC, a majority of the classified material we used was classified Secret or Confidential, however, there were times when Top Secret documents regarding on-going operations crossed our desk. Almost always, the classified documents contained the restrictive caveat NOFORN, which meant the information was not to be disclosed to foreign nationals. Classified documents had to be stamped with the classification of the highest level of information they contained on the cover sheet and at the top and bottom of each page. Additionally, each paragraph of a classified document also had to start with the letters (i.e. TS, S, or C), indicating the classification level of the information.

ABCCC received classified documents by two methods. Top Secret material was delivered to the squadron by courier either from Blue Chip or the Air Attache in Vientiane, Lao. Most times, the documents were delivered to our radio shack via secure teletype. In both instances, once the material was delivered to the Alleycat shack, it was signed for, and a record of the receipt of the document was established. When not in use, the material was stored in a secure file cabinet in our shack. An inventory of each classified document was maintained, and members of the battle staff had to sign the inventory sheet whenever classified documents were removed and returned. During the day, while the day crew was preparing for that evening's mission, the cabinets were left unlocked. Once a classified document was judged to be of no further use, it was destroyed. We did not have document shredders at the time, and classified material was destroyed by burning. The inventory of classified documents was noted whenever a classified document was destroyed, and signatures attested to the destruction. Such documents were placed in burn bags and stored in secure file cabinets. Once or twice a week, a detail would take the burn bags to the burn barrels located on the west side of the runway, not far from the ABCCC compound.

Prior to my acceptance as a student at the Armed Forces Air Intelligence School at Lowry Air Force Base (Denver, Colorado), the FBI conducted a Background Investigation (BI), part of which included interviews with my associates and former employers. Once a security clearance was granted, I participated in a briefing regarding proper security measures and protocols and was required to sign a non-disclosure agreement (NDA). Following my deployment to Southeast Asia, I was assigned to Headquarters, Tactical Air Command (TAC), a position that required a security clearance and access levels beyond Top Secret. To obtain such clearances, the FBI conducted an EBI before I was granted access. When I separated from the Air Force, part of the out-processing was a security de-briefing conducted by FBI agents. De-briefings, I learned, served several purposes;

• Reminded me of a life-time commitment to withhold the classified information to which I had been given access;

• A formal record was established that I no longer had access to classified information (interestingly, I did not lose my security clearances but, instead, surrendered my need to know);

• I was provided with contact information in the event I was ever approached by anyone seeking classified information; and

• I signed another NDA.

BURNING CD

Throughout my deployment, I was curious about operations at ABCCC and eager to learn all I could. One of the more mundane jobs that was assigned to the radio operators was the destruction of classified waste material. We generated lots of notes, message traffic, working papers, and classified documents, which quickly became outdated. The material was collected and referred to as classified destruct (CD) material. On several occasions, I volunteered to accompany our radio operators to the burn barrels where the CD was burned. At the end of each flight, our radio operators meticulously collected all paper on which notes were taken and placed this material in a burn bag. Similarly, all CD that was generated while performing ground duties in the orbit work area was also collected. The bags of CD were secured in file cabinets, and several times a week, it was taken to the burn barrels.

The burn barrels were located on the west perimeter of the runway, not more than 20 yards from the taxiway. All Udorn based units used the area to destroy CD. To my great delight, the CD area provided a close view of the main runway, multitude of aircraft in various stages of flight operations, and nearby parking ramps. I thoroughly enjoyed helping our radio operators because the trips to the area were memorable.

On one side of the burn barrels, an Army detachment maintained a parking ramp for several different aircraft. The only aircraft I recognized was the OV-1 Mohawk. The presence of those aircraft served as a reminder of military "politics" at its worst. The call sign for those Army aircraft was Spud, and they were fragged for Barrel Roll on a fairly regular basis; two to five times a week. For years, the Army and Air Force had been having on-going "discussions" regarding each of its missions. Finally, an agreement was reached in the mid 1960's. The Air Force would accept the Army flying armed helicopters, and, in exchange, the Army would remove armaments from its fixed wing aircraft. The Mohawk had been stripped of its 50 caliber machine gun and rockets, and its role became one of gathering electronic intelligence (ELINT). To do this, Mohawk aircraft were fitted with pods that carried side looking airborne radar (SLAR) and infrared (IR) sensors. Those sensors could "look" through tree canopy and foliage and provide excellent images of enemy forces and materiel on the ground. However, the absurdity of inter-service rivalry was such that the information gathered by the Spuds was not provided to the Air Force, as far as I knew. Other than clearing Spuds into their designated target areas, ABCCC never knew how the information they had gathered was ever used. A huge advantage of Spud aircraft was that they were virtually silent and could approach target areas without being heard.

On the other side of the burn barrels, Air America maintained a large compound and parking ramp. Clearly visible were the AC-47 gunships used to train Lao pilots under the provisions of Water Pump. One day while burning CD, we observed flight of six T-28's returning to base. They flew downwind over the runway, and then one by one, broke out of the formation, descending into the landing pattern. It was fascinating to watch the aircraft land and taxi to the ramp. I waited until they left the aircraft, wanting to get a good look at the Laotian and Thai pilots.

One day, upon our arrival at the burn barrels, we discovered a load of classified flight manuals for the RF-4C. The thick manuals, which were classified Secret N/F (No Foreign Dissemination), had been thrown into the barrels and were almost completely intact. Clearly, it was a serious breach of security. After burning our material, we gathered up the documents and delivered them to the recce squadron on our way back to our shack. The master sergeant with whom we spoke didn't seem too concerned. In fact, he was a little annoyed we had returned the material. So much for being security conscious.

§

My first challenge was to learn all I could about the history and politics of Laos. That knowledge was needed to better understand and fulfill our squadron's mission and the role I was assuming. I needed to understand how Laos was connected to the War in Vietnam, a war of which I was now a part. I embarked on a crash course to understand all things Lao. It didn't take long for me to realize how little I knew about the complexity of Southeast Asian geo-politics; it was complicated.**

Once I had achieved a rudimentary understanding of the First Indochina War and the circumstances in which Laos became embroiled in the Second Indochina War, my attention shifted to learning all I could about our Area of Operations (AO), the warriors opposing the Communist aggressors, the dozens of forward operating bases from which they operated, and the unique landscape in which the war was fought.

** For a more in-depth discussion regarding the chronology of events in the First and Second Indochina Wars, refer to Appendices A and B.

— 5 —

AREA OF OPERATIONS

O ur call sign was Alleycat, and our Area of Operations was Northern Laos, which would become my "life" and night-time "home" for the next year. In 1955, Laos was divided into five Military Regions (MR). ABCCC was responsible for the command and control of all flights and operations over the country of Laos. Military Regions 1, 2, and 5 were located in northern Laos, and, collectively, those three regions were designated as Barrel Roll.

The panhandle of southern Laos was designated Steel Tiger North (Military Region 3) and Steel Tiger South (MR 4); collectively, however, it was simply referred to as Steel Tiger.

ABCCC had four orbits that controlled Barrel Roll and Steel Tiger. Each orbit had a call sign: Alleycat, Cricket, Moonbeam, and Hillsboro. From 0600 until 1800 hours, the call sign for the orbit controlling Barrel Roll was Cricket, and Hillsboro controlled Steel Tiger. After arriving on station to assume control at 1800 hours and until 0600 the next morning, Alleycat controlled the north, and Moonbeam was responsible for operations in southern Laos. Alleycat's Military Regions were 1, 2, and 5, and each was vastly different.

For instance, the vast majority of air and ground operations in Barrel Roll occurred in MR 2. MR 2 was comprised of the provinces of Xiang Khouang, Houa Phan, Bolikhamxai, and the northern portion of Vientiane Province. Xiang Khouang and Houa Phan Provinces comprised the northeast portion of Laos and included the fabled Plaine des Jarres (PDJ).

THE PDJ

The PDJ is a 500-square-mile region in North Laos that is covered with rolling hills, high ridges, and grassy flatlands. Its average elevation is 3,000 feet. The PDJ gets its name from the hundreds of stone funeral jars that dot the landscape. The jars are over five feet high and were created by an unknown Southeast Asian race of people, probably sometime between 500 BC and 800 AD. The PDJ was the center of combat operations in northern Laos, a vitally important tactical and strategic location that changed hands during the war on multiple occasions.

§

It was along the roads, trails, and waterways of MR 2 that the ebb and flow of a majority of military operations occurred. Unfortunately, the civilian population living in the numerous villages became unwitting participants and victims of the chaos and destruction of combat. In time, I would become intimately familiar with the geography of MR 2, as well as the names of those villages, rivers, and route designations.

MR 1 was the largest Military Region, and it occupied the entire northwest portion of Laos. It was comprised of seven provinces; Bokeo, Luang Namtha (which bordered China), Xaignabouli, Oudomxai, Phongsali, (with common borders with both China and North Vietnam), Sam Neua (with a common border with North Vietnam), and Luang Prabang (which bordered MR 5 to the south). Ostensibly, the Lao government had given the Chinese permission to embark on an ambitious road building program in the northern provinces of Luang Namtha and Bokeo.

Because of the Chinese presence and America's reluctance to avoid incidents with the Chinese that might widen the war, much of the northern portions of the region were, officially, declared off-limits by the Rules of Engagement (ROE). But covert operations, both in the air and on the ground, did take place in MR 1, and did so, on a fairly regular basis. The purpose of those operations, of course, was to blunt the Chinese efforts to use the roads, trails, and waterways in the area to infiltrate supplies, weapons, and materiel to support units of both the People's Army of Vietnam (NVA) and Pathet Lao (PL).

During my deployment, MR 5 was considered safely under the control of the RLG. MR 5 included the Provinces of Vientiane (southern portion) and Borikhane, the surrounding areas of the capitol city, Vientiane. Few major combat operations took place in MR 5, however, from time to time, the NVA and PL made thrusts southward toward Vientiane.

Once I attained a general understanding of the nature of military operations in Barrel Roll, I then focused my attention on some of the more practical aspects of the war. An understanding of the *L'Armee Clandestine*, and its components, with whom ABCCC interacted every day, was essential to provide them with support upon which their lives depended. *L'Armee Clandestine* was mostly comprised by Hmong hill people. At the outset of my journey to Southeast Asia, I had little knowledge about the Hmong and their compelling leader, General Vang Pao, nor any inkling about the impact these humble people would have on my life. It was also essential to fully grasp the rules that guided the conduct of military operations.

— 6 —

GROUND WARRIORS

T he Hmong hill people were fierce warriors, and they had their origins in central Asia. By the mid-1800s, pockets of Hmong had firmly established themselves in the highest elevations of Laos. Physically, the Hmong stood out as among the shortest of the tribes of Laotian hill people. The physical demands of mountain life gave the Hmong broad shoulders, strong legs, and incredible stamina.

With but a few exceptions, the ground war in northern Laos (Barrel Roll) was fought by the CIA's so-called secret army (*L'Armee Clandestine*), comprised almost entirely of Hmong hill people. The Royal Laotian Government Army (RLA) and Royal Laotian Air Force (RLAF) also participated in combat operations in Barrel Roll but at a greatly reduced level. The RLA was primarily deployed in Steel Tiger.

The Hmong's unquestioned leader was their charismatic commander, General Vang Pao. He was a fierce and courageous warrior, but more importantly, he was their inspirational leader. They called him "Txiv" or Father, and he has been recognized for leading the Hmong out of a "stone age" existence and into the modern world.

The more I read about General Vang Pao, the more enthralled I became by his life and military career. His military career began at the age of 13, working as a translator for French commandos who were in Laos to organize a resistance to the Japanese. The efficient way he performed his duties caught the attention of French officers, and following the war, Vang Pao was enrolled in the French Police Academy. At the age of 21, he graduated from the Academy and became a policeman, leading successful patrols against the Viet Minh during the First Indochina War. Based on his outstanding performance in combat, Vang Pao was selected to attend Officer Candidate School by the French and became an officer in the Armee Nationale Laotienne (ANL), the national army of Laos. He was recognized as a highly effective commander and quickly rose through the ranks, achieving the rank of Major General in 1964, the first and only Hmong to hold that rank in the Royal Lao Army.

General Vang Pao's reputation as a natural leader and fierce warrior was noted by CIA personnel who were working closely with the ANL. Bill Lair, the architect of paramilitary operations in Laos, successfully recruited General Vang Pao to join the CIA's efforts to establish a paramilitary force in Laos. Vang Pao's hatred of Communism and ability to recruit fellow Hmong to fight the Pathet Lao and Viet Minh forged a relationship with the CIA that lasted until 1975 when the CIA ceased operations and General Vang Pao left his beloved Laos. General Vang Pao was the undisputed leader of Laotian forces in Northern Laos and an inspiration to anyone with whom he had contact.

§

An essential component of the *L'Armee Clandestine*, were the paramilitary warriors who were trained personnel to control air strikes from the ground. These ground controllers were referred to as Forward Air Guides (FAGs). Lao, Thai, and Americans served as FAGs. They were fearless and courageous men who played vital roles in the counter insurgency war in Laos. FAGs served as a link between ground forces and ABCCC. They all spoke English (barely passable for some) and were the source of real-time intelligence regarding the enemy, its strength, and disposition.

FAGs were trained in Thailand at the Khao Mae Plong Camp, operated under the control of their CIA handlers. The training facility was located in Prachinburi Province, east of Bangkok. In addition to calling in air strikes, FAGs accompanied RWTs as well as advance SGU units and carried out a myriad of other special assignments. It was a FAG who directed air strikes in the event SGU forces came under attack, referred to as Troops in Contact (TIC), or located targets of opportunity. Within a short period of time, I developed a close emotional attachment to and an enduring respect for those courageous men. They lived in the field under demanding and harsh conditions and participated in extremely dangerous missions, exposing the PL and NVA to the multitude of resources the Air Force could deliver. I did all I could to provide them with the air support they needed. The call signs for those FAGs with whom I maintained daily contact were:

HILLTOP	HUNTER	POGO
BLACK LION	SHOWBOAT	RED DOG
KNEECAP	COUNTER	WHITE ROSE
REDHAT	RED MAN	RED TIGER
WATTS	LULU	BLUECAP
RUBY 52	LIMA LIMA	BLUE
MOON	QUIET MAN	POPPY

FAGs proved to be highly successful and remained in place for the duration of the Second Indochina War. While the NVA held advantages in artillery, armored vehicles, and a better standard of training, the SGU's strength was the use of air power. However, in time, SGU forces became "addicted" to air power and depended on it for the conduct of both offensive and defensive operations. Even during lulls in combat, SGU forces and FAGs felt more secure, knowing there were aircraft nearby to provide close air support.

Being a FAG was a dangerous occupation, and, sadly, some with whom we worked were killed in action. Black Lion was an African American who had served in the United States military. He had developed an affinity for the Laotian people and elected to stay in Laos, working for the CIA. He was a gentleman, always professional, and had a deep resonant voice. He was killed when he stepped on a land mine somewhere in Barrel Roll. His name was Will Green. Two other FAGs, Red Tiger and Pogo, were also killed in action, during my deployment while in service to the United States.

Other members of the *L'Armee Clandestine* who contributed greatly to its overall mission were those who served on Road Watch Teams (RWT). RWT's mission was to conduct surveillance of the movement of the NVA along the roads, trails, and rivers of Laos. Unless defending their position, members of RWTs were not expected to fight. Perched on locations overlooking LOCs, team members reported the locations of lucrative targets such as vehicle convoys, truck parks, and troop concentrations. At the height of the Second Indochina War, the CIA coordinated the work of more than 20 RWTs. The teams were comprised of between six to ten members, most of whom were Lao, however, some Thai mercenaries were also recruited. A majority of the RWTs operated in Steel Tiger, monitoring traffic along the Ho Chi Minh Trail complex, however, five or six teams were always working in Barrel Roll. It was vitally important that we knew the exact locations of all active RWTs to avoid friendly fire incidents.

In 1963, when the program was initiated, team members hiked long distances to reach their target areas, sometimes up to 30 to 40 miles. They remained in position for two months or more. By the late 1960's, RWT members were inserted and exfiltrated by helicopter. That mission was assigned to the 20th Helicopter Squadron, the call sign of which was Pony Express.

The ground war in Barrel Roll was dependent upon air power, and as the war years progressed, General Vang Pao and his army became more and more dependent upon air mobility and close air support. Before I could gain a complete understanding of the role of air power and its critical role in supporting the *L'Armee Clandestine*, I had to become knowledgeable about the Rules of Engagement (ROE).

§

Pony Express was the call sign for another very important and highly classified program. The official designation for the operation was the 20th Special Operations Squadron (SOS), and its pilots flew the Sikorsky CH-3C helicopter, a variation of the HH-3C. The helicopters had upgraded engines, sacrificed armor for airspeed, and did not display any U.S. markings or insignia. Another version of that aircraft was the HH-3C (Super Jolly Green Giant), the pre-eminent rescue helicopter in use in Southeast Asia. The 20th SOS was assigned two critical missions, both of which were cloaked in the veil of secrecy.

In an effort to improve the accuracy of air strikes in Laos and Vietnam and reduce civilian casualties, Tactical Air Navigation (TACAN) sites were installed. They provided pilots with a bearing and distance with which to locate targets. Pony Express crews flew men and materiel to install, maintain, and support the TACAN sites constructed in Southeast Asia.

The Ponies' second job was to fly missions ordered by the Director of Operations for Special Activities (DOSA). DOSA missions were exclusively clandestine operations and involved the infiltration and exfiltration of American and indigenous military personnel. Perhaps to add confusion to those missions and disguise the assets, euphemisms were used, such as Controlled American sources (CAS), Studies and Observations Group (SOG), or Road Watch Teams (RWT). Other times, they were called Long Range Reconnaissance Patrols (LURPS). The top-secret operation was a joint unconventional warfare task force created in 1964 by the Joint Chiefs of Staff to conduct cross-border operations, almost always, behind enemy lines. Operations were conducted in Vietnam, Laos, and Cambodia, and it was the Pony Express aircrews that inserted and exfiltrated teams of highly motivated and courageous men. The teams of 8-10 operators performed critically vital missions such as identifying enemy sanctuaries and base camps, bomb damage assessment (BDA), intelligence gathering, prisoner snatches, wire taps, deployment of sensors, psychological operations, the interdiction and harassment of enemy road building and construction efforts, and observing enemy troop movements.

Since they were high-risk missions, and the enemy regularly used trackers and dogs for perimeter defense, it was not uncommon for the teams to engage in contact with the enemy. If team members found themselves in a tactical emergency and were fleeing contact, a Prairie Fire emergency was declared. When the words "Prairie Fire" were heard, our first responsibility was to place a radio call to Kontum (SOG Command Post in Vietnam) and alert them to the Prairie Fire emergency. On the few occasions when I reported a Praire Fire emergency, Kontum had already been alerted. All available air assets were diverted to assist in the rescue and safe return of team members. Pony Express aircraft that were standing by at secure sites, as nearby as possible, took to the air to effect the rescue. The exploits of SOG and CAS missions are legendary and one of the great untold success stories of the Second Indochina War. Thankfully, their incredible feats and sacrifices have begun to be told.

PONY EXPRESS RIDES

Mid-way through my deployment, construction was completed on a Bachelor Officers Quarters (BOQ) on base. I, along with several other members of the squadron opted to move from our bungalows in town into the new, air-conditioned building. I moved my meager belongings into a suite that had four bedrooms, two bathrooms, and a common area. As luck would have it, one of my new suitemates, Jim Brown, was a Pony Express pilot. It didn't take long for me to prevail upon him to get me on his squadron's flight manifest to fly with the Ponies. Thanks to a friendly squadron clerk, I was approved to fly orientation flights with Pony Express to "coordinate operations between Pony Express and ABCCC". All I wanted was to get some helicopter flight time and enjoy the Thai countryside. I flew a total of three training missions with Jim and his crew and enjoyed every minute of the flight time. I sat on the floor in the back of the aircraft, looking out over the lowered ramp. I wanted to learn as much as possible regarding Pony Express operations and was fascinated to listen to the stories they shared.

The training missions entailed low level flying and combat landings to simulate insertions and exfiltrations. Emergency landings, due to the loss of power, were also practiced. The technique is called autorotation, and it utilizes the air moving up through the rotors, to turn the rotors, permitting the aircraft to settle safely to the ground. The autorotation maneuvers were practiced at a huge sprawling air base located about 50 miles south of Udorn.

The name of the US-built base was Nam Phong, and it was huge. In addition to the long concrete runway and taxiways, the base had a control tower, multiple hangars, support buildings, barracks, POL storage, and command structures. The base looked to be unoccupied, but upon closer scrutiny, I saw several vehicles parked near one of the buildings on the base's perimeter. Though not yet operational for air operations, Nam Phong was being used for other purposes. According to sources, the CIA used portions of the sprawling complex to house and interrogate prisoners.

Nam Phong Air Base was built to be the home of the F-111 (Aardvark). At the time, it was one of the newest aircraft in the US Air Force inventory. Originally designated as the TFX (tactical fighter experimental) the F-111 was the result of an initiative by Secretary of Defense Robert McNamara of the Kennedy and Johnson administrations. It was created through a joint service project, the concept of which was to develop a tactical fighter-bomber that could be used by both the Navy and Air Force. Until the Navy dropped out of the project, the F-111 was intended to land on aircraft carriers as well as to be deployed to bases with traditional concrete runways. That meant, of course, the project was doomed to fail.

The F-111 had adjustable swept wings and was the first aircraft to utilize terrain following radar, which meant the plane was capable of flying at night and/or in bad weather at high speeds and low altitude. The ground avoidance radar controlled the plane and designed to make adjustments to the plane's attitude as the terrain ahead of the aircraft changed. It was a great concept, but the plane's entry into the Vietnam War in 1968 (Operation Combat Lancer) was premature since it had not yet completed its operational test program. That was yet another egregious decision by Robert McNamara and the Johnson administration. After a squadron of F-111's deployed to Korat Royal Thai Air Base during the spring of 1968, it began flying combat missions. During its first year of combat, fifteen aircraft were lost, which resulted in the first of its many groundings. The plane returned to a combat role in 1972. Despite having flown over 3000 combat sorties, the F-111 never distinguished itself in the air war. In 1996, the plane was retired from the Air Force inventory.

One of the joys of visiting the base was the opportunity to meet with some of the locals and barter with them to purchase home-made long guns. When they saw the helicopters performing the autorotation maneuvers, groups of men would approach the base perimeter and wait for their visitors. After greeting one another with the traditional Wai (bowing slightly with the hands in prayer fashion in front of the chest), we squatted in a circle, inspecting the guns they had brought with them. They were ingenious and made the weapons out of scrap metal and other discarded military materials. The bargaining began when the Thais wrote down a number (of baht) in the sand, which represented a sum of money they knew would never be acceptable. Once their number was written, we discussed the price, shook our heads no, erased the number in the sand, and replaced it with an equally ridiculously low counter-offer. Then it was the Thais turn to discuss the offer, laugh, erase our offer, and come back with another offer.

This process was repeated several times, with each side either raising or lowering their offer. After ten minutes of bargaining, one side eventually accepted the offer and a deal was struck.

Once the money and guns were exchanged, everyone smiled, laughed, and did our best to "talk" with one another. I purchased one of the homemade long guns and gave it to my best friend, Duke Hammond, when he served as my Best Man.

— 7 —

RULES OF ENGAGEMENT

During the Second Indochina War, Vietnam and Laos each had their unique set of Rules of Engagement (ROE). The rules were one of the first topics about which I was expected to become Alleycat's expert. As Alleycat's senior Intelligence Officer, it would be my responsibility to provide accurate interpretations of the ROE to the battle staff and ensure no breaches were permitted to occur. I would also provide timely updates on changes to the ROE. In time, I learned just how consequential the ROE was to the outcome of the Second Indochina War.

The use of air power was controlled for the dual purpose of not widening the war and risking increased Russian or Chinese involvement. Air power's intention was also to prevent collateral damage and loss of life of the civilian population.

In Laos, decisions regarding the ROE were made by the Lao Prime Minister, Prince Souvanna Phouma. However, the reality was that all decisions regarding the use of air power in Laos were made by the American Ambassador to Laos, and the Prince merely rubber-stamped those decisions. The ambassador and his Air Attache were stationed at the American Embassy in Vientiane. Their call sign was Geneva, and on several occasions, I contacted the Ambassador to report significant events that were unfolding on the ground. Interestingly, on those occasions, Geneva seemed more perturbed about having their sleep interrupted than they were concerned about the events occurring on the ground in Barrel Roll.

The ROEs did not apply to Lao, Thai, or Hmong pilots. They were free to strike whatever target(s) they deemed unfriendly. All preplanning and scheduling of targets in Laos were made only with the approval of the Laotian Prime Minister, American Ambassador, and Air Attache.

After ground duty was over, I became fully immersed in my role as senior Intelligence Officer and reviewed various portions of the ROE to the battle staff during pre-mission briefings to reinforce its understanding. The controllers needed to understand the ROE since they authorized aircraft to operate in specific areas. According to the Uniformed Code of Military Justice (UCMJ), a violation of the ROE could result in disciplinary action. But in the confusion of battle, it was inevitable that breaches of the ROE would occur, and they did.

The micro-managing of the war and imposition of such limitations severely limited our ability to wage war. Ultimately, the restrictions imposed by the ROE cost our nation the lives of many of our servicemen and lives of our allies. Those layers of restrictions were constantly being updated and revised to avoid international complications. It was a challenge for me to understand and memorize all of the nuances and small details of the ROE and a daunting task to ensure all pilots and members of the battle staff were properly briefed. We carried a copy of the current ROE on all flights.

RULES OF ENGAGEMENT FOR LAOS

- *A No Bomb Line (NBL) was placed around the city of Sam Neua since it was the location of the Pathet Lao (PL) headquarters. This was particularly galling since the enemy knew the ROE and used the city as a sanctuary. Reconnaissance photos showed huge stores of materiel and troops within the city and on its outskirts, but our self-imposed rules prevented us from destroying these targets. Once those supplies and personnel left Sam Neua and began traveling down the trail system, they could then be attacked;*
- *Wats (temples), historic sites (i.e. locations of the funeral jars), and cultural centers were off-limits;*
- *Strike aircraft were prohibited from operating within 20 miles of*

China's border. In the event hostile fire was received from within that zone, special permission had to be sought and granted from the American Embassy;

- *A 25-mile NBL was placed around the cities of Luang Prabang (royal capital) and Vientiane (political capital) and a 15,000 foot avoidance over those cities;*
- *A ten-mile NBL was placed around other major cities (e.g. Pakse, Savannakhet, Thakhet, etc.) and a 15,000 foot avoidance over the cities;*
- *No ordnance could be delivered within 500 meters of any village or against any building within the restricted area. The only exception were buildings from which AAA was fired;*
- *No airstrikes were authorized more than 200 meters off major roads or trails (to protect covert teams and civilians). As the air war expanded, this restriction was rescinded);*
- *Free fire zones were established in which any type of target could be attacked;*
- *All strike aircraft had to be under the positive control of an airborne FAC or FAG or under the control of a navigational precision bombing system (e.g. AN-MSQ77);*
- *Once a month, a flight from the International Control Commission (charged with monitoring and enforcing the Geneva Convention) overflew Laos and during its flight, air operations along its route ceased and aircraft were ordered to "hide," Once the flight entered North Vietnam airspace, the air-war in Barrel Roll resumed;*
- *Surface to Air Missile (SAM) sites could not be attacked while under construction but only after they became operational; and*
- *Thai based aircraft could not deliver ordnance in South Vietnam for any reason.*

— 8 —

AIR WARRIORS

The learning curve I faced was steep. After immersing myself in the ROE, my attention turned to the air war in Laos. Air operations were conducted by pilots that were either clandestine warriors or members of the American Armed Forces.

By the mid-1960's, the CIA and Defense Department had become painfully aware of the need for close air support for *L'Armee Clandestine*. In 1968, to address that need, the comprehensive Palace Dog program was implemented. It replaced the successful but short-lived Butterfly Forward Air Controller program. Palace Dog had two components and addressed the need for close air support.

The first component, called Steve Canyon, placed forward air controllers in Laos. Their call sign was Raven and they played a significant role in the war in Laos. The CIA recruited Air Force pilots to volunteer for an assignment about which they knew nothing. They were only told it was a secret, extremely high-risk assignment that would provide them with far more autonomy from the military bureaucracy and onerous Rules of Engagement of South Vietnam. Ravens were Air Force fighter pilots or forward air controllers who had completed at least four months of their Vietnam deployment and accumulated at 750 hours of flying time.

Once pilots were accepted into the program, they were "sheep-dipped." That is, they were given temporary duty (TDY) orders to the

American Embassy in Vientiane where they were stripped of all Air Force identification, uniforms, and equipment. They were supplied with U.S. AID identification and cover stories (most were firefighters) to explain their presence in Laos. For the remainder of their deployment as Ravens, they wore civilian clothing, which was a blatant disregard of the Geneva Accords and subjected Ravens to certain death if captured by the enemy. Rumors had it that Ravens carried a lethal shellfish toxin pill in the event they were captured. Ravens performed their duties under the direction of the Air Attache (AIRA), who in turn took his orders from the American Ambassador to Laos.

Ravens flew low and slow, a dangerous mission profile that resulted in a high casualty rate. They flew anywhere from one to four daylight missions every day and accumulated close to 300 hours of flying time a month. Along with volunteering to become a Raven, they incurred a six-month deployment. Practically all the Ravens extended their tours for a second six-month tour. At any one point in time, the number of Ravens in Laos rarely numbered more than approximately 20-25. Of the 161 pilots on the Raven roster, 23 were killed during the secret war in Laos. They were elite pilots, who identified with and cared deeply for the Hmong.

Ravens were authorized to control air strikes themselves. In addition, their role included that of observation, marking targets, and reporting bomb damage assessment (BDA) following airstrikes. Ravens worked closely with ground forces, and once strike aircraft were handed off to a Raven, he identified and marked the target. After briefing aircraft commanders about the ground situation, Raven then authorized pilots to strike the target.

RAVEN AIRCRAFT

O-1 (Cessna L-19) Bird Dog

The O-1 (Cessna L-19) Bird Dog, was a small, light observation plane that was armed with only white phosphorous (Willy Pete) marking rockets. It was a short takeoff and landing (STOL) aircraft, easy plane to fly, and a tail dragger. The O-1 had a two person, in-line seating configuration, and a cruising speed of about 100 MPH and maximum speed of 115 MPH. Based on load configuration, the Bird Dog's mission could last for more than four hours. The only armor carried by the O-1 was a quarter inch below the pilot's seat. With plexiglass panels above the pilot's head, it had the best visibility of the three Raven aircraft. While the O-1 instrumentation permitted nighttime flying, typically, Ravens did not fly night missions. There were no U.S. markings on the Bird Dog.

U-17B

The U-17B was the military version of the Cessna 185 Skywagon. It was a heavier and faster version of the O-1 and could loiter for up to seven hours. Its' one downside was the tandem seating arrangement, which limited the FAC/pilot's right-hand view if a passenger was aboard. Like the O-1, it carried only marking rockets too.

T-28 (Trojan)

Some of the "lucky" pilots flew a T-28 (Trojan), a single engine plane that had been an Air Force and Navy training aircraft. Ravens flew the T-28 as a FAC platform, but it could be configured with more than just marking rockets. The plane's low wings tended to obstruct the FAC/pilot's ground visibility. Air America pilots flew the T-28 for strike missions, and for a small plane, carried a remarkably large payload. Among the T-28's arsenal was napalm, conventional bombs, rockets, and 50 caliber machine guns.

The Project 404 portion of Palace Dog was a program that recruited flight line crew technicians who maintained and serviced Raven aircraft as well as the aircraft flown by the RLG Air Force. Additionally, Project 404 personnel trained Laotians to service and maintain RLG aircraft. Like Raven pilots, whom they supported, Project 404 personnel were also sheep-dipped, wore civilian clothing, and lived in northern Laos at General Vang Pao's Headquarters in Long Tieng. They numbered approximately 100.

RAVEN 41

The ABCCC radio operators had their own shack on the flight line, and they possessed tens of thousands of hours of radio transmissions between ABCCC and pilots. They were great in capturing the tense moments during airstrike operations and SARs. Knowing my interest in learning all I could regarding the air war, Alleycat radio operators kept me supplied with recordings of what they thought were the more fascinating moments of the air war.

Raven 41 had completed his tour as a Raven pilot. He had flown his last combat mission the previous day and had just taken off from Long Tieng to begin his long journey home. He was flying to Udorn where he would hop on the Klong Hopper and make other connections that would eventually take him home.

Not more than ten minutes after taking off, his aircraft was hit by enemy AAA that shattered his canopy. He was struck by flying debris that caused serious bleeding in his arm. In colorful language, he is heard on Guard (radio frequency for emergencies) calling out his emergency. Immediately, King 1 is heard responding to the emergency, inquiring about his injury and the nature of the damage to the plane.

You can hear Raven 41 speculating about the weapon that struck his aircraft. He thought it might have been a 14.5 mm gun but acknowledged it might have been a 23 mm gun that struck his aircraft. As the pilot scrambled for something he might have used as a tourniquet, other Ravens can be heard expressing concern for their "brother" and offering their assistance.

Two Sandies (A1-E), that had been diverted by King 01, arrived on the scene and escorted Raven 41 back to Long Tieng. I have no knowledge of the fate of Raven 41, but I assume his quick return to safety and medical attention contributed to his survival.

§

The Air America operation was much larger than that of the Ravens, and conducted operations in both north and south Laos. It employed approximately 300 pilots, co-pilots, flight mechanics, and air freight specialists. Depending on their specific mission, aircrews were stationed at Long Tieng, Sam Thong, Vientiane, and Udorn Royal Thai Air Base. In total, Air America had more than 40 aircraft in its inventory and employed over 1,600 people to conduct its operations in Laos. Many Air America pilots had been long-time employees of the CIA, attracted, no doubt, by the high pay and adventure. When in Vientiane, Raven and Air America pilots stayed at the storied Constellation

Hotel, which was under contract to the CIA. In addition to providing air mobility, Air America also transported a countless number of Hmong family members, as well as their livestock. As General Vang Pao's *L'Armee Clandestine* increased its numbers, Air America grew as well.

At the northeast end of the main runway at Udorn Royal Thai Air Base, there was a nondescript compound that had no identifiable markings. Officially, the compound was designated as the 4802nd Liaison Detachment. It was the CIA's command center for operations in Laos. Nearby, adjacent to a taxiway, was the Air America parking ramp and maintenance shed, where many of its assorted aircraft were maintained and secured.

AIR AMERICA AIRCRAFT

In order to access and support the remote Lima Sites, Air America had acquired a diverse fleet of aircraft, almost all of which had a short takeoff and landing (STOL) capability as well as the ability to operate on unimproved runway surfaces. The primary STOL inventory included the Cessna O-1 (Bird Dog), the Pilatus Porter, C-7 (Carribou), Helio Courier, DHC6 Twin Otter, and Aero Commander. These were relatively small aircraft, however several of the planes had the capacity to carry up to 20 troops.

Pilatus Porter

The Pilatus Porter is a distinctive looking aircraft that was built in Switzerland for use in the Alps. It has a reversible turboprop, permitting it to land in as little as 300 feet. It is a high-wing plane with large tires and a steerable tail wheel. Its cruising speed is over 100 MPH and possesses a flight time duration of more than three hours. It was designed to carry eight or nine passengers, but oftentimes, as many as 12 Hmong crowded into the plane. Supplies were dropped from side cargo doors as well as through a floor hatch. Since the Pilatus Porter had been designed as a civilian aircraft, it did not have rocket rails for which the plane had to be ret-rofitted. Initially, Ravens had to manually throw smoke grenades out of the plane to mark targets.

Helio Courier

The military version of the Helio Courier accommodates four passengers in a side-by-side configuration and can easily land and take off on unimproved airstrips. It was a versatile aircraft and fulfilled a variety of roles. The Helio Courier was used for liaison, light cargo, supply drops, psychological operations, reconnaissance, and FAC roles. It had a cruising speed of 160 MPH and an incredible range of over 1,000 miles. The Helio Courier's biggest shortcoming was that its wings could not be configured with rocket rails.

Aero Commander

The Aero Commander was a twin-piston engine plane with retractable landing gear. It could be configured to carry up to 10 passengers, however when transporting Hmong troops, more than 15 squeezed into the plane. It had a cruising speed of over 200 MPH and was used for liaison and light cargo purposes.

Twin Otter

The Twin Otter was manufactured by de Havilland Canada, and the STOL aircraft replaced the Aero Commander. It is a twin piston engine mounted on a high wing. The Twin Otter was a workhorse making nighttime supply drops of food and ammunition to Road Watch Teams (RWT), transporting troops and parachuting commandos, and delivering cargo. The plane accommodated up to 19 passengers. To improve its night mission capability, the CIA installed a ground avoidance radar system in the Twin Otter. In one of the most extraordinary "bombing" missions that occurred during the air war in Laos, a Twin Otter attacked an NVA target in Steel Tiger by delivering two 55-gallon drums of aviation gas with thermite grenades attached. The kicker pulled the grenade pins and pushed the "bombs" out of the cargo bay.

C-7 Caribou

Another plane designed and manufactured by de Havilland Canada that figured prominently in Air America operations was the C-7 Caribou. Like the Otter, the Caribou was a STOL aircraft however on a much larger scale. The C-7 was capable of carrying more than 30 soldiers or two light vehicles and featured a rear loading ramp for parachute operations. Originally, the U.S. Army purchased 159 of the aircraft, but they were transferred to the Air Force in an agreement in which the Army relinquished fixed wing aircraft in exchange for an end to restrictions to the Army's varied helicopter operations. The Caribou was used by Air American for tactical airlift to resupply troops and evacuate casualties.

Multi-engine Planes

For the transportation of larger numbers of troops, equipment, and supplies, Air America had a fleet of larger multi-engine planes. Among those aircraft were the C-119 (Flying Boxcar), C-123 (Provider), C-46 (Commando), and C-47 (Skytrain). Towards the end of the war in Laos, Air American acquired C-130s. Helicopters were the workhorse of the war in Vietnam, as they were in Laos, playing a vital role in the insertion and evacuation of troops in the field. In the Air America inventory were two older helicopters manufactured by Sikorsky, the S-58T and S-55. Two Bell manufactured helicopters were also used extensively, the Korean War vintage UH-34 and the iconic UH-1, Huey. This collection of aircraft was used for air mobility, to re-supply troops with food, weapons, and ammunition, and to provide medical evacuation.

— 9 —

LIMA SITES
AND THE LANDSCAPE

In the early 1960s, the CIA established a headquarters for General Vang Pao and his forces in Long Tieng, a valley located at an elevation of 3,100 feet. At the time, the area was sparsely populated, but by 1964, the CIA had established a sprawling air base and constructed a 4,200-foot hard-surface runway. One of the valley's distinguishing features was a noticeable dip at its center. The air base was surrounded by mountains on three sides, and one of those imposing mountaintops loomed menacingly over the west end of the runway. This landmark was known as Skyline Ridge, and its presence challenged pilots' skills on every take-off and landing. Family members of the Hmong soldiers moved to Long Tieng, and the population of the CIA's "secret city" swelled to over 40,000, making it the second-largest city in Laos. Within a few years, Long Tieng grew into one of the largest and busiest US installations on foreign soil. During the height of the air war in Barrel Roll, Long Tieng controlled more than 400 flights every day.

In Barrel Roll, General Vang Pao's army units staged out of a network of short, primitive landing sites, called Lima (for landing) Sites. Each Lima Site was assigned a numerical designation, which followed the letters LS. Instead of using the name of the town or area in which the site was located, the alpha/numeric identifier was used. For example, LS-85, LS-108, etc. Lima Sites had been dug out of the tops and sides of mountains as well as hidden away in isolated valleys. With some exceptions, Lima Sites were located in remote areas. Almost all of the runways were dirt and unimproved, had dips and bends, and were extremely short, factors which made landing at these forward bases extremely challenging for the fixed-winged aircraft flown by Air America and Ravens. In total, there were more than 400 Lima Sites in Laos, but anti-Communist forces used less than 100 of those bases from which they regularly conducted operations or occupied as forward staging bases. A few of those landing sites had been constructed by the Japanese during its occupation of Indochina during WW II. Others were built by the French during the First Indochina War, and at the outset of the Second Indochina War, the United States constructed others.

Long Tieng had two Lima Site designations. Officially, it was LS-98, but it was more commonly referred to as LS-20A (Alternate). Most times, however, Long Tieng was simply referred to as 20 Alternate. About ten miles north of Long Tieng, on the other side of a mountain, was the second most important CIA base in Barrel Roll. It was Sam Thong, and its designation was LS-20. Sam Thong was a smaller version of 20 Alternate and served more of an administrative role for Barrel Roll operations, whereas Long Tieng was the location from which military operations emanated. LS-20 was a favorite overnight stop for Air America pilots because its "chalet," which could accommodate up to 28 pilots, had comfortable beds, provided hot showers, and served hot meals. A training facility was also located at LS-20 at which future Road Watch Team members were trained.

Forward Air Guides (FAG) staged out of Long Tieng, and between deployments, they and members of their families lived at the base. Ravens also staged out of 20 Alternate as well as Sam Thong, and for varying lengths of time, they remained in the field at Lima Sites. When they had well-deserved downtime, CIA personnel would stay at Vientiane or Udorn.

§

THE LANDSCAPE

One of the unique characteristics of the geology and geography of Laos is the dominating presence of Karst mountains, isolated ridges, and sloping hills, all of which are composed of limestone. Thousands of caves were formed when the karst upheavals were created millennia ago. In both the First and Second Indochina Wars, our opposition made extensive use of the various cave complexes throughout the country, utilizing them to serve as living quarters, hospitals, anti-aircraft sites, rest areas, and temples. The obvious advantage of the caves was the protection they afforded from air strikes. In light of the tactical importance of cave complexes, they were continually being targeted during the Second Indochina War.[*]

During the war, we knew of the tactical importance of the caves but failed to consider the caves were also used by the civilian population as refuge from American air power.

The caves at Vieng Xai presented a unique challenge. The complex, without question, was the most important cave system targeted by the United States and Laos. We knew the caves at Vieng Xai were being used by the NVA and PL as the headquarters for the Communist Pathet Lao. However, the complex was located in a series of narrow valleys amongst the limestone mountains of Houa Phan Province. Despite the dangerous target environment, Vieng Xai was targeted repeatedly for air strikes because of its strategic importance. The cave complex is located on Rt. 6, approximately 30 miles to the east of Sam Neua. These caves would become an important part of my transformative journey in later years.

§

The NVA knew its success in the war hinged on its ability to maintain a logistics supply line from North Vietnam to South Vietnam, a distance of more than 1200 miles. Col. Vo Bam was assigned the task of "organizing a special communication line to send supplies to the revolution in the South." Officially, it was called the Truong Son Strategic Supply Route, the name coming from one of the mountain ranges through which it passed. The trail was also referred to as Highway 559, which memorialized the month and year the North Vietnamese authorized Resolution 15, in which North Vietnam became committed to supporting the Viet Cong movement in South Vietnam. To Americans, Highway 559 was referred to as the Ho Chi Minh Trail.

---

[*]. Some of the most frequently targeted caves, but by no means the only ones, were Tham Piu near Muang Kham; Pathok Caves at Nong Khiaw; Pak Ou just north of Luang Prabang; Phou Khout west of Moung Soui; and the massive Vieng Xai cave complex east of Sam Neua.

The soldiers who marched along the Trail were referred to as bo dois, and they had to be resourceful and tireless. The trip was fraught with danger. In addition to the continual air strikes, some got lost while others were killed by tigers and bears. Even before the United States started bombing the Trail in 1964, cemeteries were appearing at the stations along the way. Numerous camps were located along the Trail that were operated by units called Binh trams. Binh trams supplied porters, security forces, engineers, laborers, and air defense troops. While some of those people were regular NVA troops, most of them were peasants drafted into service, farmers from coastal areas, and thousands of women who volunteered to serve their country's call. To escape the relentless interdiction of the Trail, most of the binh trams members lived underground. Some of those men and women lived and worked on the Trail for over a decade.

At the outset, Col. Vo Bam managed to transport only a few tons of supplies and war materiel down the trail on bicycles, pack animals, or the backs of porters. Within a decade, however, a network of 12,000 miles of roads, rivers, and high-speed trails was operating throughout Laos, beginning at Mu Gia Pass and crossing into South Vietnam at the A Shau Valley in the Central Highlands. An extension of the trail system went through Cambodia and channeled troops and supplies into Tay Ninh Province just northwest of Saigon. All major routes along the Trail had at least two bypasses so trucks could detour roads and trails that had been interdicted. Large portions of the trail system were hidden under a triple canopy of vegetation, and where naturally thick vegetation didn't conceal it, the North Vietnamese engineers and support personnel constructed elaborate bamboo trellises to hide the trail. While the North Vietnamese successfully transported tanks down the trail system, the primary vehicles in use were trucks. Intelligence estimates put the truck inventory in Laos at between three to five thousand. The process of moving supplies and war materiel down the trail was labor-intensive, requiring numerous transfers of cargo in and out of camouflaged storage caches along the network. We referred to those transfer stations as truck parks, and locating truck parks was a priority. Virtually all movements along Highway 559 occurred at night in a series of short shuttles from one truck park to the next. Typically, trucks began moving shortly after dusk, and traffic continued until approximately 0500.

— 10 —

ABCCC DUTY CYCLES

At full staffing, each of the four ABCCC orbits (i.e. Alleycat, Cricket, Moonbeam, and Hillsboro) were authorized to have three sets of battle staff personnel, which would facilitate a standard three-day duty cycle. Ideally, the Intelligence component would be comprised of three enlisted personnel and three junior officers for each orbit. An airman and officer would be paired and work ground duty and flights together on a three-day rotation. The reality, however, was quite different. We were always short-staffed; deployments ended at different times, replacement personnel did not always arrive to coincide with departures, personnel were granted one week R & R (Rest and Recuperation) leaves, and illness placed some personnel on Duty Not Included Flying (DNIF) status. When fully staffed, orbits worked a three-day cycle.

BATTLE STAFF

A Battle Staff capsule consisted of three radio/teletype operators, a mission commander (DABS - Director of the Air Battle Staff), assistant commander (BSOO -Battle Staff Operations Officer), four controllers (two officers and two enlisted men), and two intelligence personnel (one officer and one enlisted technician). The DABS and BSOO positions were filled with officers who had been fighter pilots in Vietnam. Most of them were finishing their year-long tours after having experienced a shoot down, in which case they were given their choice of returning to the cockpit or opting for another combat assignment. Some were extending their tours and chose ABCCC, while others, due to injury, were not cleared to return to the cockpit. Their practical experience as fighter pilots was invaluable since they understood the needs of the pilots and capabilities of the various aircraft with which we worked. The DABS position was filled by Lieutenant Colonels, and Majors, and senior Captains were assigned to the BSOO role.

§

On Day 1 of the three-day duty cycle, members of the battle staff reported to the orbit shack to perform ground duties. The Intelligence officer and technician were responsible for preparing and delivering the Intelligence briefing for that evening's flight. They assisted the Controllers to "break out" the FRAG. Officially named the Daily Fragmentary Operations Orders, which was generated by Headquarters 7th/13th Air Force, our command authority, it listed all planned targets, assigned flights, ordnance load, time on target, call sign, and any special packages that had been scheduled for our AO.* It was our responsibility to be knowledgeable about each target and post them on the plot board once the aircraft was boarded.

§

The call sign for Headquarters 7th/13th Air Force was Blue Chip, and during my year with ABCCC, we exchanged radio calls daily. Headquarters 7th/13th Air Force was located at Ton Son Nhut Air Base in Saigon, South Vietnam. As its name indicates, the 7th/13th was a combined command of two of the numbered Air Forces from the Pacific Air Force (PACAF).

Blue Chip did a great job of supporting our mission by disseminating intelligence and targeting materials (annotated photography) and did so in a prompt and efficient manner. During a typical mission, I spoke with Blue Chip, perhaps a half dozen times. We spoke so frequently that we began to recognize each other's voices. However, since our radio transmissions were in the clear, we had to maintain radio discipline and limit our "small talk."

Once control of Barrel Roll had been transferred to Cricket, it was the

---

*.   Special packages were classified operations that will be expanded upon later.

Intelligence Officer's responsibility to prepare the after-action report. The Intelligence Specialist and I collected mission summaries from the controllers, and along with the notes we had maintained during the mission, I prepared the report. A portable typewriter was used to prepare the report during our return flight to Udorn—there were no word processors or computers in those days. Mission reports summarized the targets that had been struck and resulting BDA, unusual activity or events that had occurred, and the status of FAGs and RWTs. Once completed, the report was given to the DABs for his approval and signature. Our radio technicians teletyped the report to Blue Chip. Most times, this process was completed prior to our return to Udorn. On those evenings when significant events occurred on the ground, that information was shared with Blue Chip in real-time via a secure radio link and updates were provided as they took place.

Blue Chip, Blue Chip, This is Alleycat

Almost 40 years after my deployment to Southeast Asia, I was living in the Pacific Northwest and joined a VFW Post in Edmonds, WA. One of the members of the Post, Don, and I started a conversation about our service during the Second Indochina War. Like me, he was Air Force and our tours had overlapped. In what was a remarkable coincidence, he served as Blue Chip Intel, worked nights, and he and I had engaged in radio transmissions on numerous occasions.

In the event the need arose to support friendly forces on the ground or attack targets of opportunity that had been identified, Intel needed to know the type of assets available in order to make informed recommendations to the DABS. During the pre-flight briefing, the Intel officer was responsible for providing an overview regarding the assigned targets, special operations taking place, recent operations in Barrel Roll, high priority threat locations and assessments, locations of road watch teams, recent shoot downs, and any on-going SAR operations. Once the briefing for that day's mission was delivered and the aircraft was safely in the air, the responsibilities of the ground crew were completed. Safes were locked, the building secured, and personnel were off for dinner and an evening of fun in town.

On Day 2 of the three-day cycle, members of the battle staff were assigned to fly. Personnel were required to report no later than 1400 hours, which meant an opportunity for sleeping-in. After lunch, at either a restaurant in town or the Officer's Club, those scheduled to fly reported to the shack to participate in the planning for that evening's mission and to attend the pre-flight briefing. Usually, the briefings lasted about an hour, after which the Intel personnel reviewed recent intelligence reports and on-going operations in Steel Tiger. It was important to be prepared to assume responsibility for Steel Tiger in the event Moonbeam experienced mechanical problems and needed to return to base. At approximately 1600 hours, one hour prior to take-off, Alleycat Intel gathered up the materials needed for that evening's mission and made their way to the BEMO shack to pick up survival gear. In addition to a survival vest, each crewman signed for a pistol and blood chit, and tested the operation of the survival radio. Once personal equipment was inspected and secured, members of the battle staff were driven to the flight line in one of Alleycat's step-vans.

Day 3 of the three-day duty cycle was a day of rest. After breakfast at either the Officer's or Enlisted Club, crewmen returned to their bungalows in town for some much-needed sleep. Battle staff members who had flown the previous evening had no official duties for the remainder of the day. The three-day cycle would then be repeated.

However, the reality was such that the squadron was always short of personnel. In those instances, which accounted for more than half of my deployment, we worked a two-day cycle, which meant flying every other day. Under those circumstances, on days you were scheduled to fly, Intel staff were required to report to the orbit no later than 1200 hours. With but two hours, we had to perform the normal ground duties that an Intel officer and technician would be required to perform in a normal eight-hour workday. Since that was an impossible challenge to complete in a professional manner, and the lives of so many depended on a Command Post fully prepared to provide the support operations properly, I made it a point to arrive by 0900 hours on those days I was scheduled for a two-day cycle. The extra time was needed to properly prepare for the pre-flight briefing and that evening's flight. The warriors on the ground in Barrel Roll deserved our best effort.

Upon returning from a mission the following morning, we had the rest of the day off. The cycle was repeated every two days. The two-day cycle was tiring, however the pace kept me fully engaged with the Squadron's mission and more closely connected with our comrades on the ground. I absolutely loved my job, looked forward to each flight, and never objected when I had to work two-day cycles, which proved to be not quite half of my year-long deployment.

— 11 —
ATTENTION TO DETAIL

O n the day of my first mission, as I was preparing for the flight, a familiar feeling from my days of athletic competition took hold of me. Only now it wasn't a matter of winning or losing an athletic contest, it was a matter of "competing" in a combat environment. I didn't know it at the time, and it would take me years to realize it, but my life was about to change forever.

As I always did on game days, I paid close attention to the details of preparing for the mission, checking and re-checking equipment, ensuring all was in order. It was a routine I followed prior to each of my 116 missions. The flight suits we wore were sanitized; there were no unit patches, name tags, or rank insignia. This was done so that in the event of a shootdown, our captors wouldn't be provided with information regarding our unit and mission. I also checked to ensure the personal survival knife I carried was securely attached, with parachute cord, to the small pocket along the inside of the right thigh. The dog tags I wore were covered in a plastic case, which would reduce the sound of the metal tags in the event we were forced to evade capture. I made sure I had extra pens in the pocket on the left shoulder pocket of my flight suit and that the plastic case containing ear plugs was secured to the zipper. Despite the fact that temperatures at Udorn were usually in the 90's, I always carried a flight jacket. I did that because there were times when the on-board air conditioning worked too well, and it was uncomfortably cool in the capsule. Another of the life lessons I learned from my year in Southeast Asia was the importance of attention to detail.

Mixed in with the familiar feelings of excitement and exhilaration, there were new feelings of anxiety and fear. The "competition" in which I was about to be engaged, was not a game. The thought was not lost on me that for the first time in my life I was about to enter the world of "life and death." I was preparing to enter the world of combat, and while I did not know exactly what to expect, I was satisfied I had done my best to prepare for my first flight.

I arrived at the Alleycat shack at mid-morning, several hours earlier than expected. I wanted to be sure I was prepared for my first flight. Truth be told, my anxiety was running rampant, and I was impatient for my childhood dream to become a reality. Finally, the day had arrived. I reviewed the mission report from the previous evening's flight making note of any unusual activity that had occurred. I also wanted to be sure I knew the current locations of the FAGs who would be active that night. After checking the frag to review the missions scheduled for Barrel Roll, I read the message traffic from Blue Chip. Even though the duty officer had already accomplished the task, I checked the Intel bags to ensure they contained all the resources we were expected to carry and might need, always checking and re-checking. It was as if I was a child again, having great difficulty waiting to open presents on Christmas morning. I left the air conditioning of the shack and walked to the Day Room to check for mail. As usual, a ping pong game was underway. You could always tell who had been on isolated tours because they were highly skilled and played with intensity. A letter from Mom was usually waiting for me. During my year in Southeast Asia, a great source of strength was from my mother's daily letters. I knew she was praying mightily for my safe return home.

LAOS CALLING

During my year in SEA, thanks to our terrific radio operators, I spoke with my parents once. It was in the fall of 1969, and my parents had just retired and were making plans to move to their childhood town of Wellsboro, Pennsylvania. I was surprised to learn that some members of the squadron were making "calls" to family members back home, a process about which I knew nothing. One of our radio operators tried to explain the process to me and wanted to know if I would like to place a call.

Our radio operators would broadcast a radio call, and if the atmospheric conditions were favorable, the radio signal would "bounce" off layers of the atmosphere and be received by a ham radio operator somewhere in the United States. Contact information (i.e. name and phone numbers) for the family were broadcast to the ham operator who then, at their own expense, placed a telephone call to the family. Once a connection was made, the ham operator served as a relay, repeating the message from overseas radio transmission to the family in the States and then reversing the process for the reply. The conversations, of course, were broadcast in the clear and anyone monitoring the frequency could hear what was said.

To this day, I feel those ham radio operators deserve special recognition and our sincerest thanks for connecting our active-duty personnel with family members back home. They don't receive the recognition they deserve. Unlike today, there were no cell phones or Internet/WIFI to connect with loved ones.

I have few regrets in life, but I do wish that during that phone call I had asked my Mom that as she was preparing a moving sale to save my baseball card collection.

When Jim arrived, we retrieved a couple of cold drinks from the refrigerator and sat down to review the procedures we would follow once we boarded the aircraft. As we talked, one of our radio operators stopped by to take our box lunch order. Jim quizzed me on the radio frequencies we would be using to contact the FAGs (i.e. VFH 121.1 and 123.5) and the names and locations of those who would be active that evening. He quizzed me on the ROE, asking me to recite things like the stand-off distances for NBLs in the PDJ. I responded to each of his questions confidently and correctly. I was prepared.

During the pre-mission briefing, I did my best to appear attentive. However, I was nervous. For sure, it was a concern about the unknown, but lingering beneath my conscious thought was an element of fear. Fear about flying over areas controlled by enemy forces; fear about being shot down; fear about being captured; and fear of dying. Like many, I repressed those thoughts and, instead, exhibited a casual disregard for and denial of the risks we assumed, but fear was always just below my conscious thought. In fact, I never expected to survive the war.

As soon as we left the shack, events sped up. Everything moved quickly, and the feeling of being overwhelmed began to take hold. We stopped at the BEMO shack, and Jim led me through the pre-mission routine. He handed me a survival vest that I donned and zipped up. Next, we were given survival radios, and Jim demonstrated how we tested it for proper functioning. Signatures were required for a pistol and blood chit as well as the serial numbers of each.

A blood chit was written in 13 languages and identified the downed airman as an American who needed assistance. Every Air Force rescue helicopter carried a quantity of gold on board, used to reward indigenous people who provided assistance to downed aircrewmen.

Once outfitted with our gear, we boarded a van for the five-minute drive to the flight line. As we passed the north end of the runway, Jim pointed out some interesting artifacts from the Japanese occupation of Udorn RTAB during WW II. The Japanese used the air base at Udorn from which to fly combat missions, attacking allied targets in China, Burma, and Vietnam. Several wooden aircraft hangars, built by the Japanese, were still standing, although no longer in use. The hangar doors stood wide open. Further along the runway perimeter, there was a control tower, also built by the Japanese. It was painted green, surrounded by sandbags at its base. It was no longer in use for the purpose for which it was intended. Instead, the old control tower was being used by Thai and Air Force Air Police as an observation post of the northern perimeter of the base, a look-out for enemy infiltrators. During my year of duty at Udorn, the perimeter fence was breached on several occasions.

In what had to be one of those ironic occurrences that occur in warfare and life, a member of our squadron and a good friend, Lt. Col. Paul (Shorty) Hartz, was stationed in Hanoi during WW II and took off from Hanoi to bomb the Japanese at Udorn. Almost thirty years later, Lt. Col. Hartz was now taking off from Udorn to control missions that were striking targets in and around Hanoi. Prior to his arrival at ABCCC, he flew bombing missions over Hanoi while flying F-105s out of Tahkli Royal Thai Air Base.

We arrived at the flight line, passing the Air America, Pony Express, and Super Jolly Greens parking ramps as we drove down the taxiway. I was usually standing up, looking out the front windshield, not wanting to miss anything. I never tired of the excitement of the activity on the flight line, noise of aircraft operations, and the distinctive odor of jet fuel and aircraft exhaust. When performing ground duty, I took advantage of every opportunity to visit the flight line and coordinate operations with other units, participate in training flights with Pony Express, or assist with the burning of classified material.

ABCCC aircraft were kept in revetments, where the grounding crew performed aircraft maintenance. The squadron did have a maintenance shack, but it was too small to accommodate a C-130. Each aircraft was surrounded by six-foot-high steel blast walls on three sides, which protected the aircraft within the revetment as well as surrounding aircraft. Upon our arrival, two C-130s, one for Alleycat and one for Moonbeam, had been moved out of the revetment area and onto the apron. Members of the ground crew were the unsung heroes of ABCCC. They worked long hours, night and day, to maintain the aircraft, always working under ever-present deadlines. Since the aircraft sat under a blazing sun all day, the inside temperature of the command capsule was well over 100 degrees. To make the environment in which we would be working a bit more comfortable, the ground crew ran a large hose from a portable air conditioning unit into the capsule. It helped a lot, however, once airborne, it took the aircraft about 15 minutes to become fully pressurized to create a comfortable environment. On many nights the flight jacket I carried was put to good use.

Members of the flight crew, who had departed the shack earlier, had already completed their pre-flight inspection of the plane. The radio operators had arrived early, after picking up box lunches for the crew and battle staff. By the time the battle staff arrived, the radio operators had already performed radio checks. Once we were fully loaded, the paratroop door was secured, and the flight deck crew began engine startup. Members of the ground crew stood by with huge fire extinguishers as each of the four engines was started.

C-130 (HERCULES)

The aircraft in which we flew were C-130's (Hercules), which had been modified with long-range fuel tanks, a multitude of radio antennas, and to accommodate the command capsule. A vast array of radios, teletypes, and encryption devices were located at the front of the capsule, just behind the flight deck. The plotting boards were displayed on the left side of the capsule, and along the right-side wall were 8 stations at which the battle staff sat and worked. Each station had access to UHF, VHF, and FM radios, and the radio operators could dial in any radio frequency we needed to accomplish our mission. At any one time, we had access to over a dozen different radio frequencies, which we constantly monitored. At the rear of the capsule there was a bunk, latrine, several seats for VIP's and guests, and a kitchen area (refrigerator, coffee pot, hot plate, and juice dispensers). The squadron had seven aircraft, four of which were flying every day, and two which served as spares. A seventh aircraft was rotated to Ching Chuan Kang (CCK) Air Base in Taiwan for comprehensive maintenance. The squadron also had a maintenance staff, members of which maintained the planes and were present on the flight line to facilitate takeoffs and landings. These men, a majority of whom were young Airmen, were highly dedicated and worked long hours to properly maintain the aircraft that were continually being stressed due to an overwhelming workload. Their "reward" was a monthly flight so they could qualify for flight pay.

The C-130 was introduced into the Air Force inventory in the mid-1950s. As of the early 2020s, the aircraft was still being manufactured by Lockheed. The plane was primarily used as a transport, but, over the years, it has been modified to fulfill a variety of roles. It has four turbo-prop engines mounted on high wings and has been designed to operate from short, rough, dirt airstrips. It has proven to have been one of the most versatile and dependable airplanes in the Air Force inventory, and it is widely exported to countries around the world. During the Vietnam War, C-130's were used to perform roles as gunships, flare ships, special operations, refueling, and command and control. Without a doubt, the C-130 is the most versatile aircraft in the Air Force inventory and is projected to continue in those roles for decades to come.

— 12 —
UNPREPARED FOR UNCONVENTIONAL WARFARE

As I continued to read more about the Second Indochina War, it became painfully apparent that the United States was woefully unprepared for unconventional warfare. During the intervening years between the Korean War and the Second Indochina War, the Air Force had evolved into a strategic deterrent force with an emphasis on "higher and faster." Other than its bomber force, most of the "fighter" aircraft in the Air Force inventory were designed for either high-altitude long-range interception missions or the delivery of strategic and tactical nuclear weapons, and those platforms were totally inadequate for close air support.

The Air Force lacked a precision bombing capability and did not have an aircraft in its inventory designed specifically for close air support, nor did we have an aircraft specifically designed for air-to-air combat. Among the obsolete aircraft that were pressed into service was the single engine Cessna aircraft that assumed the role of Forward Air Controller (FAC). The RF-101 Voodoo, a plane introduced into the Air Force inventory in 1954 was our sole photo reconnaissance platform. Our two primary fighter aircraft, the F-102 Delta Dagger and the F-104 Starfighter were totally unsuited for close air support and interdiction missions. Both planes had been designed for the single purpose of intercepting Soviet Union TU-95 Bear long-range bombers before they could get close enough to US airspace to drop its nuclear weapons.

The F-100 Super Sabre was the only legitimate jet fighter bomber in Southeast Asia capable of flying both bombing and close air support missions. The "Hun" also flew MiG combat air patrol (MiG CAP) missions.

In 1964, the F-4 Phantom and F-105 Thunderchief arrived in Southeast Asia and immediately became the workhorses of the Air Force inventory. Though not designed to do so, the F-105 and F-4 flew and excelled in a variety of daylight and nighttime roles; bombing missions, close air support, combat air patrol (CAP), and air-to-air combat.

Military planners understood the futility of attempting to locate targets along the Ho Chi Minh Trail complex during nighttime hours, and Air Force planners came to the realization they needed low and slow platforms capable of lengthy loiter time with the ability to locate and strike enemy targets at night as well as during inclement weather. Recognizing its shortcomings, the Air Force embarked upon two important initiatives that, ultimately, defined the air war in Laos.

Having recognized its need for aircraft that could perform interdiction and close air support missions, the Air Force sought to revitalize its inventory by visiting the "Boneyard" at Davis Monthan Air Force Base near Tucson, Arizona. The base was home to the 309th Aerospace Maintenance and Regeneration Group (AMARG), a storage and preservation center for aircraft that had been retired from Air Force, Navy, Marine Corps, and Army inventories. As needs arose, planes were refurbished and returned to active duty.

Thanks to the forethought of military planners, the Air Force brought hundreds of planes out of retirement and created an inventory that addressed the challenges of unconventional warfare. Resulting was an Air Force that was a mix of old and new, fast and slow, and bomber and fighter. Planes retrieved from the Boneyard included the C-47, A1E, C-121, A-26, B-57, T-28, and B-66, each of which had its unique capabilities and specific roles. When combined with our highly skilled, motivated, and professional flight crews, the Air Force produced a lethal fighting force.

The Air Force's second initiative, called Operation Shed Light, sought to use technology to improve the performance of aircrews and aircraft. Operation Shed Light was tasked with the challenge of pursuing a variety of research projects, monitoring, testing, and evaluating those that were the most promising. Operation Shed Light focused on several critical needs, such as improving navigation aids, all-weather and night flying capabilities, and precision bombing. Battlefield illumination and the development of equipment that would permit aircrews to "see" through clouds, foliage, structures, and darkness were also goals of Shed Light. While not all of the projects proved successful, Operation Shed Light resulted in the implementation of many effective technological innovations, weapons platforms, and tactics that dramatically improved performance and defined the air war during the Second Indochina War.

Upgrades and improvements were made to Long Range (LORAN) and Tactical Air (TACAN) navigation systems. Additional navigation sites were established in Vietnam and Laos to provide full coverage of the areas over which American aircraft flew. Precision bombing was greatly improved with the introduction of Bomb Directing Central Radar, referred to simply as MSQ (Miscue). MSQ sites were established throughout Vietnam and Laos, and approximately 75% of all bombing missions in Southeast Asia utilized MSQ technology. Those missions, in which ground controllers used MSQ site data to determine the location, airspeed, and altitude of the strike aircraft, were called Combat Skyspot missions, and they proved effective during daylight missions, and for the first time, Combat Skyspot provided aircraft with an accurate nighttime and foul weather capability.

As a result of the Operation Shed Light research, improvements were made to night vision devices (NVD), and the technology was modified for use in aircraft, providing pilots, for the first-time, real-time imagery during nighttime operations. Pilots now had the ability to "see" through clouds, foliage, and structures. Along with other innovations, the era of the gunship was born, changing air warfare dramatically.

Shed Light research also provided a long-sought capability, battlefield illumination. A new generation of flare illumination was developed. Called the Briteye Flare, it burned at 5 million candlepower for over five minutes. It produced a signal indicating its burn was about to end, which prompted the release of another flare. Its descent was slowed by a parachute. That research produced a new generation of airborne battlefield platforms, the flareship.

Arguably, the single greatest contribution to air war resulting from Shed Light research was the revolution of precision weaponry. New technology was utilized to guide maneuverable bombs directly to the target. The technology was called Light Amplification by the Stimulated Emission of Radiation or LASER to the layperson. The concept consisted of two components. The first was a device that focused a beam of LASER energy on the intended target. The second component was a bomb equipped with an "eye" that could see the energized target and guide the ordnance to the illuminated target. That revolutionary technology introduced Pave Way munitions, or smart bombs, into the Air Force weapons inventory.

— 13 —

"Anything, Anywhere, Anytime, Professionally"
Motto of Air America

Even though the chapter title was the motto of Air America, the sentiment expressed in the slogan could well apply to all American aircrewmen who engaged in the air war during the Second Indochina War. Each branch of the American Armed Forces contributed to our efforts to deny the Communists from seizing control of South Vietnam, Laos, and Cambodia. The air war was a well-coordinated collaborative effort of hundreds of thousands of crewmen and support personnel who were fearless and dedicated to their mission.

In fulfilling my role as an Air Intelligence Officer, it was imperative that I fully understood the various air assets that were available to support the ground war. It was incumbent on me to know the call signs, weapons systems, tactics, and capabilities of each aircraft we controlled.

FORWARD AIR CONTROLLERS

Forward Air Controllers (FAC) played a significant role in the Second Indochina War, flying low and slow in light weight propeller drive aircraft. During the beginning years of the war, FACs flew the Cessna O-1 Bird Dog. It was a two-seater with several important limitations. It was slow, lacked instrumentation for night operations, had a limited payload (i.e. marking rockets), and had access to only one radio channel at a time.

The Cessna O-2 Skymaster was a modified Cessna 510 and intended as an interim FAC platform, replacing the O-1. It was faster than the O-1, modified to have four hard points for an increased rocket load, and had a seven hour loiter time. Like the O-1, it was a two-seater.

The OV-10 Bronco was the first American plane specifically designed to assume the FAC roles. It had a two-propeller design (puller-pusher) and flew at twice the speed of the O-1. The Bronco entered Air Force service on 6 July 1968 much to the approval of FAC pilots. The new plane provided pilots with excellent sight lines and avionics that included eight secure radios and an array of flight instruments. The OV-10's five ordnance hardened points made it a lethal combination of serving as FAC and providing close air support.

The FACs working in Barrel Roll and Steel Timer had call signs of either Nail or Covey. Usually, calls signs designated the base at which the aircraft were stationed. For example, Nails flew out of Nakon Phanom Royal Thai Air Base and Coveys were stationed at Da Nang, South Vietnam.

Flying in steep banked turns, FACs moved along LOCs performing visual reconnaissance in search of the enemy and targets of opportunity. Usually, FACs were assigned to the same AO and with a growing familiarity of the area, they became quite good at noticing the subtlest of changes in the jungle terrain below. The "tells" they identified, often times, uncovered troop concentrations, truck parks, trails, weapons caches, and underwater bridges.

In addition to flying visual reconnaissance missions, FACs were also fragged to control air strikes on designated targets. Once the assigned strike aircraft arrived on station and checked in with ABCCC, they were "handed off" to a FAC, already on station. The FAC briefed the pilots on the target, provided a threat assessment, marked the target with white phosphorous rockets, and then cleared the strike aircraft to attack the target. Depending on the strike aircraft's weapons load, the FAC might authorize multiple runs on the target. When the strike was completed, the FAC would make a bomb damage assessment (BDA) and report it to the strike aircraft. After checking out with their FAC, strike aircraft pilots reported BDA to ABCCC before receiving clearance to leave the area and RTB.

FAST FACS

As interdiction efforts along the trail complex continued to improve, the NVA responded by reinforcing its defenses with antiaircraft artillery (AAA) and surface to air missiles (SAM). As threat environments around important sections of the Ho Chi Minh Trail became more deadly, losses of slow moving FACs increased to the point of being unacceptable. Commando Sabre was the Air Force response and introduced the Fast FAC program. It was thought the increased speed of jet aircraft might improve the survivability of FACs along key passes from North Vietnam into Laos and the more heavily defended portions of the trail. The two-seater F-100F Super Sabre was selected to be the first fast FAC and was flown by all-volunteer crews of seasoned fighter pilots. The demanding mission required the full attention of the pilot since the fast-moving aircraft flew at low levels, flying tight steep banked turns, and constantly jinking (i.e. rapidly changing altitude and direction) to avoid ground fire. The mission became even more dangerous at night. The "guy in the back" (GIB), usually a navigator, was responsible for navigation and communicating, authorizing, and coordinating with assigned aircraft. The program was initiated in June 1967. Their call sign was Misty, and they flew out of either Phu Cat or Tuy Hoa in South Vietnam. Flying inverted, at times, the more than four-hour missions required multiple refuelings. Misty pilots performed visual reconnaissance, but since they also carried a weapons load, they were free to strike targets of opportunity they located.

COLONEL "BUD" DAY

Colonel "Bud" Day was the first Misty commander and was shot down early in the program's existence. He was held as a POW for the remainder of the war. The definitive story about the Misty program is documented in the book *Bury Us Upside Down*, written by Rick Newman. To learn about the brilliance of Colonel Day and how he shaped Air Force doctrine and future aircraft design, the reader is urged to read *American Patriot* by Robert Coram. During the last quarter of 1968, the Fast FAC program was introduced in Laos, and Misty's regularly flew missions in Steel Tiger and Barrel Roll. Misty's were legendary for two "truck massacres" they controlled in Laos, once in 1968 and a second time in 1970. As the casualty rate among

Misty pilots exceeded 25%, the F-100F was gradually phased out of Commando Sabre and replaced with the F-4 Phantom. The F-4 Fast FACs had several call signs; Wolf and Night Owl (Ubon RTAB), Gunsmoke and Manual (Da Nang), Laredo (Udorn RTAB), and Tiger (Korat RTAB).

WATER PUMP

Water Pump was created in 1964 when a 40-man detachment settled into its compound at Udorn. The operation continued until the truce of February 1973. Its first assignment was the training of Air America pilots who were transitioning to the T-28, a role in which it would continue to serve to include Raven pilots as well. Waterpump's primary mission was to train pilots for the Royal Laotian Air Force. The casualty rates for Laotian pilots was so high, that Waterpump struggled to train replacement pilots in sufficient numbers. In light of that shortage, Thai mercenaries were recruited for the pilot training program.

In March 1969, Waterpump's role was expanded to include the training of pilots and air crewmen for AC-47 gunships. At the time, the Air Force had a squadron of 16 C-47 gunships (call sign Spooky) stationed at Udorn. As Laotian gunship crews were trained, the United States transferred aircraft to the Royal Laotian Air Force.

About mid-way through my year at Udorn, 11 of the 16 Spooky aircraft were turned over to the Royal Laotian Air Force. The expectation was that Laotian aircrews would fly air support missions for ground operations in Barrel Roll and Steel Tiger. One of our great frustrations was that the RLAF pilots rarely answered their radios during evening hours. When that occurred, American aircrews responded to our calls for assistance. The continued reluctance of RLAF gunship crews to fly night missions led me to question their level of commitment to fight for and defend their own country. It was disheartening to witness, firsthand, the sacrifices made every day by highly motivated Air Force personnel who flew dangerous missions, worked long hours, and were fully committed to their respective missions. It was as if we cared more for their cause than some of the Laotians did. We talked about it amongst ourselves, and for the first time, I began to question the rectitude of our mission.

GUNSHIPS

Gunships served two vital roles in the air war in Laos: interdiction of troops, vehicles, and materiel along roads and trails and close air support for friendly forces engaged in contact with the enemy. A gunship was always the first request for air support by FAGs.

The year was 1964. Recognizing the need for a close air support platform, the Air Force embarked on an initiative called Project Gunship I. The result was the AC-47, a modified C-47, the military version of the C-3 passenger plane of the 40's and 50's. This first-generation gunship had the call sign, Spooky. Spooky carried three gatling-type mini-guns, which fired 7.62 mm rounds at the rate of 6,000 rounds per minute. Every fifth round was a red tracer that assisted with aiming the weapon. A full load of ammunition was 16,500 rounds, and the C-47 gunships could remain on station approximately 6-7 hours. The guns were installed in a fixed position, pointing out of the left paratroop door. While flying the aircraft in a tight banked left turn, the pilot aimed the guns by adjusting the aircraft's attitude. Firing from a pylon turn permitted the gunship to focus fire on a target for a much longer time than from a conventional strafing run. The guns were fired downward and actuated by a control on the pilot's yoke. The guns could be fired individually or all at once. Once a FAC or FAG identified/marked a target, several test rounds were fired to ensure the target had been accurately located. When battlefield illumination was required, crewmen could hand launch flares.

Within months of the initial work on Project Gunship 1, the first two AC-47s arrived at Bien Hoa Air Base in South Vietnam in December 1964. The initial call sign was Puff, and the newest strike aircraft in the Air Force inventory kept busy providing air support for several Special Forces outposts under attack by Viet Cong. In the space of 11 days, Puff flew 16 missions, each of which successfully broke off enemy engagements. Those initial gunship trials were so successful that the decision was made to convert additional C-47s into gunships. Eventually, two squadrons of AC-47 gunships, each consisting of 16 planes, were formed, one based at Nha Trang, South Vietnam and one at Udorn Royal Thai Air Base. The new call sign for the gunships was Spooky.

Udorn was selected because of its location to northeastern

Laos. The base was equidistant from Barrel Roll and Steel Tiger, which facilitated arrival on station in the shortest possible time.

While AC-47 gunships were flying air support and interdiction missions in South Vietnam and Laos, the Air Force was busy with Project Gunship II, converting the C-130 platform into a gunship. Using night vision and Forward Looking Infrared (FLIR) technology, the AC-130 was equipped with two 20 mm Vulcan cannons, one Bofors 40 mm cannon, and one 105 mm howitzer, all of which combined to produce a lethal and deadly accurate weapons system. With the call sign, Spectre, the new gunship arrived in Southeast Asia on 21 September 1967. The new platform greatly improved mission endurance, fire power, munitions load, and accuracy. Similar to the AC-47s, Spectre guns were fired by the pilot from a fixed position on the left side of the aircraft and carried flares for battlefield illumination. A squadron of AC-130s was assigned to Ubon Royal Thai Air Base, and those crewmen and aircraft continued to fly throughout the duration of the war. By mid-1969, Spectre aircraft had replaced AC-47s. Spectre aircraft were fragged for nightly missions in Barrel Roll and Steel Tiger and served a dual purpose. They performed armed reconnaissance missions along LOCs and served as a FAC for the strike aircraft assigned to them. Spectre gunships were also on stand-by alert at Ubon in the event they were needed for an emergency. However, in light of the nearly two hours it took to arrive in Barrel Roll, we usually looked for other options.

SUPER SPOOKY

One evening, I took a call from a FAG who reported TIC, and he requested a Spooky. The only available gunship was a Spectre, a C-130 gunship about which the FAG had no knowledge or previous experience. In my best pidgin' English, I told him, "We send you Super Spooky. You work with big Spooky, he help you. He big, big Spooky". Clearly, despite my best efforts to advise the FAG about the differences between a Spooky and Spectre gunship, my message was not being received or understood. Nevertheless, the FAG gladly accepted the gunship. As I often did, I listened in on the strike frequency as the Spectre pilot contacted the FAG and began the process of getting set up on the intended target. The FAG described the area in which the enemy was located and autho-rized the pilot to begin shooting. As gunship pilots always did before commencing to "hose down" an area, the pilot fired a single round after which he would be instructed how to adjust his aim. The FAG had never experienced an exploding 40 mm round before, which, evidently, got a little too close to the friendlies. The first round scared the hell out of the FAG. Immediately, he screamed, "Spooky go home, now", "Spooky no good." That was the first time a FAG had ever released a gunship before it had expended its full ammunition load. The pilot was just as amused by the incident as I was. For the remainder of the evening, the FAG's site was silent.

FLARESHIPS

Among the significant achievements of Operation Shed Light, was the newly developed capability to provide battlefield illumination through the conversion of transport platforms into flareships. The new technology proved to be a critical factor and dramatic improvement in the Air Force's ability to interdict the movement of vehicles along the trail complex at night. For the FAGs, RWTs, and SGU forces who operated at night, the air support provided by battlefield illumination became a life-saver. In light of the frequent TIC calls we received and requests for support, flareships were used extensively in Barrel Roll and Steel Tiger.

Two aircraft were converted for the sole purpose of dropping flares during nighttime operations. Candlestick was the call sign for C-123's (Provider), and they flew out of Nakon Pahnom (NKP) Royal Thai Air Force Base. C-130 flare ships were stationed at Ubon Royal Thai Air Force Base and answered to the call sign Blind Bat. One or more flareships were fragged to Barrel Roll every night and were on stand-by to respond to emergencies declared by ground forces. Flareships provided illumination around the perimeters of their positions, which limited the enemy's movement and made them vulnerable to sniping. When lucrative targets were located and reported to Alleycat Intel, flareships were assigned to provide battlefield illumination while strike aircraft engaged the targets.

Candlesticks could loiter for several hours and Blind Bats even longer. Usually, the supply of flares was exhausted before they reached bingo fuel, necessitating a return to base (RTB).

A SPECTACULAR LIGHT DISPLAY

It was not uncommon for us to have more than a half dozen gunships and flareships working targets in Barrel Roll at the same time during a single evening. Along with the regularly fragged strike aircraft, it all presented a spectacular light display. Several of the Alleycat pilots and I became friends, and if there was a particularly good "show" occurring, they invited me to the flight deck to enjoy a few minutes of the display. The flares were incredibly bright and lit up the sky in different portions of the PDJ as they drifted slowly to earth. The gunships fired what appeared to be little fingers of light interspersed by the red tracer rounds. On several occasions, I observed secondary explosions, indicating the gunships had struck an ammunition cache.

The success of North Vietnam's goal of seizing control of South Vietnam to "reunite" the country, was contingent upon its ability to maintain the continued flow of men and materiel through Laos. American military planners devised numerous tactics and weapons systems to interdict the flow of those men and supplies. One of the tactics was a concept called Armed Reconnaissance. Rather than attacking pre-designated targets, pilots were authorized to perform armed reconnaissance missions. Once they identified a target of opportunity in their designated AO, they were authorized to attack the target. The innovative tactic provided an immediate response to enemy activity, eliminating built-in time delays in attacking fragged targets (i.e. checking in with the FAC, target marking, and authorization).

Armed reconnaissance missions were fragged to Barrel Roll every evening and attacked enemy targets along the most used LOCs; Routes 6, 7, and 13 and the Nam Ou (River). Aircraft fragged for armed recce missions included gunships, slow movers (e.g. A-26, A-1E), and fast movers (e.g. F-4, F-100). Armed recce missions proved to be quite successful, and on occasion, when lucrative targets were identified, we diverted additional resources to the location and reported the target to Cricket the following morning, so the attack could continue.

— 14 —
ENEMY ORDER OF BATTLE

O ne of Intel's responsibilities was to prepare the daily pre-mission briefings, and one of the most important portions of the briefing was the assessment and identification of threat locations. In official military jargon, it is called Order of Battle and refers to the identification of enemy command structure, strength, and the disposition of units and weapon systems. Due to the dynamic nature of operations in Laos, the Order of Battle was continually being revised and altered. Intelligence analysts at Blue Chip, methodically interpreted reconnaissance photography and poured through after-action reports to maintain a comprehensive and as accurately as possible, precise listing of enemy threat locations. I then had to pore through the massive amount of information to identify new threat assessments in Barrel Roll and update our Order of Battle. My biggest fear was that a weapon system had been moved to a new location and was overlooked by the analysts, thus, placing aircraft and air crewmen at risk, including ourselves.

§

Surface to Air Missile (SAM) sites were high priority targets. The SA-2 (Guideline) missile was manufactured in the USRR and China, and both countries provided the weapon to North Vietnam. It was a radar guided system that could be deployed singly from a mobile launcher or from a fixed position. Fixed SAM sites were easy to identify in reconnaissance photography by its classic star-like formation, almost always in a group of six missiles mounted on launchers. Control and support vans were located nearby as well as two radar dishes. All facilities were connected by a maze of cables. Spoon Rest was a search radar that detected approaching aircraft from as far away as 70 miles. The Fan Song guidance radar system had two functions; it acquired the target and guided the missile to the aircraft. Several seconds or more were needed by the missile controllers to use the radar to first locate an aircraft and then illuminate the target (lock-on to the plane).

The dependence on radar to acquire and fire its missiles made SAM sites vulnerable to attack. To take advantage of this "weakness", aircraft were equipped with Radio Homing and Warning (RHAW) receivers that detected the electronic signals emitted by the Spoon Rest and Fan Song radar systems and alerted aircraft crewmen whenever a site was actively illuminating their aircraft. The RHAW equipment detected the various sequences of search, lock-on, and firing and a series of flashing warning lights and buzzing tones warned pilots (and/or Electronic Warfare Officers) who would then take evasive action. The NVA took counter-counter measures by using radar intermittently, using short bursts of energy to acquire, lock-on, and fire a missile. At times, the NVA just shut down the radar altogether to avoid an attack on their site.

The NVA were experts in the use of camouflage, and they constructed well-camouflaged SAM sites. A favorite tactic was moving its missiles and support equipment between established sites. However, SAM sites could not be permanently camouflaged since the radar needed clear "views" of targets and missiles could not be fired from under tree canopy. That made them somewhat vulnerable to visual and photo detection. SAM sites were almost always ringed with Anti-Aircraft Artillery (AAA) with overlapping fields of fire, making SAM sites a most dangerous and difficult target to attack.

When locations of SAM sites were established, either through intelligence sources, visual contact, or recce photographs, strike missions were fragged to attack those high priority targets. Wild Weasel was the term used by the Air Force to refer to those missions.

WILD WEASEL
In 1965, the Air Force developed a strategy to attack SAM

sites, tactics that remained in place into the 2000's. It was called Wild Weasel, and its objective was to render the SAM site useless by destroying its controlling radar. Once the site was shutdown, through the successful launching of an anti-radiation missile (ARM), the missiles, launchers, and support facilities could then be attacked without fear of missile attack, however the presence of AAA made such missions extremely dangerous.

Initially, the AGM-45 (Shrike) missile was used to attack SAM sites, since it was the only ARM in the military inventory. However, due to its small warhead, limited range, and poor guidance system, a new ARM was quickly developed and used for the first time in 1968. While Shrikes continued to be used against SAM sites, the AGM-78 (STARM), which featured a blast fragmentation warhead, was the preferred weapon of choice.

A Wild Weasel mission was a two aircraft mission (sometimes four) in which one plane trolled suspected SAM locations, serving as a decoy target, while its wingman did his best to hide from the search radar by flying below nearby ridge lines. The most renowned terrain masking feature used by not only Wild Weasel aircraft, but all aircraft assigned to strike targets in and around Hanoi, was a 5,000-foot-high ridge line located 15 miles northwest of Hanoi. Officially, it was called the Tam Dao Range. Pilots called it Thud Ridge, and its unique terrain feature served as a waypoint for ingressing aircraft. Eventually, the North Vietnamese installed AAA on the Thud Ridge.

Once a site came up and initiated a radar search and lock-on sequence, the wingman would pop-up and launch an ARM. As long as the radar remained illuminated, launches were usually successful.

After one year of experimenting with the F-100, the role of Wild Weasel was assigned to the F-105D Thunderchief. The Thud is a supersonic aircraft that was originally designed and built for one mission only, to deliver a single nuclear device while performing a pop-up maneuver.

Like SAMs, the Anti-Aircraft Artillery (AAA) used by the NVA and PL was also manufactured and distributed by China and

Russia. Instead of interdicting this hardware at the point of entry, along the border with China or in the port of Haiphong, the ROE precluded air strikes at the border crossings and North Vietnam's major port. Throughout the war, reconnaissance photography confirmed the presence of large military depots in North Vietnam, just inside its border with China. It was a major frustration for us all to see train cars loaded with hundreds of AAA guns and SAMs sitting in the open and knowing the ROE prevented the weapons from being attacked.

AAA weapons included the 12.7, 14.5, 23, 37, 57, 85 and 100 mm guns. The higher caliber guns were effective up to 50,000 feet. The 23, 57, 85 and 100 mm guns were controlled by radar control systems (the 23 and 37 mm guns were also optically aimed). The large caliber weapons were towed. The 85 and 100 mm guns, because of its' size, were usually deployed in or around larger cities in North Vietnam.

Since the trail system through Laos and Cambodia provided the lifeblood of personnel, food and materiel for the war in South Vietnam, the NVA made heroic efforts to protect the trails and truck parks in Barrel Roll and Steel Tiger. Somehow, the NVA and PL maneuvered heavy and bulky 23mm, 37mm, and 57 mm guns up the sides of hills, through dense vegetation, and used natural caves in the ubiquitous karst formations to shield and camouflage gun sites and create ambush locations. When necessary, guns were dismantled and carried, piece by piece, up steep mountain terrain. The NVA and PL were ingenious, industrious, tireless, and totally dedicated to their cause.

Since the SAM air defense system was most effective at higher elevations, its major influence was that it forced strike aircraft to lower altitudes (i.e. treetop level and up to 4,000 - 10,000 feet). Flight at those lower levels made aircraft vulnerable to the 23, 37, and 57 mm guns. The more maneuverable 12.7 and 14.5 mm guns were much easier to move, and those two weapons accounted for most of the battle damage to our aircraft and shootdowns.

It was challenging to maintain an up-to-date and accurate order of battle of enemy SAM and AAA threats, but that was our job. Based on the reports of FACs, strike aircraft, RWTs, and FAGs, the order of battle was continually being updated, even during our missions, in real time. It was with a deadly seriousness of purpose that many personnel worked long hours to ensure the enemy Order of Battle was current and correct.

MiG aircraft was a family of Soviet fighter aircraft designed and built by Mikoyan Aircraft and exported to North Vietnam (China exported MiG 19's to North Vietnam). The aircraft were designed by Artem Mikoyan (M) and Mikhail Gurevich (G) (the "i" in MiG means "and" in Russian). The North Vietnamese flew MiG 17's (Fresco), 19's (Farmer) and 21's (Fishbed). The MiGs flew out of three major air bases in North Vietnam, Phuc Yen, Kep, and Gia Lam.

Like AAA and SAMs, MiGs presented a threat source for which ABCCC aircraft had no active defense. Our one and only defense was to avoid those areas in which MiGs were active. College Eye was an airborne EC-121 that flew out of Korat Royal Thai Air Base. One of its missions was to monitor MiG activity at the North Vietnamese airfields and alert Allied aircraft whenever MiGs were detected starting engines and taking off. Once detected, College Eye then broadcasted a Bandit Call on Guard (UHF 243.0), which ensured all airborne aircraft and most ground stations received the warning. The call reported the direction and distance from Bullseye (i.e. Hanoi) in which the MiG was located/ flying. During my year-long tour, Bandit Calls occurred frequently. Generally, we were never in imminent danger from a MiG attack; however, there were several occasions when we flew near the border with North Vietnam to support on-going operations and were forced to take precautionary evasive maneuvers. On at least one flight, we entered North Vietnamese airspace. On those occasions, we donned our parachutes, and the Intel technician and I prepared to shred classified documents.

— 15 —

DUMB BOMBS AND SMART BOMBS

In 1965, a bombing campaign called Rolling Thunder commenced. For the first time, Air Force, Navy, and Marine Corps fighter-bombers attacked targets in North Vietnam. The Thanh Hoa Bridge (Dragon's Jaw Bridge) was one of the first targets because of its strategic importance in providing the only railroad connection between Hanoi to the panhandle in the south. From the outset, it became readily apparent we lacked conventional weapons that combined accuracy and power. Incredibly, our munitions inventory was comprised of iron bombs (i.e. dumb bombs), similar to what had been used in WW II. The first attack on Dragon's Jaw Bridge was conducted by 31 F-105s carrying 750-pound iron bombs and 250-pound Bullpup wire-guided missiles. Follow-on reconnaissance aircraft indicated there was no appreciable damage done to the bridge. The next day, a flight of 46 F-105s struck the bridge again, dropping over 300 dumb bombs, and, again, the bridge sustained no significant damage.

At the time, under the research umbrella of Operation Shed Light, the Air Force was conducting research into the development of a smart bomb. The goal was to develop a munition that could be guided to its intended target. The first generation of Pave Way munitions was born and combat testing took place in 1968. The new technology involved the use of two aircraft. A spotter aircraft directed (illuminated) a concentrated beam of laser energy on the intended target. The second aircraft released a bomb that had been modified with a guidance system that could "see" the illuminated target once it entered the cone of laser energy. Modification kits were used to transform 750- and 2,000-pound dumb bombs into smart bombs. Initially, two F-4's, based at Ubon RTAB, were paired to deliver the Pave Way munitions, and bombing accuracy improved significantly. Initially, one Pave Way bomb kit cost in excess of $100,000, but as production increased, the cost per unit decreased to less than $2500. As the price of Pave Way bomb kits decreased sharply, the number of Pave Way missions increased. In time, the Mark 84 2,000-pound bomb proved to be a superior weapon. It was effective against cave complexes, cratering roads, and causing earth slides to block roads and trails.

In 1970, the Air Force introduced a modification to smart bombing. Called Pave Nail, the illumination pods were placed on OV-10 FAC aircraft. It made sense inasmuch as the number of the F-4 aircraft delivering Pave Way munitions was doubled. The FACs were already flying in the vicinity of designated targets and could easily illuminate the target. The FAC's call sign was changed to Pave Nail.

§

Our inventory of air delivered munitions fell into three categories: general purpose (GP) bombs, napalm, and cluster bomb units (CBU). Napalm and CBUs were considered anti-personnel munitions and were the weapon of choice during TIC. Subsequent to the war, the use of those munitions became a subject of controversy as the public learned of the nature of its destructive force, and CBUs, in particular, were decried because of continued injuries to civilians long after hostilities had ended.

As aircraft checked in with Alleycat, it was important for me to be aware of the munitions they carried in the event close air support was needed. General Purpose bombs were our last choice in air support munitions for our ground forces, however, when no other ordnance was available, those flights were diverted and cleared to check in with our FAGs.

Some bombs were fitted with retarding devices to increase the bomb's drag. After aircraft release, the air stream released a set of tail fins on the bomb, slowing its descent. The slower descent permitted for low-level bombing runs and improved accuracy. Those munitions were called Snakeye and proved to be effective in a close air support role. General purpose bombs were also modified by the installation of fuse extenders. The two-to-three-foot extenders were installed onto the nose of the munition, which produced an above ground detonation, improving both its blast and fragmentation effects.

Napalm was an incendiary device, originally used in WW II. It was a mixture of a gelling agent and a combustible fuel that was delivered at low levels. Its clamshell container opened and as the mixture was spread over a wide area, it ignited. Napalm generated temperatures in excess of 1500 degrees F, and the burning gel stuck to the skin, with no practical means of removing it. Victims suffered serious burns that were prone to infection. The burning napalm also created an atmosphere in excess of 20% carbon monoxide and firestorm winds in excess of 70 miles an hour. Napalm also proved to be effective against enemy soldiers who sought refuge in trenches and underground bunkers. The burning gel flowed into the bunkers, and victims succumbed to asphyxiation. Napalm canisters were configured with and without fins. Finned napalm had a more predictable delivery pattern and provided better penetration of tree canopy while unfinned napalm tumbled during descent and was less accurate.

Cluster Bomb Units (CBU) was a class of weapons that were highly effective as anti-personnel and anti-armored vehicle weapons. There were several different types of CBUs, each with unique features and designed for unique roles. After release, CBU munitions ejected sub-munitions or explosive bomblets from a clam-shell container. As the bomblets fell, they became armed. Most CBU munitions were intended to explode upon impact, but some had delayed fusing.

HUNG ORDNANCE

We had just arrived at our parking ramp on the flight line and were preparing to board the aircraft for our evening's mission. Members of the ground crew told us about an impending emergency landing. Word was out that an F-105 was preparing to land with hung ordnance. While on a bombing mission in Barrel Roll, a 500 lb. bomb failed to leave the rails after having been "released". Since the bomb had been released, it had also become armed. Unless there were mechanical problems or damage to the aircraft that prevented them from doing so, all returning aircraft with remaining ordnance would release their weapons at designated bomb dumps (e.g. free fire zones) prior to landing. Air Force policy was that returning strike aircraft were not permitted to land still laden with bombs. The pilot of the Thud was very professional and greased the landing. As soon as he tapped the brakes, the bomb flew off the rails. The braking action had propelled the bomb forward as the plane suddenly decel- erated. With our mouths open and staring in disbelief, we stood on the taxiway and watched the bomb porpoise down the runway. Clearly, the pilot wanted to avoid the errant bomb and quickly decelerated his aircraft, bringing it to a screeching halt. Ahead of him, the porpoising bomb bounced high into the air and exploded on impact with the runway. The pilot had successfully cratered his own runway! Taxiways were used for flight operations while repairs were being made to the newly cratered runway. By mid-morning the following day, full operations on the main runway had been restored.

THUD ACCIDENT

We were preparing to leave for the flight line when word spread that an F-105 was on approach to final, making an emergency landing. Due to battle damage, the plane's hydraulic system had been lost, and the Thud would be landing without brakes. We boarded a van and stopped short of the north end of the runway until the emergency was over. Sure enough, roaring down the runway came the Thud trailing its drogue chute. Somehow, the crippled aircraft missed the barriers and with sparks flying, came to a skidding halt in a ditch at the end of the runway. We were not more than 50 yards away as we watched the crash landing. After coming to a stop, the plane immediately burst into flames, the canopy popped open, and the pilot scrambled to safety. Pedro, the call sign for firefighting helicopters, had been circling overhead and went to work to extinguish the flames and save the aircraft. As additional rescue crews arrived at the scene, we drove on to the ABCCC parking ramp.

APRIL-MAY
1969

§

— 16 —

FIRST FLIGHT

During my inaugural flight, I followed Jim's lead but always seemed to be a minute or so behind him. Events moved quickly. I donned a parachute and fumbled with the straps as I tried to make the necessary adjustments. By the time I accomplished that task, Jim was already working with the controllers to chart the night's missions on the plotting map/board. Using grease pencils, the call signs for each aircraft scheduled to work Barrel Roll that night were written on small, color-coded plastic arrows. Different colors identified fast movers, slow movers, FACs, gunships, flareships, and "special packages." They were placed in chronological order on the upper right-hand corner of the board. When each aircraft checked in, a controller placed the arrow at the intended target's location. Similarly, when missions were completed and the aircraft left our control, the arrow was removed from the board. By using the color-coded arrows, a quick glance at the plotting map/board indicated all on-going air operations in Barrel Roll at any moment in time. Call signs also told us the type of aircraft and its weapons load that were available in the event resources needed to be diverted to support TIC.

It was Intel's job to plot the locations of Forward Air Guides FAGs who were active that evening as well as the intended targets/routes for any special package(s). Usually, by the time the plotting map/board was updated, our aircraft had already taxied to the end of the runway, performed its engine run-up, and began its takeoff roll. We sat at our work-stations and assembled the resources we would be using and went to work.

Next came an introduction to the radios at our consoles. I put on a headset and plugged it into the console. Each member of the battle staff had long extension cords, which permitted us to move about the capsule as needed and still be able to monitor the radios. Jim introduced me to the three radio operators, and they provided a quick explanation of the equipment they used and how they supported the battle staff.*

As soon as we "crossed the fence" (Mekong River), Jim began calling FAGs to establish contact and conduct radio checks. It was reassuring for them to know we were on station and prepared to provide the air support they might need. I could hear it in their voice. The VFH radios used by the FAGs were line of sight, and for us to be able to communicate effectively we had to be flying directly overhead or in a nearby location with no mountains or hills between our positions. There were times when FAGs or RWTs were in remote locations, which forced us to alter our flight plan in order to establish and maintain radio contact. When requested to do so, our pilots were always cooperative and made the necessary adjustments.

After that first flight, I always made a point to introduce myself to any radio operator with whom I was working for the first time. They provided critical support to our mission, often changing frequencies to our consoles under fast-moving and stressful situations.

MEKONG RIVER

The mighty Mekong is the world's 12th-longest river and the 7th longest in Southeast Asia. It is more than 2,700 miles long, and its source is in the mountains of Tibet. According to the season, its flow varies greatly. The Mekong River has served as a major navigation and trade route in Southeast Asia for centuries and sustains the lives of millions as a fishing resource and for the irrigation of crops. In Lao and Thai, the name means "mother of waters."

The Mekong River's lower basin forms the borders of China, Thailand, Laos, and Myanmar (formerly, Burma), an area referred to as the Golden Triangle. Before the river flows into the South China Sea, it forms the extensive Mekong Delta region of Vietnam.

I listened and learned as Jim spoke with each of the FAGs. They exchanged messages such as "5 by 5," "4 by 4," "4 by 3," and so forth. Jim provided an explanation of the numbers. On a scale of one to five, with five being the best, the numbers reflected the volume and clarity of the radio contact. For example, a response of "5 by 3" indicated the message was received loudly but the clarity was only average. Once we established radio contact with each FAG, they provided a status report.

Events moved at a fast pace, and once I had internalized one task, Jim was addressing another of our responsibilities. Thankfully, as the night progressed, the pace of operations slowed down a bit, which provided time for me to ask questions about what was taking place. As the mission unfolded, Jim had me speaking with FAGs, checking on their status, and responding to their radio calls. I alerted the DABS and BSOO of impending special missions. Thanks to Jim's leadership, I was so fully engaged in the job that, never once, did any of the fear and anxiety I had experienced at the start of the mission enter into my conscious thought.

As our time on station was ending, I listened to Jim as he briefed Cricket Intel about the evening's operations. Another lesson learned. Once Cricket had assumed control of Barrel Roll, Jim pulled out a portable typewriter and methodically reviewed the information we had accumulated during the evening. I was told to organize and type the mission report. I had read enough after-action reports to know the format. As I prepared the report, one of the radio operators began to collect all of the papers and notes the battle staff had generated during the mission. The working papers were placed in a CD burn bag. The bags were returned to the shack and secured in a file cabinet until they were taken to the burn barrel for destruction.

I was still on an emotional high when we landed. It was an exhilarating learning experience for me, and although I knew I had much more to learn, it was with a sense of accomplishment when we returned to the Alleycat shack. However, there was one more lesson to learn. After a post-mission briefing, the lock was removed from the refrigerator and most of the members of the battle staff grabbed a cold beer. Blame it on my inexperience and naivete, but I couldn't imagine drinking beer that early in the morning. But that was about to change! It took but a few missions before I, too, found out how good a cold beer tasted in the morning after working all night.

Prior to my second training flight, Jim informed me he would be an observer and I would be expected to perform all duties and responsibilities. I had worked hard to prepare myself for the challenge but wasn't sure if I was ready. Prior to the pre-mission briefing, the excitement I had felt prior to my first flight returned. In fact, for the remainder of my deployment, I felt that same excitement and nervous energy every day I flew. I reveled in each adrenaline-charged mission and remained energized and focused throughout the year. Each day presented new challenges in the ever-changing and dynamic nature of the war in Barrel Roll.

My final training flight proceeded without incident, and when needed, Jim was there to assist. Since it was Jim's Sawatdee flight (last flight), upon our return to the flight line, I was introduced to an Air Force tradition. As the battle staff exited the aircraft, our colleagues hosed us down with water from a fire truck that was standing by. And when we returned to the shack we found several bottles of champagne waiting for us. Our Squadron Commander congratulated Jim for his outstanding service to ABCCC, and we all delighted in toasting my mentor.

Jim's deployment was over, and he returned home. Incredibly, within several weeks, I became the Alleycat Intelligence Officer in charge, and that steep learning curve I faced upon arrival loomed even larger. There was so much more to learn and experience, and the work was anything but routine. I embraced the challenge and fully committed myself to our mission. I was fascinated by what I had learned about General Vang Pao and the CIA's so-called "secret" army. Considering the very public proclamation that the United States did not have any forces stationed in Laos nor did America conduct military operations in that country, our missions were even more alluring.

— 17 —

THE EBB AND FLOW OF BATTLE

Without intending to do so or even aware I was doing so; my life had become totally absorbed into the world of *L'Armee Clandestine*. I had become solely focused on our mission, and as the days passed, I identified more and more with the Hmong. Time passed quickly, and my daily life had fallen into a routine that was anything but dull.

During the first half of my deployment, I was living in town, in a bungalow I shared with three other members of ABCCC. On the days I was scheduled to fly, I usually arrived at the base a little before Noon and had lunch at the Officer's Club (OC). I almost always arrived at the shack earlier than required and immediately immersed myself in intelligence reports and mission planning. I developed a thirst for knowledge that I never seemed able to satisfy. It was a positive addiction.

Typically, the ground war in Northern Laos was fought on a seasonal basis. During the dry season, which lasted from November through April, the NVA and its allies, the Pathet Lao, launched their campaigns and went on the offensive, overrunning friendly locations and making significant advances in the PDJ. May through October marked the rainy season and that was when the anti-Communist forces, taking advantage of Air America air mobility, used guerilla tactics to make its advances and re-claim territory lost during the dry season. The war in Laos was a mirror image of that in Vietnam. In Laos, Communist forces conducted operations in a conventional manner and relied on fixed supply lines, armored vehicles, and artillery. General Vang Pao's SGU forces countered with guerrilla tactics.

During my year-long deployment, Alleycat supported a series of operations and counterattacks conducted by Vang Pao's troops. There would be one constant, the ebb and flow of opposing forces across the PDJ. My year in Southeast Asia was measured not by months but by the names of a succession of major combat operations.

Before he left ABCCC and returned home, Jim had briefed me on the most recent operation being waged in Barrel Roll, Operation Rain Dance. Prepared or not, I was now responsible for supporting Operation Rain Dance. The operation involved a massive bombing campaign in Barrel Roll that produced one of the most memorable air strikes of my year-long deployment occurred during my first month of serving as Alleycat Intel. On 21 April 1969, a flight of F-105's struck a cave complex and a nearby town in the Muang Ngan Valley with Bullpup missiles. The area is located east of the PDJ, about 20 kilometers from Phonsavan. During a day-time strike, one of the Bullpups entered the mouth of a cave, resulting in huge explosions coming from its mouth as well as ventilation shafts at the top of the mountain. At the time of the strike, a village a half mile away also erupted in flames, indicating the Communists had dug access tunnels from the cave complex to the town. The explosions and fires lingered, which prompted me to ask our pilot to overfly the area that night to provide us with a view of the spectacle below. The fires continued for almost 20 hours.

General Vang Pao resumed his ground offensive on 29 April 1969; three battalions left the security of their mountaintop positions at Long Tieng and entered the PDJ. The 1,000 Hmong warriors entered the target rich town of Xieng Khouagnville and regained control of the town and the fertile rice growing area in the Muong Ngan valley for the first time since 1962. Much of the town had been destroyed by a 21 April air strike. The Hmong encountered no enemy resistance. In fact, the NVA and PL had withdrawn its defenders. The Hmong found two armored cars, 18 trucks, twelve 37mm AAA guns, and a 75 mm howitzer, all of which had been destroyed by the fleeing NVA. A cave complex was discovered just outside the town, which contained 300 tons of medical supplies, and in an adjoining cave, they discovered a 1,000-bed field hospital that had an operating theater and two X-ray machines. The next day, Air America flew in a huge quantity of explosives and combat engineers destroyed the cave complexes.

Air strikes continued to attack designated Barrel Roll targets, and impressive BDA was reported day and night. By mid-May we began receiving RWT reports of heavy enemy movement from Sam Neau in the north, along Route 6, and from the east along Route 7. Clearly, the NVA were preparing for a wet season offensive campaign. Based on the FAG and RWT reports, we diverted flights to cut the critical Lines of Communication (LOCs).

Just as General Vang Pao's dry season operation, Pig Fat, was a departure from past tactical planning, the North Vietnamese impending wet season attack was a deviation from its past practice. By the end of May, Xieng Khouagnville was surrounded by PL and NVA. Our evenings were devoted to providing the defenders of the ancient city with flareships and gunships, to counter the probes to which they were being continually subjected. In a battle that claimed the lives of over 200 Hmong fighters, the NVA finally overran Xieng Khouagnville. The impressive gains Vang Pao and the Hmong had achieved in Operation Stranglehold, just six weeks earlier, had been reversed. Such was the ebb and flow nature of the war in Barrel Roll.

American air power continued to attack NVA targets but were forced into an air support role as General Vang Pao withdrew the remainder of his three battalions. Air America pilots were kept busy flying non-stop missions to ex-filtrate our friendlies. FAGs were under continual pressure during the night, and we did our best to provide non-stop gunship and flareship coverage. There were, however, two bright spots amid the gloom; air strikes continued to amass impressive BDA and amid the Communist pressure LS-108, Muong Soui, was successfully defended. During my year with Alleycat, control of this strategically important Lima Site changed hands on multiple occasions.

JUNE-SEPTEMBER
1969

§

— 18 —

JUNE 1969

By the beginning of June 1969, the NVA and PL had gradually made its presence known in and around the PDJ. Our evenings were kept busy with reports of TIC and responding to requests for "Spooky." Reports from RWTs indicated there was increased enemy activity along Route 7. Despite our continued efforts to disrupt NVA efforts to improve Route 7 to all-weather status, the NVA engineers persevered and made major improvements to the road surface. Among the sightings were reports of armored vehicles, which, if true, would have been a first for the Communists. Those reports were promptly forwarded to Blue Chip and Geneva.

Since the Communists had always eschewed wet season campaigns, initially, the reports were met with a degree of skepticism. However, continued intelligence gathering confirmed the sightings. Clearly, the NVA were preparing for an offensive operation. It was called Campaign Toan Thang (Total Victory). To determine what the Communists were planning, additional FAGs were activated and inserted into the hills surrounding the PDJ. In time, and thanks to the intelligence gathering skills of those FAGs and RWTs, military planners concluded Moung Soui, LS-108 was the NVA's target.

Only after the Communist offensive unfolded and, in its aftermath, did we learn the details of Campaign Toan Thang. Reverting to their penchant for guerilla operations, the NVA and PL successfully circumvented the string of Lima Sites that ringed the hillsides overlooking the PDJ and were poised to launch its first-ever wet season offensive.

By mid-June 1969, three enemy battalions, estimated to be approximately 1,200 soldiers, had advanced to Moung Soui, occupying the high ground surrounding one of Vang Pao's most important bases on the PDJ. Its hard surface runway made it the only forward operating base from which RLA forces could launch T-28 strikes. In anticipation of an attack, the number of defenders of the town swelled to more than 4,000 troops, most of whom were RLA soldiers. Those troops, however, were not battle-tested and notoriously unreliable. Among the defenders was a 300-man Thai artillery battalion and approximately 100 Hmong "regulars."

Campaign Toan Thang was launched 18 June 1969, as the NVA and PL launched its first assault against an SGU unit located on a mountaintop overlooking Moung Soui. The radio call came to us several hours after we had arrived on station on the 18th. An excited FAG (I cannot recall his call sign) advised us of TIC, and we responded by providing gunship and flareship coverage for the remainder of the evening. Over the next several evenings, that pattern was repeated as the enemy tightened its stranglehold hold on Moung Soui. By 24 June 1969, LS-108 was completely surrounded, and as expected, the major attack took place that evening. Sappers preceded the assault, which was led by six PT-76 tanks. Despite being struck by more than 70 strike aircraft and gunships during the evening, the Communists prevailed.

Foul weather precluded air strikes the following day, which surprisingly, was a quiet day. On the evening of 25 June 1969, Alley-cat circled the Lima Site all night, prepared to provide cover in the event the Communists resumed its offensive. On the following day, Geneva made the decision to evacuate RLA dependents from the base. In an operation called Swan Lake, a fleet of 24 helicopters from several different sources (i.e. Air America, Pony Express, and Jolly Greens) was organized, and removed family members. Once their family members had been successfully evacuated, many RLA troops began to leave the base, moving off to the south. That evening, approximately 500 Laotian troops remained to defend the base. By morning, that number dwindled to 300 after more than 200 troops abandoned their comrades.

On the morning of 27 June 1969, only the Thais and Hmong were willing to remain at Moung Soui to make a stand and fight. The generals thought otherwise. Under enemy fire, the remaining defenders were evacuated in the early evening. Shortly after Alleycat assumed control, the last of the troops defending LS-108 departed. In their retreat, they left behind three 155 mm and five 105 mm fully functioning artillery pieces. Moung Soui had fallen, again. Campaign Toan Thang was an overwhelming Communist victory not because of its military superiority but due to the inability of RLA troops to be an effective fighting force. It was a disheartening loss.

Often after a mission, several friends and I enjoyed a cold beer at the shack after the post-mission briefing and then headed to the OC for breakfast. Upon returning to the bungalow, it was immediately to bed, but sleep was usually difficult in the swelter of hot and humid Thailand. I had only an oscillating ceiling fan to stir the air. During the six months I lived in the bungalow, I never had to cover myself with anything when sleeping, not even a sheet. My "roommates" were geckos that crawled along the ceiling and walls, but I never bothered them since they did a great job of controlling the mosquito population.

When I had a day off, I enjoyed exploring Udorn, delighting in the scenes of the townspeople going about their daily lives or running headlong into water buffalo being herded down a street. It was a joy to experience Thai culture, although I didn't do so well with the Thai street food. The people of Udorn were very friendly and curious about life in America, and I took advantage of several opportunities to visit and enjoy meals with local families.

On duty days when it was my responsibility to prepare for that night's mission, I arrived at the base early and after breakfast at the OC, I was among the first to arrive at the shack. I worked throughout the day, rarely taking time for lunch. During the evenings, I headed to town for dinner and an evening of relaxation at one or more of the numerous clubs.

On night's off, I usually visited downtown Udorn for dinner and some nightlife. One of my favorite restaurants was owned and operated by five Chinese sisters and was named Five Sisters (but in Thai). Typically, I enjoyed noodles, vegetables, or fried rice. One of the more unusual sights was when a customer ordered a snake dish. One of the chefs would bring the snake out and hold it up for the customer's approval and then disappear to prepare the delicacy. Another favorite hangout of mine was Ciro's, a GI bar, of which there were many in Udorn. GI bars typically consisted of a live band playing loud music, Go-Go dancers, and plenty of bar girls.

Ciro's served a good personal pan pizza. I walked everywhere and always bought a flower lei from the ubiquitous barefoot street children with dirty faces. They were adorable. Worn around the neck, the flowers provided a wonderful fragrance (similar to that of a gardenia) and cost but five cents.

FALLEN COMRADE
LT. LLOYD M. SCOTT, JR.

During pre-mission briefings, we included a summary of major events from the previous day, including shootdowns and SAR activity. On 10 June 1969, I was listening to the pre-mission briefing and was stunned to hear the name of a dear friend who had been killed the previous day. We attended OTS together and were members of a 16-person flight that survived the three-month experience by working together in a spirit of cooperation. Following his commissioning in November 1967, Scotty departed for pilot training. After advanced pilot training in the A1-E Skyraider, he was stationed at Nakon Phanom (NKP) Royal Thai Air Base and was a member of the 56th Special Operations Wing. His call sign was Zorro, and he flew close air support missions in Northern Laos and over the Ho Chi Minh Trail complex in Southern Laos. After completing more than a dozen daylight missions, on 9 June 1969, Scotty was fragged to fly his first solo night mission. Shortly after taking off from NKP, for unknown reasons, Scotty lost control of his aircraft, it rolled over, and flew into the ground. 1st Lieutenant Lloyd M. Scott, Jr., was killed instantly.

In addition to the Vietnam Service and Campaign Medals, Scotty was awarded the Air Force Presidential Unit Citation, Air Medal, and Vietnam Gallantry Cross.

On days when I was scheduled to fly, I usually had lunch at the Officer's Club. It was convenient and quick. Usually lunch started with a salad, but after discovering an inchworm crawling among what was supposed to be salad greens, I didn't order another salad for the rest of my tour. It didn't take long for the waitresses to learn that for me, a salad was cucumber slices and shredded cheese. Like many of the Thais I met, the waitresses had a great sense of humor, and we enjoyed playing practical jokes on one another. One very hot afternoon, I sat down to enjoy a glass of cold iced tea. I took several long swallows before I noticed several waitresses standing against a nearby wall with their eyes glued on me. I knew something was amiss but didn't know what. After another sip of iced tea, I glanced at the glass and staring back at me, among the ice cubes, was a small frog. The waitresses roared with delight.

The OC was also a convenient location for breakfast on mornings after a flight. Still on an adrenaline high, it wasn't unusual to stop at the bar for another beer or two. Usually, a dozen or more aircrewman were at the bar, still in their flight suits. We fed the jukebox with quarters and played, over and over, what became an anthem for us. It was a song by Blood, Sweat, and Tears titled, "And When I Die." The song summed up our feelings regarding what we thought was our reality, we wouldn't survive the Second Indochina War.

§

To cope with the dangerous missions upon which we embarked, we exhibited a casual disregard and denial of the risks involved. Fears were, mostly, kept below our level of consciousness. Each of us developed our own means of managing the fear and anxiety we all experienced. Some engaged in self-destructive behavior and sought peace through the haze of alcohol and drugs, while others depended on their religion. A few went "native" and moved in with a telak (i.e. darling, lover), establishing a family life while on their remote assignment.

I chose to compartmentalize my life. While on duty, I immersed myself in all things regarding ground and air operations in Barrel Roll. I pored over the daily and weekly intelligence summaries and the after-action reports for both Barrel Roll and Steel Tiger. I volunteered for extra flights and reported early for ground duty. I was the one who was usually the first to report and the last to leave our shack. I was continually in search of ways in which I could, in some small measure, support our beloved Hmong warriors.

Whatever free time remained was devoted to reading and recording music. With my newly purchased Teac A-1500 reel to reel tape player, I recorded many hours of music at the base library. The squadron had a library, of sorts. One could borrow and return books. New books were added each month when one of the squadron's seven C-130's returned from Taiwan after a major overhaul of its engines. Since Taiwan did not recognize copyright laws of the United States, newly released books could be purchased for less than a dollar. The paper was exceedingly thin, but the books were readable. Crewmen also brought back news magazines, and we roared with delight when we read the repeated Government denials of any ground or air operations taking place in Laos.

Beneath the surface of whichever coping mechanism we used, there was an underlying sense of melancholy. The death of American servicemen and Hmong warriors never ceased, and while we were reluctant to express it publicly, we knew the Communists would prevail. Something else no one ever admitted was that for some, the news of another's death brought a sense of relief that it wasn't you who was killed. Such feelings of survivor's guilt were quickly followed by an overwhelming sense of shame, guilt, and remorse for having harbored such unspeakable thoughts and feelings. For others, a sense of guilt developed because they blamed themselves for not doing more to either prevent a shootdown or to save the life of a comrade. It was a complicated array of emotions, a challenge for me to which I had no experience. Sadly, for some who experienced such emotional trauma in "that world", they were never able to leave that suffering behind. In a sense, they never came home.

For the rest of us, we experienced the euphoria of "surviving the war"; or so we thought. In time, I learned that the combat experience to which I had been exposed would always be with me and become a significant part of my persona. The year in Southeast Asia changed me in countless ways and has had an all-encompassing impact on my identity and greatly influenced my personal and professional lives. The crucible of combat provided wonderful insights into what is important in life and provided a road map as to how to live my life.

— 19 —

JULY 1969

The timing couldn't have been worse. It was the end of June 1969, and the NVA wet season offensive was poised to achieve its objective of overrunning Moung Soui and seizing control of the strategically vital forward operating base. Despite my objections, I was a part of a small detachment of Alleycat personnel that was assigned to a temporary duty (TDY) assignment to Korat Royal Thai Air Base. We were sent to Korat to fly three missions with College Eye (call sign Bat Cat) aircraft. Alleycat personnel included one DABS, one BSOO, four controllers, and one Intel Officer. Our flights took place between 23-26 June 1969.

The purpose of the mission was to participate in a feasibility study to determine if the ABCCC mission could be accomplished while flying with Bat Cats. For two years, College Eye aircraft were flying racetrack patterns over Steel Tiger, receiving and relaying information provided by the sensors along portions of the Ho Chi Minh Trail in southern Laos. Headquarters 7th 13th was planning to insert sensors in Barrel Roll in August 1969, which would require additional aircraft to monitor the new strings of sensors. Since Bat Cat aircraft would have to overfly Barrel Roll to monitor the sensors, it made sense to determine if one platform could perform both College Eye and ABCCC missions.

The "test" proved to be complicated. Apparently, the test was intended to investigate more than just combining the Barrel Roll missions of ABCCC and College Eye. While we flew with Bat Cat, a down-sized Alleycat crew flew with Moonbeam on the first night of the test. Evidently, the decision-makers were investigating the feasibility of combining ABCCC orbits into one day mission and one night mission as well as checking out the practicability of flying all ABCCC missions on Bat Cat aircraft. From its outset, the test was, at best, an error in judgment. In reality, it was a fiasco.

The combined Alleycat/Moonbeam flight compromised Moonbeam's ability to perform its mission, since it had to move its orbit further north, limiting its ability to communicate (i.e. control) with aircraft and ground personnel in Steel Tiger. Similarly, Alleycat's ability to communicate with its resources was also compromised. That portion of the "test" lasted just one night. Additionally, the capsule just wasn't big enough to comfortably accommodate extra members of the battle staff, and the workload was overwhelming to the point that it compromised the safety of the aircraft fragged to Barrel Roll and Steel Tiger and fell far short of addressing the needs of the FAGs and RWTs. The following evening, Alleycat and Moonbeam flew its normal missions.

In Korat, we were woefully unprepared to assume any sort of control of aircraft in Barrel Roll. We carried no resource material and did not have access to that day's Frag. Apparently, our only task was to conduct radio checks throughout the evening with aircraft operating in Barrel Roll, FAGs, and RWTs. While the Bat Cats contained a variety of radios in sufficient numbers to accommodate our needs, the orbit the aircraft flew was too far removed from the ground personnel with whom we needed to communicate. This was true for the controllers as well as Intel.

Following our initial flight, the Alleycat crew met to discuss our experience. To a person, we thought the concept of combining missions was ill-advised, and the experiment was a failure. It was decided that only the DABS and two controllers would participate in the remaining two missions. With my portion of the assignment completed, that afternoon, I caught the Klong flight to Udorn and was able to "witness" the evacuation of LS-108. Upon his return, Lt. Col. Hartz, our DABS who participated in the TDY assignment to Korat, prepared and submitted his report. We never heard anything more about combining College Eye and ABCCC missions.

Following the loss of Moung Soui, the area became somewhat of a free-fire zone. During daylight hours, Cricket controlled armed reconnaissance missions in the area and Ravens trolled the area in hopes of luring the enemy out of hiding. RWTs continued to monitor enemy movements in the environs of the PDJ. It was estimated that almost NVA battalions occupied the PDJ. At night, overlapping gunship coverage was fragged to Barrel Roll for the purpose of responding to the needs of FAGs who still operated in the area.

§

General Vang Pao began making plans to avenge the loss of Moung Soui before the sun set on 28 June 1969. He hoped that a prompt counterattack would surprise the NVA. Hastily, a plan was patched together and christened Operation Off Balance. Despite Vang Pao's reluctance to work with RLA troops, he was forced to include two battalions in the attacking force. Two Hmong battalions, totaling more than 600 soldiers, also participated in the counterattack. The final force included in the battle plan was a battalion of the RLA paratroops. They were considered to be the best of the RLA. The Air Force responded by fragging over 120 daily Barrel Roll air strikes to support the operation. A three-pronged pincer operation was planned, with units approaching Moung Soui from the north, west, and east. Units were helicoptered into place by Air America pilots. On 1 July 1969, three days after Operation Off Balance was first proposed, it launched.

ABCCC had not received prior notification about Operation Off Balance. However, once the Frag was opened, we noted the dramatic increase in the number of strike aircraft scheduled to Barrel Roll. We assumed a special operation was underway but did not know its specifics. All we could do was monitor strike frequencies and respond to calls for assistance.

MAJOR LEE LUE

On 12 July 1969, a Hmong fighter bomber pilot, Major Lee Lue, was shot down while flying in support of Hmong ground forces participating in Operation Off Balance. His T-28 was hit by 37 mm AAA. No parachute was observed as his plane broke up as it went straight in. Prior to volunteering for flight training in 1967, Lee Lue was one of only a handful of Hmong teachers in his country. He enrolled in the six-month

Waterpump flight training program in Thailand and started flying combat missions by the middle of 1967. It was not uncommon for Major Lee Lue to fly as many at 12 missions in a single day. Stories were told about his courage and heroics. On occasion, he was so exhausted from flying all day, he had to be helped out of the cockpit by his ground crew. During his nearly two years of flying T-28s for the Royal Laotian Air Force, he accumulated more than 5,000 missions, an incredible feat that earned him the respect of Lao and American pilots. The motto, "Fly 'til you die" was attributed to Major Lee Lue. He was posthumously promoted to Lieutenant Colonel. His death was a major blow to Hmong morale.

At best, Operation Off Balance was an overly optimistic attempt to re-take an important forward operating base. At worst, it was a disastrously mishandled operation. As General Vang Pao's inserted his forces, clear skies allowed over 100 Air Force sorties to attack NVA troop concentration in and around Moung Soui. Good BDA was reported to Cricket. During the evening, gunships and flareships were kept busy, attacking NVA targets and providing support to the friendly forces. Tiger Mobile, Pogo, Red Hat, and Rainbow were the most active FAGs during the operation, which continued through the first two weeks of July 1969. From the outset, one of the RLA battalions refused to fight and a week later, a second RLA battalion withdrew. With air support and clear skies, the Hmong and the paratroop battalions advanced to within three miles of LS-108 and fought to a stand-off. While the operation unfolded, RWTs observed eight tanks and over 1000 trucks advancing towards the PDJ. Clearly, the North Vietnamese were calling in reinforcements and doing so at unprecedented levels. On 15 July 1969, the hastily planned Operation Off Balance ended, having not achieved its goals of retaking Moung Soui nor preempting the Communist advance on the PDJ.

POGO

On one memorable evening, towards the end of July 1969, I was talking to Pogo, who was another one of our very dependable and loyal FAGs. In mid-sentence, his transmission abruptly ceased. Immediately, a member of his team came on the radio, speaking extremely loud and fast, in a language I did not understand. I had no idea what was being transmitted. Another FAG, White Rose, came to our rescue and translated for us. White Rose explained that while talking on the radio, Pogo had been shot in the forehead and died instantly.

In subsequent briefings, we learned Pogo and his team were reconnoitering a suspected prisoner of war (POW) camp about 25 miles west of Hanoi. Due to Pogo's death the operation to raid the POW camp, and, hopefully, liberate captured American airmen, was delayed. Originally, the raid was to have taken place in May 1970. The POW camp was Son Tay, and the eventual raid, while technically a success, found that the prisoners had been moved from the facility several weeks prior to the raid. The raid was conducted on 20 November 1970. Had Pogo and his team not been compromised, perhaps the Son Tay Prison Raid would have been executed according to the original timetable, and a different outcome might have occurred. In recognition of his courage, loyal service, and ultimate sacrifice, the call sign Pogo was retired, never to be used again.

Readers can learn about this brave attempt to rescue captured American crewmen in a book by Col. Arthur "Bull" Simmons titled, *The Raid*. The raiding party staged out of Udorn, and had the raid been successful, the aircraft and rescued POW's would have returned to Udorn. The raid, which resulted in over 100 enemy killed while only one member of the raiding party was injured (a broken ankle), prompted the NVA to consolidate their prisons and move all American POW's to two central locations in Hanoi. The other effect the raid had was that once it had become known to our POWs, their spirits soared, knowing they had not been forgotten.

— 20 —

IGLOO WHITE

In light of the success of the NVA's first wet season offensive and its use of tanks on the PDJ for the first time, Blue Chip and Geneva made a momentous decision to insert sensors along the major LOCs in Barrel Roll. For almost two years, the "electronic fence" had been used in Steel Tiger and proved to be an effective real-time intelligence gathering capability. To further disrupt the flow of materiel into Laos, portions of the Nam Ou and Nam Et (rivers) were seeded with air-delivered mines.

Igloo White sensors were inserted in Barrel Roll during the first week of August 1969. Initially, three stings of sensors were established along portions of Routes 6 and 7, the two primary NVA infiltration routes. In time, additional sensor strings were added. To assist with the transition and establish protocols on how we would interface, two representatives from TFA, flew to Udorn to brief Cricket and Alleycat Intel on the sensor program. They also flew orientation flights with us.

Task Force Alpha was an Air Force unit assigned to the 56th Special Operations Wing at Nakon Phanom Royal Thai Air Base. It was a top-secret electronic warfare operation called Igloo White. The operation utilized electronic sensors, state of the art IBM System 360 Model 65 computers, and communications relay aircraft. The sensor program was a concept that emerged from a think-tank in the early 1960's and became known as McNamara's electronic fence. McNamara was, of course, the Secretary of Defense, first, under President John Kennedy and then President Lyndon Johnson. The electronic fence was comprised of hundreds of strings (usually 4 -14 sensors per string) of sensors that would detect the flow of vehicles and troops along the Ho Chi Minh trail along the eastern border of Laos. Igloo White was comprised of three major elements. The first was a delivery system to insert the sensors. The second element was an airborne platform that flew over the electronic "fences" to receive the signals from the sensor strings and served in a signal-relay function. Finally, a command element was needed to receive and interpret the information and, ultimately, deliver real-time intelligence to appropriate air assets. Once the data was "interpreted" by the IBM computers, TFA analysts radioed the information to ABCCC. The call sign for TFA was Sycamore, and we received reports of enemy movement every night.

There were two types of sensors. The most common was the Air Delivered Seismic Intrusion Detector (ADSID), which detected vibrations on the ground made by the movement of vehicles and/or personnel. The other type of sensor was the Acoustic Intrusion Detector (ACOUSID), which recorded sounds in the area. Often, the ACOUSID's detected the sound of vehicles, but they also detected voices and conversations.

The sensors were three to four feet in length, camouflaged and had an antenna. They were made to look like jungle foliage. The sensors were dropped by several different means. Air Force F-4's dropped a majority of the sensors, but helicopters were also used. A modified Beech Bonanza (QU-22B), call sign Pave Eagle, also seeded sensors. On some occasions, the sensors were placed on the trail network by SGU soldiers. When delivered to its point of insertion, the seismic sensors embedded themselves into the ground. Acoustic sensors were designed to be caught in the tree canopy. The life of the sensor was about four weeks, but some had the capability of being turned on and off, which extended battery life. When placed in a string, the activation of succeeding sensors indicated the number of vehicles and the direction of travel. Since the location of the sensor strings was known, the exact location of the vehicles (troops) was known in real-time. More importantly, however, was when the sensors indicated the traffic had stopped. That usually indicated one thing, a truck park, staging area, or transshipment point, all of which were lucrative targets. When attacked, those sites usually yielded impressive BDA. The sensors transmitted its electronic signals, and those signals were received by EC-121R aircraft (Super Constellation), which flew missions around the clock in the vicinity of sensor locations. The call sign for those aircraft was Bat Cat, and they flew out of Korat Royal Thai Air Force Base. The radios on the Bat Cats automatically transmitted the signals they received to Task Force Alpha (TFA). Using the most powerful computer at the time, IBM's 360/65, intelligence analysts at TFA interpreted the data and provided the location of the target (s) directly to ABCCC Intel via radio. We then advised the DABS of the newly acquired real-time target information. It was important for Alleycat Intel to be aware of all assets that had been fragged to Barrel Roll. Knowing the various call signs, we immediately knew the type of plane and its weapons load that were either on station or would be checking in with us. With that information in mind, along with information regarding the newly acquired target of opportunity, we also provided the DABS with alternative recommendations. It was the DAB's responsibility to then render a decision regarding the allocation of assets. In other words, should a flight of strike aircraft be taken off its fragged target and diverted to this newly identified high value target? Most times, the DABS with whom I worked trusted my recommendations and diverted flights to attack the vehicles/personnel. At times, however, there were compelling reasons for strike aircraft to attack its assigned package.

The actionable intelligence generated by TFA occurred almost exclusively during the night, since enemy traffic usually only moved under the cover of darkness. During daylight hours, the traffic (which could be trucks, tanks, bikes, and people on foot) usually rested at truck parks hidden by the jungle canopy. Rarely did traffic move along the roads and trails during daylight.

TFA FUNNIES

In one memorable incident, one of the acoustic sensors transmitted the sound of a bad guy urinating on or near the sensor. On another occasion, an NVA NCO was heard instructing a soldier to climb a tree to get the parachute that had delivered the sensor. He wanted to give the material to his girlfriend so she could make a dress. The incident continued with a work crew that was heard chopping down the tree to obtain the material and sensor that had been caught in the foliage. That was followed by the sound of a crashing tree and screaming as the tree, apparently, fell on one or more of the soldiers.

ATTACK ON KHANG KHAI

During the brief planning phase for Operation Off Balance, the Prime Minister of Laos, Souvanna Phouma, in his determination to punish continued North Vietnamese aggression, sought a major strike that would "send a message" to the NVA. It was his desire to remove all restrictions from the village of Khang Khai and conduct air operations against the entrenched North Vietnamese forces. It was no secret that the ROE maintained an NBL around Khang Khai because of the presence of a Chinese Cultural Center. Discussions between officials in Washington, D.C. and Vientiane took place, but the two governments arrived at an impasse. Not wanting to offend the Chinese and fearful of repercussions, ultimately, the U.S. State Department denied the request for the retaliatory air strike. It was agreed to discuss the matter at an upcoming meeting (11 August 1969) regarding the ROE for Laos. However, the matter was resolved prior to the scheduled meeting.

In early August 1969, radio intercepts revealed a PL radio station operating on the outskirts of Khang Khai. The building was located several hundred yards from the Chinese Cultural Center. The radio station was approved for attack, and plans were made to preclude any short round that might damage the cultural center. The plan, which was scheduled for a daylight strike, was for a Raven FAC to identify and mark the target after which two F-4s would strike the target with a 1,000-pound smart bomb. The attack did not proceed according to plan. The three planes arrived on station, and once the radio shack was illuminated, the laser guided bombs were released. The Communist communications center was destroyed as planned; however, the Chinese Cultural Center was destroyed as well. The official explanation was that a "cloud drifted into the area, scattering the light beam. Confused, the smart bomb followed the strongest ray, straight into the cultural center". Not surprisingly, numerous secondary explosions emanated from the cultural center. The NVA and PL had been using the Chinese Cultural Center to store munitions, which confirmed our belief they knowingly used our ROEs to their advantage. No mention of the attack was ever made by the Chinese nor were charges ever brought forward for the violation of the ROE. From that point forward, Khang Khai was subjected to attacks on NVA and PL positions in and around the village.

— 21 —
THE BALLET OF BATTLE RESUMES

With the failure of Operation Off Balance, the mood in Barrel Roll was glum. Intelligence reports confirmed the Communists had amassed close to 20 battalions in and around the PDJ, the strength of which was estimated to be more than 8,000 combat troops and close to 4,000 support personnel. At the time, the composition of those battalions had not been identified, however, it was known that elements of the NVA's elite 312th Division were present. Sightings of close to 60 tanks were also reported by RWTs and confirmed by photo reconnaissance. Heavy traffic along major roads leading to the PDJ was confirmed by Sycamore. Based on prisoner interrogations, it was thought the NVA's next objective was to move west and cut the road between Vientiane and Luang Prabang, thus isolating the royal and administrative capitals of Laos. All indications were that the Communists would continue its wet season offensive.

General Vang Pao named his new offensive Kou Kiet. In the Lao language, it means Redeem Honor. American advisors referred to it as About Face. Not surprisingly, General Vang Pao was anxious to reverse the loss of the PDJ following the NVA's successful Campaign Toan Thang and the disappointing results of his latest operation, Operation Off Balance. As the English translation indicated, the Hmong

General was also seeking redemption. ABCCC was advised of the upcoming operation, which commenced on 6 August 1969 and ended on 30 September 1969. Coinciding with the start of the operation, and for the duration of the operation, the Air Force, Navy, and Marine Corps were fragged to fly an astounding 150 daylight and 50 nighttime missions in Barrel Roll each day. The airborne armada was comprised of a mix of fast movers, slow movers, armed reconnaissance, and FACs. In addition, three Spectres and three Candlesticks were ordered to Barrel Roll every night to be utilized at the discretion of Alleycat.

§

The monsoon rains that hampered air support during Operation Off Balance continued into the month of August at a rate that was nearly double the normal rainfall. The heavy rains forced the cancelation of some missions, but Combat Skyspot, Commando Nail, and Loran precision bombing techniques permitted most of the strikes to be conducted as fragged. The rain also hampered North Vietnamese logistics. With its supply lines already stretched thin, NVA convoys became bogged down by road conditions.

Despite the heavy rain, Air America inserted Hmong units at various locations in and around the PDJ, all in preparation for Operation About Face. Units were inserted into the hills north of Route 7, from Ban Ban to Nong Pet, near the border with North Vietnam. A second task force was inserted to the south of Route 7. They were poised to perform a pincer movement, cutting the NVA supply line, and seizing control of the vital LOC. Other units were inserted around Moung Soui, Khang Khai, and southeast of Xieng Khouangville, and they too, were prepared to launch attacks on those strategically important locations. At the time those locations were under Communist control. Phase One of Vang Pao's offensive commenced on 6 August 1969 as planned. As SGUs began to advance on enemy controlled positions in the PDJ, more and more strike missions were diverted from its fragged targets in order to support TIC.

Cricket and Alleycat noted several indications that Operation Redeem Honor was going well. We began receiving incredibly positive BDA reports. As the numbers began to accumulate, it was readily apparent that, once again, air power was taking a significant toll on the enemy. The newly inserted sensors indicated a reduced level of enemy activity. Another indication the offensive was going well, was that requests for air support to blunt TIC dropped significantly.

SEPTEMBER 1969 - JANUARY 1970

§

— 22 —
BARREL ROLL DEJA VU

September 1969

On 9 September 1969, reports reached us that Hmong forces had re-captured Phong Savan and Khang Khai and were moving across the PDJ virtually unopposed. Three days later General Vang Pao's army, using captured PT-76 tanks as its spearhead, walked into Xieng Khouangville. The increased number of air strikes scheduled for Barrel Roll continued through the month of September. Like clockwork, RF-4C aircraft from Udorn checked in with Alleycat every day, an hour or so before we left station. They were there to take post-strike photographs of the air strikes flown during the evening hours.

Military planners at 7th/13th Air Force, working with the 432nd Reconnaissance Wing at Udorn, devised a new tactic to attack enemy troop concentrations. It was called Snare Drum. Knowing the NVA were most active along the trail during the hours just before dawn and after sunset, flights of 16 to 24 F-4s attempted to catch the enemy by surprise by delivering a lethal concentration of anti-personnel munitions over a wide area. An RF-4C from Udorn, call sign Bullwhip, followed each mission to assess BDA. The first Snare Drum mission was flown on 11 September 1969, and the missions were conducted at the rate of one or two a week. Snare Drum proved to be so successful that the missions were repeatedly scheduled for the next two months, through the month of November 1969.

By the end of September 1969, Moung Soui was, once again, under the control of friendly forces as were the important LOCs of Routes 6 and 7. Building upon his initial success, General Vang Pao continued his offensive against the NVA and PL into October, and by the end of the month, the RLG had regained complete control of the PDJ. The NVA had abandoned the area as well as their PL allies who dispersed into the hills. The Communists forfeited an unprecedented amount of war materiel.

After action reports, indicated that, surprisingly, the Communist forces offered little resistance. Evidently, the Air Force bombing campaign that had preceded the operation had overwhelmed the enemy's ability to supply its troops and, in many instances, its will fight. Incredibly, General Vang Pao's forces advanced on its assigned targets, virtually unopposed.

During Operation Redeem Honor, we often monitored strike frequencies, and I was always impressed by the extraordinary professionalism of our pilots. They flew in weather conditions and low ceilings that, at times, would have been considered marginal at best. Nevertheless, they supported our ground forces, delivering life-saving close air support. They were always courteous and displayed considerable patience when working with our FAGs. I was privileged to "observe" Air Force pilots at their best and to have the opportunity to play a small role in the war in Barrel Roll.

Most of the NVA units retreated to its sanctuaries in the north, but one small group of soldiers established defensive positions in the hills to the west of Xieng Khouangville, at Thong Hai Hin. It was one of several locations of the famous funeral jars for which the PDJ was named. Enemy forces stubbornly held onto the hills surrounding Thong Hai Hin. After repeated air strikes, SGU forces successfully took control of the area. Unfortunately, in the skirmishes and air attacks on dug-in troops in trenches at the top of the hills, some of the ancient treasures sustained damage.

It took several weeks for ABCCC to learn the full extent of the success of Operation Redeem Honor. In terms of captured materiel, the operation resulted in the greatest haul of enemy supplies during the Second Indochina War. Analysts concluded that the relentless air strikes had prevented the NVA from distributing supplies to its forward units. Among the abandoned Communist materiel were:
- 6,000,000 rounds of ammunition;
- 6,400 weapons;

- 25 tanks;
- 113 trucks;
- 300 tons of medical supplies;
- 215,000 gallons of fuel; and
- Five days of food rations for over 16,000 troops.

Operation Kou Kiet, the brainchild of General Vang Pao, was a major victory for the Royal Lao Government, the Hmong Commander, and *L'Armee de Clandestine*. The PDJ and surrounding Lima Sites were under the control of the Lao government for the first time since 1960. However, questions persisted. The Communists had suffered a major loss, but unlike the Hmong, the North Vietnamese had reserves to replace its losses. As the war in Laos progressed, it took a toll on the ranks of Hmong fighters, while at the same time, the pool of Hmong recruits dwindled. Vang Pao's forces were war-weary, and the number of Hmong guerillas had been reduced to between 5,500 to 6,000 warriors. Additionally, the effectiveness of the RLA as a dependable fighting force in Barrel Roll was still in question, and without that, control of the PDJ was in serious doubt. Despite the overwhelming success of Operation Redeem Honor, the dry season loomed and with it, the uncertainty of whether or not the coalition of Vang Pao's army and RLA could successfully defend against the Communist attack that was sure to come.

RAVEN ESCADRILLE

Several weeks after the conclusion of Operation Redeem Honor, one of the oddities of the two-month campaign was revealed. Referred to as the "Raven Escadrille," it was an example of the bravery and commitment of Ravens to the Hmong cause. Born from the need to do whatever they could do to support Hmong ground forces, some Ravens used marking rockets as weapons against the enemy. They also carried hand grenades and 20-pound fragmentary bombs that were dropped out the windows of their planes. Eventually, some Ravens transitioned to T-28s for the purpose of flying strike missions.

— 23 —
VIP VISITOR AND SQUADRON RECOGNITION

November 1969

In early November 1969, we learned that a very important individual would visit the Squadron. General Vang Pao, accompanied by several aides, wanted to personally thank Alleycat and Cricket for the critical support we had provided to *L'Armee Clandestine* during Operation Redeem Honor. For us, it was a huge honor; we were thrilled to have the opportunity to meet this incredible leader, a living legend. General Vang Pao brought gifts. He presented our Squadron with a captured Soviet-made 12.7 mm AAA gun and several cases of ammunition. In addition, General Vang Pao delivered AK-47s, mounted on display frames, to the Alleycat and Cricket orbits.

General Vang Pao took time to personally greet and shake the hand of each of us who had assembled in our compound. He had a warm and genuine smile, looked directly into our eyes, and with a firm handshake, expressed sincere words of thanks. General Vang Pao had a regal presence about him and exuded a genuine sense of brotherhood throughout his visit. I "felt" his charisma and force of personality and knew, at once, why so many Hmong were inspired to follow, fight, and die for this iconic leader. Despite his short stature (perhaps, he was a little over five feet tall), General Vang Pao presented a giant presence.

I had one more opportunity to speak with General Vang Pao, but that would be under entirely different and very dire circumstances.

One of our field grade officers, a former fighter pilot, removed the gun powder and fired the primer for each 12.7 mm cartridge, rendering them inert. Thanks to Lt. Col. Brothers, we each received a remembrance of General Vang Pao's visit, a gift I have treasured ever since.

§

After General Vang Pao's visit, our Squadron Commander, Col. Jack, received a classified message from Headquarters 7th/13th Air Force. The message from General Bevan read, "Continued observation for the past two weeks indicates that Alleycat has played an indispensable role in guiding support for various Lima Sites in Barrel Roll, guaranteeing that those sites remain in friendly hands. Activity during that period has been extremely high and Alleycat's response has continually been immediate, timely, and correct. I wish that you would convey to all personnel on Alleycat my deep appreciation for such a manifestation of outstanding command and control procedures." We were humbled to have Headquarters 7th/13th Air Force recognize our support of General Vang Pao and the *L'Armee Clandestine* in their time of need. I had developed a deep affection for the Hmong and cared deeply about their fate, and the simple message from General Bevan had a profound impact on me. It validated my efforts to support our FAGs and SGU forces and reinforced my commitment to the mission.

The sentiment in the message confirmed and reinforced our efforts to make positive and tangible contributions to Barrel Roll operations and Laotian sovereignty. I was extremely proud and humbled to know the small role I had assumed in the Second Indochina War was recognized and appreciated. I approached my responsibilities with a renewed sense of dedication and commitment. The message also served as a wonderful lesson in leadership; find ways to recognize the contributions of team members and let them know you appreciate their efforts to support the organization's mission.

A month after General Vang Pao's visit, 7th ACCS was notified we had been awarded the Outstanding Unit medal for our support of and involvement in *L'Armee Clandestine* operations. In a ceremony conducted by the Wing Commander, we each received a medal in a presentation case. He advised us that we were authorized to wear the medal with a "V" device. That simple recognition meant the world to me, and of the awards and recognition I received over the years, it was the most impactful and meaningful. The "V" device, stood for Valor.

It wasn't until several years later, upon my separation from the Air Force on 29 February 1972, that I learned 7th ACCS had also been awarded the Presidential Unit Citation. Authorization to wear the PUC ribbon was a complete surprise and another humbling experience.

— 24 —
SPECIAL PACKAGES

One of Intel's responsibilities was to provide support, as needed, for "special packages." The operations were classified and scheduled for Barrel Roll throughout my deployment, the knowledge of which was based on the need to know. Some took place on a recurring basis, appearing regularly in the frag. While the controllers recognized the call signs, they were not read in on the exact nature of the missions. Others were commonly known "secrets." For some, the season determined when they were conducted. And then, there were the one-offs, highly inspired and dangerous missions, about which we knew very little.

In September 1969, Intel officers from Cricket and Alleycat were ordered to attend a briefing at Squadron Headquarters. A man in civilian clothes greeted us. We were there to be briefed about an operation that was scheduled to begin in several days, and he shared with us an overview of the operation. It was a highly classified and sensitive operation that took place in Military Region 1, the northernmost section of Laos near the border with China. It was called Operation North Wind.

Operation North Wind was a mission intended to disrupt the flow of supplies coming into Laos from China on the backs of pack animals. The operation took place near the border town of Muang Sing. It was to be a surgical strike, one in which maximum damage was to be inflicted followed by a swift extraction. At the time, Chinese workers were engaged in a road-building program across northern Laos to construct new roads and improve the surfaces of existing trails.

Our role was simple. We were given a radio frequency, which we were instructed to monitor for the next several weeks. If we received a radio transmission, our orders were to forward the message to Geneva. Neither Cricket nor Alleycat ever received any message traffic on the assigned frequency. Several weeks after being briefed about the mission, we were advised that Operation North Wind had been terminated. I never heard anything more about Operation North Wind until my next duty assignment at Headquarters Tactical Air Command. Curious about the operation, I researched records to which I had access and found just a few lines about the operation. "The operation had moderate success. Friendly forces were inserted, but strong resistance from a larger-than-expected enemy presence limited their effectiveness. The operation foundered and, ultimately, was cancelled."

During my year with ABCCC, several other similar operations took place in MR 1. Mostly, those operations involved the insertion of a "team" for the purpose of intelligence gathering, river mining, hostage taking, and sabotage.

By far, the most frequently occurring special packages were Buffalo Hunter missions. During the dry season, they were fragged several times a week. They were considered "secret" missions, but it was a poorly kept secret. Buffalo Hunter was a remotely piloted vehicle (RPV) or drone, the forerunner for the RPVs that saw extensive use in the wars in Iraq and Afghanistan and used by our military today. It was the Firebee target drone, designed and built by Ryan Aeronautical Company and used extensively by the Air Force and Navy. The Firebee airframe was approximately 30 feet in length and modified to contain Doppler radar and Loran, a precise navigation system. They were also equipped with reconnaissance cameras, capable of recording video and taking photographs. The video could be transmitted to control aircraft in real time.

The drones were launched from modified C-130's, capable of carrying and launching four Buffalo Hunter drones. Mission profiles were pre-programmed; however, if necessary, the drone could be "flown" by a pilot from the control aircraft. As modifications were made to the drones, the missions they flew also changed. Buffalo Hunter drones were used to jam enemy radars, for leaflet dropping, perform BDA, and to serve as decoys.

In its role as a decoy, they were programmed to overfly know SAM and radar-controlled gun sites. When the enemy radar illuminated the drone, attack aircraft, which were loitering in the area, would launch anti-radar missiles. On its return to a designated recovery area, a braking parachute was deployed, and as the vehicle slowly descended, it was snared out of the air by a recovery helicopter. It was Intel's responsibility to post those missions on the plotting board, alert our controllers to its presence to ensure separation with other aircraft, and monitor the missions to determine when they had ended and the aircraft were prepared to leave Barrel Roll.

Motor Pool was another special package. One of the primary infiltration routes from the north was Rt. 6. The unpaved road connected Sam Neua to the PDJ, however, major portions of the trail narrow, and wound around mountain sides. At particularly steep locations, Rt. 6 was susceptible to landslides. Photo interpreters devoted considerable time identifying potential choke points, which became the intended "targets" for Motor Pool missions.

During the rainy season, Motor Pool missions were fragged to Barrel Roll every day. "Officially", the C-130 and RF-4 aircraft were designated for weather reconnaissance. Once they checked into our area, their missions lasted from one to two hours. The real purpose of those flights did not become public information until many years after the war. The actual mission of Motor Pool aircraft was to "seed" the clouds over the Ho Chi Minh trail system with silver iodide. The theory, which was the result of an early 1960's CIA project named "Popeye", was that silver iodide created ice particles, which would stimulate precipitation. The resulting increase in rainfall created muddy conditions and landslides along vulnerable trails and roads, thus slowing the movement of men and materiel. The clouds over choke points were high-priority targets since mired vehicles created backups, making the vehicles easy targets for gunships and other strike aircraft. When vehicles were stopped and caught in the open due to road slides, Air Force tactics called for attacks on the lead and trail vehicles. Once immobilized, the lead and trail vehicles trapped the remaining convoy, which were repeatedly attacked, until all elements of the convoy were destroyed. The Air Force achieved success with this tactic, and over 13,000 Motor Pool sorties were flown during the Second Indochina War.

Another special package, called Ranch Hand, was fragged infrequently. The planes were specially modified and equipped C-123s and had the call sign Hades. Ranch Hand was an herbicidal warfare program. While the program was widely known to be in operation in Vietnam, very few knew about the use of chemical defoliants in Laos. Overall, less than 70 Ranch Hand missions were flown in Laos, mainly targeting enemy rice crops in northern Barrel Roll, however, the defoliant was dropped on portions of the tree canopy of the Ho Chi Minh Trail complex in Steel Tiger.

Without a doubt, the most intriguing operation in which Alleycat was involved took place in October 1969, at the start of the dry season. Inspired, no doubt, by the likes of James Bond or other intrepid "special agents", the highly classified operation unfolded flawlessly and was a resounding success.

Coinciding with the start of the dry season, as the expected Communist offensive began, Alleycat and Cricket were advised to prepare for a "special package". We were briefed on an operation called Traveling Salesman, and our orders were quite simple. Similar to Operation Northwind, we were provided with a radio frequency and ordered to monitor that frequency every night for the next several weeks. We were to listen for a specific message that would be transmitted in the blind. If we heard the words "traveling salesman", our orders were to relay that message via another designated discrete frequency. After monitoring the frequency for several weeks with no contact, one evening, I was startled to hear the transmission we thought would never arrive. In heavily accented English, I heard the words, "I am traveling salesman". Immediately, I requested our radio operator to dial up the specified frequency and transmitted the message, "I have a traveling salesman". I repeated the message and then heard an acknowledgment, "Roger, Alleycat, we copy". Alleycat was playing a minor role in a truly inspired counterinsurgency operation that rivaled other clandestine operations in past wars. A controlled American source had been imbedded within a convoy of regular NVA troops traveling down Route 6. That brave warrior carried a small transmitter with limited range. Since we orbited the PDJ, Alleycat was the ideal platform to receive the transmission.

As first light was approaching, it was typical that such convoys stopped and bivouacked at one of the truck parks along the trail. Once the Traveling Salesman's convoy had stopped and the troops had spread out for much needed rest, he transmitted his message, turned on the beacon he had been carrying, left his pack amongst the soldiers, and left the area. The beacon transmitted a signal that direction finding (DF) equipment easily located. Shortly after the transmission was made, two Spectre gunships checked in with us. Like us, they had been on alert every night, waiting for the mysterious Traveling Salesman. Immediately after the gunships arrived on station, Cricket also arrived, and control of Barrel Roll was turned over to them.

Once I had "passed off" my report to my Cricket counterpart, I asked him to keep me advised of the developing situation. On our RTB, we monitored Cricket strike frequencies as the gunships located the beacon and proceeded to hose down the area. Later, we learned that after working the area for more than an hour, the BDA reported by the Spectre pilots included numerous secondary explosions and fires. Traveling Salesman had been a major success. I often wondered about the fate of the brave and courageous Traveling Salesman. Who was he? How did he leave the area? Did he have anyone providing support? Did he survive the mission?

— 25 —

SEARCH AND RESCUE

On the morning of 6 December 1969, the longest and most famous search and rescue concluded with the rescue of one of two downed airmen. One of the sad realities of my new "world" was that a shoot down occurred nearly every day. Pilots who were forced to bail out in the vicinity of cities in North Vietnam (e.g. Hanoi, Vinh, or Haiphong) were usually captured immediately after landing on the ground. The best chance for a successful rescue was for pilots to get feet-wet (over water) or to head to Laos. While portions of Laos (specifically, over the trail system) were heavily defended, there remained many areas of Barrel Roll and Steel Tiger that were occupied by friendlies. Often times, however, pilots had no choice as to the location of their ejection. When a shootdown occurred, the air war, at least in the general vicinity of the crash site, stopped. Several things happened immediately. The pilot or GIB (guy in the back) would make a "may-day" call on guard, which would override all UHF frequencies and was heard by all planes and ground bases in the area. The wingman who observed the shootdown would also make a radio call to report the event. If a parachute was deployed, an emergency beeper (beacon) automatically began to transmit so that even as a pilot was descending in his parachute, his emergency was being reported.

Whenever a "may-day" call or beeper was heard, a definite physical and emotional response occurred. Your pulse quickened and an immediate adrenaline flow focused your attention on the emergency. Instinctively, you reached to turn up the volume on your radios, listened intently for the call sign of the aircraft, and all thoughts were directed as to how you could help. Our command post was poised to provide whatever information and/or assistance was needed to affect a successful SAR. Utilizing directional finding (DF) equipment, the beeper provided a means of identifying the location of the downed pilot. Once settled on the ground, if the pilot(s) was (were) physically able, they established voice contact with their survival radio. Thus, within minutes of a shootdown, a SAR began.

Command and control of the SAR was assumed by King, an orbiting HC-130, one of several that flew 24/7. The King, flying closest to the SAR location, was designated King 01 and diverted to loiter above the location of the downed airmen or as close to the scene as safety permitted. From that point forward, until the SAR was officially terminated, King 01 was in full command and control of SAR operations. When King 01 had to RTB, the replacement HC-130 became King 02. After establishing contact with the FAC aircraft that were in the vicinity of the crash site, King 01 designated one of them as the temporary on-scene commander who was now responsible for establishing radio contact with the downed airman, identifying his location, and observing what was happening on the ground in the vicinity of the crewman. King 01 then ordered the scrambling of an impressive array of rescue aircraft (rescue helicopters, FACs, and slow movers) so that when and if they were needed, they would be loitering near the scene. A schedule of needed air assets was generated to ensure the continued arrival of assets for as long as the SAR was active. King also served as an airborne tanker and refueled those rescue aircraft that had refueling capabilities.

Slow mover FACs were preferred during SARs because they could remain on station for extended periods of time, carry a large supply of marking rockets, and make steep banked turns to maintain eye contact with the survivor's location as well as with the bad guys. A major disadvantage, of course, was that slow movers made easier targets for enemy gunners.

Super Jolly Greens responded immediately to SARs, and its mid-air refueling capability meant they could remain on station for long periods of time. Once the controlling FAC judged a rescue attempt should be attempted, the Super Jolly Greens were prepared to respond.

During a SAR mission, King 01 acquired air assets to suppress enemy gun fire and hostile activity in the vicinity of the survivor so the rescue helicopters could safely approach the survivor and attempt the rescue. King would coordinate with various base operations to divert strike aircraft to the SAR and ensure those planes were loaded out with the proper ordnance and launched in proper sequence. Such coordination assured needed assets would be arriving on station in a timely manner throughout the SAR. King 01 controlled the holding patterns of assets and passed the planes off to the FAC on-scene commander as they were requested/ needed. FACs oriented the new arrivals and identified the locations at which ordnance should be targeted. If feasible, the FAC marked the target with rockets. Hard bombs were used against gun emplacements, and a variety of anti-personnel weapons were used against troop concentrations. That class of weapons included CBUs, napalm, rockets, smoke, guns, and Vodka (a reference to several types of riot control agents such as tear gas).

Without question, the best suited plane in the Air Force inventory to support SAR operations was the A-1E Skyraider. In addition to the plane's long loiter time, it had redundant systems and could withstand extensive battle damage and still complete its SAR mission. The plane was legendary for being capable of returning to base despite having huge holes in its wing, tail, or flight control surfaces. During combat missions other than SARs, the A-1E used Zorro, Hobo, and Firefly as call signs. While participating in a SAR, the call sign was either Sandy or Spad.

§

Officially known as the "Rescue at Ban Phanop", the 51-hour long SAR took place approximately 10 klicks (kilometers) southwest of the Mu Gia pass in Laos, near the border with North Vietnam. It was an area in the middle of the Ho Chi Minh trail system. The dramatic SAR is referred to as the Rescue of Boxer 22. It was the longest and largest SAR operation during the war, and it resulted in the successful rescue of the Boxer 22 Bravo (the back-seater who was the weapons system officer (WSO)). His name is 1st Lt. Woody Bergeron, and he successfully evaded capture for 51 hours. Boxer 22 Alpha, the pilot, was Major Benjamin Franklin Danielson, and he was killed by the enemy sometime during the second day of the SAR. They were flying an F4-C from the 558th Tactical Fighter Squadron in Cam Ranh Bay, Vietnam. At 1000 hours on 5 December 1969, the Boxer flight of two F4–C's, took off for an interdiction mission on Rt.

23 of the trail system, one of the most heavily defended portions of the trail. After refueling, the flight began their bomb runs on a fragged target. Boxer lead executed a successful run, and at 1127 hours he observed his wingman commence his bomb run. Almost immediately, the plane began violent pitching motions. He heard the pilot (Boxer 22 Alpha) issue a bailout command. Two good chutes were observed by Boxer lead, and the aircraft was seen impacting the ground just several meters short of the intended target. Alpha and Bravo landed about 40 meters apart but on opposite sides of a river. Major Danielson landed in an area that contained only a few clumps of trees in which to hide. Lt. Bergeron had a bit more foliage to provide cover. Voice contact was immediately established with both Alpha and Bravo, and both indicated they were in good shape.

With King 01 in charge, a SAR was immediately initiated, and for the next 51 hours an incredible drama unfolded. Three hundred and thirty-six sorties were flown by FAC and strike aircraft, and 24 Super Jolly Green missions were flown for the sole purpose of rescuing Boxer 22 Alpha and Bravo. Pilots displayed incredible acts of bravery and courage to support the SAR, and numerous aircraft sustained significant battle damage. Remarkably, only one rescuer was killed during the SAR. A PJ (pararescue jumper) aboard a Super Jolly Green was killed by small arms fire during an aborted rescue attempt on Day 1. On that day, the Jolly's made four attempts to effect a rescue, but withering fire from 23 and 37 mm guns shot up the aircraft. At 1755 hours the SAR was called off for the night. Even though no strike aircraft could work the area at night, FACs remained on station to observe the area and maintain radio contact with the survivors.

§

At first light on 6 December 1969, the SAR resumed. In his debriefing after being rescued, Lt. Bergeron reported that on that morning, Alpha had communicated with him with several beeper signals, a pre-arranged signal that the bad guys were too close for voice transmission. He could observe bad guys searching the area in which Alpha was hiding, and after a short period of time, he reported that he heard voices, a volley of automatic weapons fire, and a scream that he believed was that of his pilot. During day 2 of the SAR, repeated sorties targeted gun sights, some of which were located in caves above the river. Vodka was used on days 2 and 3, some of which was blown across the river and effected Bravo. The Jolly Greens attempted six more rescue attempts but were driven off by unrelenting gun fire. Bravo had to spend his second night on the ground, surrounded by the enemy.

On day three, 7 December 1969, strike aircraft softened up the surrounding area and riot control agents were dispersed. At approximately 1200 hours, after six hours of dropping ordnance in the area and several aborted pick-ups, Boxer 22 Bravo was rescued. News of the rescue quickly spread among those of us who had been monitoring the SAR. There was a collective sense of pride in the teamwork, sacrifice, and incredible courage that was displayed to rescue Lt. Bergeron. At the same time, we mourned the deaths of Major Danielson and the Air Force PJ. Throughout the SAR, I monitored the operation, listening to the radio transmissions and reading message traffic. Alleycat radio operators provided me with an edited recording of the Rescue of Boxer 22.

In a footnote to the Rescue at Ban Phanop, it took 37 years, but finally, Boxer 22 Alpha returned home. His remains were recovered in an excavation effort that occurred in March 2006 and later verified through DNA testing. The remains were returned to his family in Kenyon, Minnesota. Major Benjamin Franklin Danielson was buried with full military on 15 June 2007 in his Minnesota hometown.

— 26 —
NIGHT'S OFF AND R&R

(December 1969 – January 1970)

ven before General Vang Pao had completed his operation to seize control of the PDJ, General Giap was already
planning the NVA dry season counter-offensive. It was
called Campaign 139 and once again, the vaunted 312th Division
would lead the invasion of Barrel Roll along with the 316th Division.

As the dry season approached (November 1969), General Vang
Pao's forces continued to hold the PDJ and the surrounding areas they
had seized during Operation Redeem Honor. In anticipation of the
expected dry season Communist offensive, friendly forces positioned
themselves to disrupt the return of enemy forces to the PDJ. Ambush
teams, some of which had up to 200 members, were inserted into positions along Rt. 6 to the north of the PDJ, along the Ban Ban Valley,
astride Rt. 13 north of Luang Prabang, and along Rt. 7, as far east as
Nong Het, just a few miles from the border with North Vietnam.

Phou Nok Kok, a strategically important mountain overlooking the
intersection of Routes 6 and 7, was critical to the defense of the PDJ.
About 600 Hmong were dispersed on the mountaintop and along the
approaches to the mountain and in the town below, Muang Kam. They
were to serve as a blocking force in the event the Communists approached

the PDJ from the north or east. Additional preparations included increasing the number of sensor strings, and the additional mining of rivers.

Not unexpectedly, once the rains ended, enemy activity increased. Road Watch Teams and FAGs reported an increase in truck traffic and the presence of road repair crews on all major roads. Alleycat noted a dramatic increase in vehicular traffic on the major routes, based on the seemingly endless Sycamore reports we received every night. During the months of November and December 1969, sensors detected more than 3,000 vehicular movements, an incredible number. The Air Force continued to fly day and night strike missions in Barrel Roll but at reduced levels from those flown during Operation Redeem Honor. However, our nights were hectic, gunship missions were still being sent to Barrel Roll, and we were kept busy hunting trucks and providing close air support as needed. Most nights, after exhausting our fragged missions, we requested additional gunship and flareship assets.

By late November to mid-December 1969, NVA plans were immutable. Campaign 139 was intended to seize control of the entire PDJ and capture the strategically vital bases at Long Tieng and Sam Thong. 7th/13th Air Force increased the number of Barrel Roll missions, and, once again, airpower produced significant nighttime BDA. During the last two weeks of December, aircraft reported 320 trucks destroyed, 294 road cuts, 364 structures destroyed, and 1,412 secondary explosions. I missed most of the action during those two weeks because I was enjoying R & R in Australia.

Other significant changes were being made by 7th/13th Air Force to blunt the NVA operation. One was a modification to the ROE. The size of the buffer zone along the border with North Vietnam was reduced to four miles, and strikes were permitted under the control of any FAC and not just Ravens. The other change pertained to tactics. Up to that point, road interdiction missions were planned for only a few on only several of the most vulnerable sections of roads and trails. In hopes of forcing the NVA and PL to increase the number of road repair crews, thus increasing the number of "targets," many widely dispersed road Interdiction missions were scheduled. Those simple changes produced improved BDA.

R and R (24 December 1969 – 1 January 1970)

Everyone serving in a combat zone was entitled to a one-week Rest and

Recuperation (R & R) leave. R & R's were conducted at a variety of loca-
tions; Hawaii, Taiwan, Maylasia, Bangkok, Japan, and Australia. Hawaii,
Japan, and Bangkok seemed to be the most popular locations, especially for
married servicemen, because it was a convenient location to meet up with
spouses and family members. Once my superiors had explained the R &
R program to me, I immediately knew my first choice: Sydney, Australia.
Typically, R & R was scheduled to be taken midway through your tour.
I kept delaying my option to select a site, holding out for Sydney. The
selection process criteria to determine who would get which R & R site
was a combination of time-in-country and seniority. Being a junior officer
placed me at the bottom of the pecking order, but my patience paid off.

On the morning of 24 December 1969, I boarded a World Airways
charter flight. We landed in Darwin, on the north coast of Australia. Since
flights were not permitted to land in Sydney from midnight until 0600, we
had a layover of several hours. In typical military style, everything was well
organized upon landing in Sydney. After reporting to the R & R Center and
presenting my travel orders, I was assigned transportation. I elected to stay
in a suburb of Sydney called Coogee Beach and checked into a hotel called
Miller's Oceanic. Within an hour I was lying on the beach, celebrating
Christmas by enjoying the warm summer sun. However, I didn't venture
too far into the ocean because the water was ice cold, and the surf was rough.

I watched a lifeguard competition taking place on the beach. Teams
of lifeguards from different beaches competed in several events involving the
use of surfboards, rowing through the surf, and racing on the sand. The lifeguards took the competition very seriously, and I enjoyed the competition.
My first day in Australia was spent hanging out on the beach, drinking beer,
luxuriating in the sun, and eyeballing the young women in skimpy swimsuits.

The folks at Miller's Oceanic created a welcoming environment for their American guests. They provided an R & R party room
that was reserved exclusively for GIs. They made us feel welcome and
appreciated. The hotel scheduled a mixer on the day after Christmas
that provided the opportunity to meet and talk with some of the
locals as well as other military personnel. At the time, Australia had a
large contingent of combat soldiers in Vietnam, and the citizens were
quite supportive of our cause. The Australian people were friendly and
eager to learn about life in the United States. I had the good fortune
of meeting a local teacher (a niece of the hotel's owner) who agreed to

serve as my companion and tour guide during my time "Down Under".

Over the next several days, we visited the Taronga Park Zoo and attended a Cricket test match where I was introduced to meat pies - a "fast food" that had meat and veggies in a wrap. While in Australia, it became a favorite of mine. While on a ferry to the zoo, we passed the famous Sydney Opera House (which at the time was under construction). I watched lawn bowling at a private club and visited several neighborhood pubs.

At a park not far from the bowling club, young men were playing a pick-up game of cricket. I stopped to watch the play and slowly walked toward the action. Suddenly, I became aware that play had stopped, and the participants were all looking at me. I didn't know what was happening until one of the blokes shouted to me that I was on the field of play and to kindly remove my arse. Unlike baseball, which is played in a 90-degree arc, in cricket, the ball is in play 360 degrees from the point where the batter stands. Essentially, the entire field is in play. Embarrassed, I made a hasty retreat.

I stopped at several neighborhood pubs. At the time, most of the pubs were divided into two. On one side, women were welcome and could sit at the bar or at a table and drink with their friends. The other side, however, was reserved for men only. I met several blokes who had left their girlfriends or wives on one side of the pub in order to drink beer with their mates. During my time in Sydney, I practically drank for free. Once the Aussies heard me talk and discovered I was American, they quickly introduced themselves, bought me a pint, and saw to it that my glass was always filled.

My last night in Australia was New Year's Eve 1969, and I spent a quiet night at Coogee Beach. I visited several pubs but was back in my room before midnight. The following morning, I caught my return flight to Saigon. R & R was over. It had been a wonderful diversion from the everyday realities of the air war in Barrel Roll; however, I was anxious to return to work.

January 1970

As much as I enjoyed my week in Australia, I was anxious to learn about what had occurred on the PDJ during my nine-day absence. I was scheduled for ground duty on the day after my return and was an early arrival at the Alleycat shack. With the approval of our Commander, I scheduled myself to fly every other day for the next two and a half months, the remainder of my tour. During my absence, Vang Pao's forces, aided by close air support, had repelled two attacks on Phou Nok Kok by the NVA. I was pleased to learn that Laotian AC-47s flew regular missions to assist in defeating the initial Communist attacks. In the days to come, Laotian Spookys proved to be one of the mainstays in the defense of Phou Nok Kok and Muang Kham.

Intelligence reports estimated the number of NVA and PL troops participating in Campaign 139 numbered in excess of 16,000, while the defenders of the PDJ numbered no more than 6,000. As much as we hoped it would not be the case, the success of Operation Redeem Honor would be short-lived. In hopes of blunting the expected Communist onslaught, 7th/13th Air Force increased the number of air strike missions to Barrel Roll.

The NVA artillery bombardment of Phou Nok Kok began on 2 January 1970. Desperately, Hmong guerillas clung to portions of the base of the mountain and received desperate support from nightly flareship and gunship sorties.

During the evening of 7 January 1970, a first-ever sighting was reported. While working portions of Route 61 in the Ban Ban Valley, a Blind Bat reported seeing a helicopter. Our controller transferred the call to me. The pilot observed flashing red lights and was adamant that he saw a helicopter profile in the ambient moonlight. Nearby FAGs couldn't confirm the sighting, and no known friendly helicopters were working in the area. I immediately reported the sighting to Geneva and Blue Chip. No positive identification was ever made nor were there any further reported sightings.

On 10 January 1970, NVA sappers climbed the north face of Phou Nok Kok Mountain and aimed mortar fire and flamethrowers on the friendlies below the summit. Defenders withdrew and Communist forces now controlled the mountain and the vital intersection of Routes 6 and 7.

Even though the dry season had arrived, a weather anomaly hampered close air support efforts from the outset of the Communist offensive. A stubborn low lying ground haze mixed with the smoke produced by slash and burning farming obscured most of the PDJ. Usually, the haze cleared for short periods in the afternoon, but January produced only 12 days in which the ceiling was above 5,000 feet, the normal requirement for close air support missions. The challenge of the haze and smoke made it impossible for fast movers to provide close air support. When they were able to, gunships had to be painstakingly patient and use an abundance of caution when working with FAGs.

FEBRUARY
-MARCH 1970
§

— 27 —
B-52S ARRIVE IN BARREL ROLL

February - March 1970

The pressure of the Communist forces on the PDJ was relentless. Despite the significant increase in the number of air assets assigned to Barrel Roll, General Vang Pao's forces were outnumbered and simply no match for the Communists. Thanks to Air America's air mobility, SGU forces engaged in a tactical retreat from the PDJ, merging its forces, moving to ground more easily defended, and setting ambushes. By the beginning of March 1970, friendly forces consolidated their positions on the western edge of the PDJ, creating what was referred to as the "Vang Pao Line." While in theory, the Vang Pao Line made sense, strategically and tactically, it proved to be ineffectual against the NVA and PL onslaught.

The enemy easily advanced westward on Rt. 7 and seized control of the important intersection of Routes 7/13 near the town of Phou Khoun. With Route 13 under their control, the NVA severed the only road connecting Vientiane and the ancient Royal Capital City of Luang Prabang. Luang Prabang became further isolated when, to its north, along Rt. 13, the NVA/PL captured LS-01, Muong Ngai, located near the picturesque town of Nong Khiaw, lying astride the Nam Ou. The Nam Ou had been used as a major LOC by the NVA and had probably been the route they had used to infiltrate troops into the region.

As NVA and PL soldiers moved to attack and bypass the Vang Pao Line, Hmong warriors were bravely and valiantly clinging to three SGU strongholds on the PDJ: LS-108 (Muong Soui), LS-22, and Khong Khai. Up until the day Muong Soui was abandoned on 20 February 1970, T-28 sorties were still being launched from the Lima Site.

Lima Site 22 was located near Xiang Khoaungville. Simply referred to as Lima Lima, it served as a forward command base on the PDJ, and had a concrete runway, one of only a handful in all of Laos. Surrounding its barbed wire perimeter, the base was protected by howitzer and mortar pits. The SGU stronghold was located at the site of an old French fort. As was often the case with many Hmong warriors, families often followed their warrior husbands/fathers to what were considered to be "secure" locations and lived with them. With the presence of family members, Lima Lima was a moderate size city. On 4 February 1970, Air America began a large-scale evacuation of family members, which was followed by repeated enemy probes. Initially, close air support successfully defended the position. Well placed road mines success- fully thwarted armored assaults. But, the fate of Lima Lima had been sealed, and we all knew it. Continued NVA pressure successfully routed the defenders, and the site was abandoned two days after Muong Soui.

With the fall of Lima Lima, the village of Khong Khai was the last stronghold of General Vang Pao's forces. Khong Khai was always a village that demanded our full attention. During March 1970, SGU forces made a final stand at Khong Khai against enemy troops. The battle lasted several days, and in our attempts to support Vang Pao's troops, the village sustained considerable damage, and many villagers were among the casualties.

In light of the rapidly deteriorating situation in Barrel Roll and to avoid a total rout of RLG and Hmong forces, the Air Force implemented several significant changes in February 1970. We were advised, via message traffic that a detachment of OV-10 FACs was being sent to Udorn Royal Thai Air Base to fly daylight FAC missions and provide some relief to the overworked Ravens. While breaking out the Operations Plan, we also discovered that three AC-119K gunships were also being assigned to Barrel Roll for nighttime interdiction and close air support. T-28s, flown by Royal Lao Air Force pilots from other military regions, were transferred to Moung Soui and flew close air support missions from the forward base until LS-108 was abandoned on 20 February 1970. Three Spectre gunships and three Candlestick flareships continued to be fragged to Barrel Roll every night.

Without a doubt, the biggest change in Air Force doctrine and tactics was the use of B-52s in Barrel Roll for the first time during the Second Indochina War. Flying from Anderson Air Force Base in Guam, B-52s were first used against targets in North Vietnam in 1965. By 1967, over 5,000 Arc Light missions were regularly flown in Vietnam and Steel Tiger. Eventually, B-52 and KC-135 aerial refueling crews were assigned TDY at U-Tapao Royal Thai Air Base in southern Thailand. The B-52 could carry eighty-four 500-pound bombs internally and twenty-four 750-pound bombs on wing pylons for an incredible weapons load of 60,000 pounds. Most of the B-52 missions flown in Southeast Asia utilized Combat Sky Spot ground-directed bombing technology.

The standard Arc Light formation was a three-plane cell, flown individually or in multiple cells, referred to as a wave. One B-52 cell was capable of the saturation bombing of an area 1.2 miles long and .6 miles wide. Each cell had its own call sign. All B-52 operations were controlled and conducted by the Strategic Air Command (SAC). While all operations were coordinated with 7th/13th Air Force, SAC planners ordered air reconnaissance missions, selected targets, and scheduled the missions.

At various times during 1969, requests had been made to the State Department to use our strategic bombers in Barrel Roll, however, each time, the requests had been denied. Unknown to us at ABCCC, planning for an Arc Light mission in Barrel Roll had already begun. Air reconnaissance missions had been flown, targets had been identified, and the State Department approved Operation Good Look, the first usage of B-52s in Barrel Roll. On the evening of 17-18 February 1970, a flight of 36 B-52s, organized in 12 cells, struck the suspected headquarters and staging area of the NVA 312th Division. I was scheduled to fly on that historic night, and, as usual, arrived early. Upon entering the shack, there was a "buzz," and I knew immediately something was up. The Intel duty officer shared the amazing news with me; our oft shared hopes had become a reality. In addition to the destructive power of Arc Light missions, planners were also counting on the psychological effect such missions might have on both the friendly and Communist forces. The battle staff was looking forward to the "fireworks." Just prior to the pre-mission briefing, I grabbed a copy of the Frag and read the entries for the Arc Light mission. As I reviewed the call signs of the cells that would be flying that night, I was shocked to see that the call sign for one of the twelve cells was Apgar!

Operation Good Look continued to support Barrel Roll operations for the next three years, until the war ended in 1973. During that time, 2,518 B-52 sorties were flown in Barrel Roll, dropping 58,374 tons of munitions on suspected NVA and PL targets.

GREETINGS FROM RODNEY!

Somewhere in my archives, I have a portion of the page from the frag that contained the B-52 call sign "Apgar." Immediately upon seeing my family name in the classified document, I knew the source. One of our former Alleycat Intelligence Officers had left us for an assignment at Headquarters Strategic Air Command (SAC) at Offutt Air Force Base in Omaha, Nebraska. It was Rodney's way of saying "Hello" to an old friend. I saw Rodney one more time during a random airport encounter.

All of the success in regaining control of the PDJ from the previous summer had been reversed. Thanks to Air America, the only consolation was that the recent NVA offensive had not come with a larger loss of friendly casualties. Air American pilots were stellar in their non-stop flying to evacuate Hmong warriors and members of their families. The vaunted "Vang Pao Line" was gone, and the intentions of the North Vietnamese were clearly evident, Long Tieng and Sam Thong.

As my year-long deployment was drawing to a close, it was distressing to monitor the dramatic change in momentum of combat operations in Barrel Roll. Despite our best efforts, we just weren't able to provide the Hmong troops with the air support they needed to defend the PDJ and remain on the offensive. I celebrated their victories and mourned their losses. When FAGs declared TIC, assets were always diverted to provide them with the close air support they needed. My ultimate frustration was when we had no resources to allocate. For one year, we had played an important role in each other's lives, and, within a few weeks, I would be leaving them and their war. As my date of estimated return from overseas (DEROS) approached, my total focus was on the distressing events that were unfolding in Barrel Roll.

— 28 —

ATTACK ON LONG TIENG
AND SAM THONG

I t was a quiet night during the second week in March 1970 when, suddenly, all hell broke loose on the radios. Out of breath and clearly stressed, Hilltop called to inform us that Long Tieng was under attack. He reported rocket and mortar fire landing on the base. Numerous buildings had been damaged as well as aircraft on the flight line. Hilltop indicated he and others were leaving the base, seeking refuge in the surrounding jungle. He said he would continue to monitor his radio and direct aircraft to strike enemy locations. I wished him Godspeed and was sobered by the fact that Hilltop was in mortal danger and the realization I might never speak to him again. I assured him helicopters would be available at first light to pick him up. We quickly lost radio contact, and I would not speak with him again for the remainder of the night. However, while Annon could not hear me, I could clearly hear him directing aircraft against enemy locations in and around Long Tieng.

During the initial confusion, a stern voice suddenly came on the air. In an abrupt and gruff manner, the man behind the voice ordered Alleycat to provide flare ship and gunship support throughout the night. I then heard him demand to have his jeep brought to him. It was the second time I had the opportunity to speak with General Vang Pao, but this time, the circumstances were entirely different. I assured him we would provide his forces with the support they needed.

Almost immediately after Hilltop's frantic call, we received a similar call from Sam Thong, and they too, were under attack. Obviously, the NVA and PL had unleashed a well-coordinated attack. During the evening, gunships, flare ships, and fast and slow movers were diverted to provide relief to General Vang Pao's forces at LS-98 and LS-20. With the direct approval of the General, gunships destroyed the ammunition dump at Long Tieng.

While the attacks on the Lima Sites were unfolding, I used the secure radio to place a call to Geneva, the air attaché in Vientiane. It was my duty to alert the Ambassador, G. McMurtrie Godley III, of what was unfolding at SGU Headquarters. Incredibly, the embassy staff seemed irritated to be awakened in the middle of the night. Blue Chip, on the other hand, was highly interested in the ongoing battles and requested regular updates. With the attacks on Long Tieng and Sam Thong, coupled with their seizure of the PDJ, the NVA, and PL were now on the threshold of controlling Barrel Roll in its entirety. The situation was critical.

As soon as we received Hilltop's initial call, the Battle Staff immediately went into action, diverting resources to Long Tieng and Sam Thong, and requesting additional assets. Our biggest challenge was to locate a FAG at LS-20 who could direct air strikes. Our ABCCC pilot altered the orbit and we moved to the western portion of the PDJ to improve radio reception. The radios were alive with non-stop traffic all night.

I listened intently as Hilltop furiously controlled airstrikes. I marveled at this man, his cool and in control demeanor, directing air strikes against the invading NVA troops as he was fleeing for his life. He was decisive in providing clearly understood instructions to the various strike aircraft with which he worked and did so throughout the night. His first priority was to destroy the AAA gun at the west end of the runway. After the gun was destroyed, Hilltop then located the ammunition dump for the pilot. While the ammunition dump was providing numerous secondary explosions, Hilltop then directed gunship fire on the enemy poised along Skyline Ridge One. While working with gunships throughout the night, Hilltop also worked with flareships to provide battlefield illumination for the defenders of LS-98. The battle staff monitored the strike frequencies Hilltop used throughout the night. As the night turned into daylight, I could hear Hilltop's labored breathing, obviously fatigued from the frantic pace of defending Long Tieng.

Had it not been for the seriousness of the situation, we might have had a chuckle at the Spectre command pilot's attempt to have Hilltop authenticate his identity. Normally, such an authentication procedure between a FAG and a pilot would involve the use of the "Wheel." In the emergency in which we found ourselves, it was completely understandable why Hilltop was not carrying a Wheel with him. I was able to hear the exchanges between Hilltop and the pilot, but I wasn't able to speak directly with my friend. I confirmed with the pilot that he was speaking with the "genuine article" and then had a thought. I suggested to the pilot that he ask Hilltop to provide him with the name of the man in Alleycat with whom he speaks. Immediately, Hilltop responded, "Fred," and that satisfied the need to authenticate Hilltop's identity.

As morning approached, the destructive fury being delivered by American pilots began taking its toll on the invaders. Eventually, contact was broken, and the Communists withdrew to the safety of the surrounding mountains. Hilltop remained in the field that night, and at first light, he and several of his fellow survivors were rescued by Air America helicopters and returned to the base. The NVA/PL were expected to initiate another ground assault, but it didn't materialize, at least not immediately.

Subsequent to the attack, we learned the NVA had infiltrated and seized control of Skyline Ridge One, the westernmost ridge line overlooking the base. From that strategic location, the enemy fired rockets and mortars onto the base, infiltrated a 20-man sapper team, and managed to set up a 23 mm AAA gun at the west end of the runway. The gun was used to destroy aircraft and buildings and target SGU forces and civilians.

The next day, Hilltop was back on the job leading a patchwork of SGU forces, Thai regulars, CIA irregulars from Steel Tiger, and RLA regulars. They managed to re-take control of Skyline Ridge One and secure Long Tieng. Once again, 20 Alternate was under Royal Government control, and a counter-offensive was launched against NVA/PL forces at Sam Thong.

I didn't learn until several days after the coordinated attacks on Long Tieng and Sam Thong, that a powerful weapon system, Commando Vault, had been used in Laos for the first time. The weapons system proved to be a significant factor in motivating the NVA/PL to break off its well-coordinated attack. Nick-named "Big Blue", it was a 15,000-pound bomb, comprised of a gelled explosive slurry, which produced massive overpressure and destruction over a wide-spread area. The weapon was successfully dropped on an NVA troop concentration on a mountain top overlooking Sam Thong.

Big Blue succeeded in breaking the enemy's presence at Lima Site 20.

The Communists had come close to destroying the Barrel Roll SGU command center, which would surely have hampered, if not doomed, American and allied operations in Barrel Roll. In response to the attack on Long Tieng and Sam Thong, 7th/13th Air Force significantly increased the number of air strikes in the upcoming days. While the NVA and PL occupied the PDJ, its supply lines were being disrupted, a large number of enemy combatants had been killed and injured, and the awesome might of American Air Power negatively impacted NVA and PL confidence and morale.

However, Campaign 139 had taken its toll on the Hmong as well. It wasn't until more than three months after I left Southeast Asia that I learned just how depleted General Vang Pao's forces were in terms of number and spirit.

After reporting for my next duty assignment as an Air Intelligence Officer at Headquarters Tactical Air Command (TAC), I would once again have access to classified briefings and information regarding the Second Indochina War. I would follow the Second Indochina War from afar.

NEGOTIATIONS WITH THE PATHET LAO

Several years would pass before I learned that during my last month in SEA, March 1970, the Royal Lao Government had entered into peace negotiations with the Pathet Lao, seeking a cease-fire and permanent end to the war. Ultimately, those discussions were unproductive. Also, during that fateful month, distraught that the number of soldiers in his Hmong army had dwindled to approximately 5,500 effectively, General Vang Pao had considered removing his guerrilla force and family members from the north and relocating to relative safety near the Thai/Lao border. Reports indicated it was not the first time General Vang Pao considered leaving his homeland. He had been having ongoing discussions with the Hmong Council of Elders regarding the fate of the Hmong and over the next two years, General Vang Pao engaged PL representatives regarding a cease-fire. The goal of the Hmong Council of Elders was to live in peace in a secure homeland in northern Laos.

Two days after the attack on LS-98, one of our radio operators stopped by our shack and gave me a recording of the fateful night's activity. Aware of my passion for the Hmong and interest in Barrel

Roll operations, from time to time, my friends in the radio shack gave me edited tapes that captured significant events and highlights from our event-filled missions. I will always be grateful for their thoughtfulness and kindness by providing me with the thrill of hearing Hilltop's voice once again. Hilltop was a warrior, and I have been blessed to have had the paths of our lives cross during my year in Southeast Asia.

My year of serving as Alleycat Intel was near its end. After the memorable night of the coordinated attacks on LS-98 and LS-20, I was scheduled to fly just two more missions. The hectic pace never let up. During daylight hours, civilians were being frantically evacuated from both locations. A 300-man Royal Thai artillery battalion was moved to a fire base on the perimeter of Long Tieng. T-28 strike missions were, once again, being flown from 20 Alternate by Lao and Raven pilots. One Hmong pilot flew an incredible 31 missions in one day. FAGs were active and went in search of enemy targets and once located, they were relentlessly attacked, day and night.

— 29 —
GOODBYE TO MY WARRIOR FRIEND

I was scheduled to fly my last mission on the night of 16/17 March 1970, St. Patrick's Day! Three of us (Lt. Col Paul "Shorty" Hartz and Captain Tom Borre) shared the same DEROS and would be celebrating our Sawatdee flight together. After out-processing, we would also return to the USA on the same "Freedom Flight" on 25 March 1970.

It was with mixed emotions when I reported to the shack for my final flight. I was happy, knowing the end of my tour was near and within a week, I would be reunited with family and friends. However, I was concerned about the safety and future of the courageous Hmong warriors and the fate of their homeland. For their survival, they would need to continue an aggressive pursuit of the retreating enemy. Additionally, they would need continued close air support and the continual disruption of enemy supply lines. The situation was approaching desperate; the NVA and PL had seized control of the PDJ, the Vang Pao Line had been bypassed, and Luang Prabang had been cut off from Vientiane. It was with a sense of guilt that I was abandoning their cause.

When I boarded the flight for my last mission, I thought about my first flight, taking orders from my training officer. Now, my replacement, whom I had been training for the past ten days was on board for his final check flight. As Jim had done with me, I permitted our newest Intel officer to handle the bulk of mission responsibilities. Back in the shack, someone had put several bottles of champagne on ice, and I noticed a couple of those bottles had somehow made their way onto our plane. To celebrate St. Patrick's Day, those of us who were short timers wore bright green shirts under our flight suits. Overall, it was a quiet night. Everyone knew that at some point soon, the Communists would renew their attacks on Long Tieng and Sam Thong, and in hopes of delaying that inevitability, non-stop air strikes were being sent to Barrel Roll, day and night. Thankfully, no TIC was reported on my final flight.

Once Alleycat had assumed control of Barrel Roll, I took the opportunity to contact those FAGs with whom I had worked closely for the past year. I explained that while this would be the last time I spoke with them, Alleycat would be flying every night to provide assistance, as always. I thanked them for their great work and told them how honored I was to call them my friend. I told them, each, goodbye and I would always remember the experience we shared in Laos. Next, I contacted Sycamore and Blue Chip. Over the past year, we called ourselves friends, talking every day and recognizing each other's voices. My last radio contact was with Hilltop. We had forged a special relationship, a brotherhood. When we signed off, I was quite certain it would be the last time I would have the privilege of speaking with my warrior friend. My respect and admiration for Hilltop had grown throughout the year as did my emotional attachment. I was in awe of his courage and valor and very concerned about his future well-being. He understood it would be the last time we would be speaking with one another, and he was profuse with his praise and thanks.

As first light was approaching and once Cricket assumed control of Barrel Roll, we engaged in some on-board hijinks. The bottles of champagne were opened, cups were filled, and a series of toasts were made as we crossed the fence. And the silliness did not stop there. The three short-timers had the honor of de-planing first and were the first to be welcomed by a traditional last mission hosing. After our drenching, we celebrated with more toasts and champagne on the flight line. I made a point to shake the hand of each member of the ground crew and thank them for their great work in maintaining our aircraft. It was an emotional experience and military bonding at its best. The day crew was waiting for us at the shack and joined in the celebration. We had a quick after-action briefing, and then, as our flight suits were drying, we walked around in our underwear and consumed copious amounts of beer.

With my duties at Alleycat officially over, the next few days were devoted to out-processing. We were required to have a physical examination, return issued equipment to BEMO, and check out with CBPO to receive travel orders and pick up payroll records. Arrangements were made to have my belongings packed and shipped to my next duty station.

My time in Southeast Asia was ending, but the war would continue. Each afternoon, I visited the Alleycat shack to obtain updates regarding the status of our forces and Barrel Roll operations. I read after-action reports, message traffic from Blue Chip, and the daily intelligence summaries. It was difficult for me to "let go" and regretted by decision to not extend my tour when offered the opportunity. Many years passed before I realized I would never able to let go of the bonds that had formed during my year in Southeast Asia. It took a long time to realize those feelings and emotions had become an important part of my persona and would remain within me throughout my lifetime.

Every month, each of the four orbits held a Sawatdee party for those whose deployments were ending. It was a military tradition, one in which we recognized the contributions of our squadron mates, thanked them for their service, and said goodbye. We wore our red party suits, drank a lot of adult beverages, and had a great time. My squadron mates toasted those of us who were leaving, and we had the opportunity to express our thoughts about all that had taken place during the past year, express our appreciation for the friendships we had developed, and to say goodbye.

Shortly after we had gathered at a local restaurant in town, I was shocked to see Hilltop walking into the room. I was humbled that he had gone to the trouble to find out the date and location of our Sawatdee party and scheduled time off to fly to Udorn just to say goodbye to me. Like me, he valued the bond and connection we had established during our year of working together. I was humbled by his presence. Hilltop's heroic reputation and status had preceded him, and, deservedly so. He immediately became the center of attention and deservedly so. He received a standing ovation, and his presence was an honor for all of us.

I was grateful to have the opportunity to talk with Hilltop in person one last time and to embrace this fine young man and brave warrior. As the evening progressed, many toasts were offered, and we all engaged in well-intentioned and spirited banter. Hilltop was among one of the last to speak. In his near-perfect English and quiet manner, he expressed his grateful appreciation for the support our Squadron had provided to Vang Pao's ground forces and singled out Alleycat for the life-and-death role we had played in Barrel Roll operations. As a token of his friendship, Annon gave me two photographs of himself and a very special gift. They were gifts I will treasure forever.

One of the photos was of Hilltop, carrying an M-16 rifle, as he walked in front of a barracks at Long Tieng. He was on his way to work. On the back of the picture, Annon had written, "My Dear Fraid, You're my friend forever." The other picture was of Annon and a comrade sitting atop captured Russian-made PT-76 tanks. Hilltop and his team had conducted a successful ambush of NVA forces as they approached the PDJ from the north, along a trail system to the east of Route 6 in the Ban Ban Valley. Annon presented me with the watch he had taken from the body of the tank commander who had been killed in the ambush. The watch had been made in Russia. After the Sawatdee party, I accompanied Hilltop, one last time, to his part of Udorn.

Each departing member of Alleycat received a wooden Alleycat carving inscribed with the dates of our service. While it is only a piece of wood, to me, it symbolizes a transformative life experience. It represents the accomplishment of my childhood goal of serving in the military and participating in combat operations. I was honored to be one of the more than two million men and women, of varied backgrounds, who used their talents and skills and committed themselves to the missions to which we had been assigned. I was privileged to "observe" ordinary men display extraordinary acts of valor. Every day, incredible acts of bravery and courage were on display by those men who, in their words, "were only doing their job."

The more than 58,000 combat deaths that occurred during the Vietnam War represented the ultimate sacrifice by those who chose to protect the lives of their brothers in combat. It was an honor and humbling experience to have had the privilege of serving with those patriots and heroes and to have had the opportunity to play a minor role in the war.

Two days after the Sawatdee party, the day of my departure arrived. I gave my flight cap to our house-girl, Dang, and with tears in her eyes, she gave me a beautiful Thai flower lei, a symbol of good luck in your travels. The fragrance was wonderful and reminded me of similar leis I had purchased from the street children of Udorn. Dang also gave me a very special gift, a one baht note, a bill rarely found in circulation. I signed out at the Squadron and said goodbye to my squadron mates. The three of us, "Shorty" Hartz, Tom Borre, and me, were driven to the terminal where we boarded the Klong Hopper for the flight to Bangkok. We didn't speak much, each seemingly lost in our own thoughts. That evening, we stayed at the Chao Phraya Hotel in Bangkok, which served as a Visiting Officers Quarters (VOQ) for the military. Before leaving the hotel the next morning, I cut and trimmed my handlebar mustache and sideburns. Like most other military personnel leaving Southeast Asia, it was time to adhere to regulations regarding personal grooming. Then it was off to Saigon where we connected with our chartered flight to CONUS.

— 30 —

GOING HOME

During the long flight home, I had ample time to reflect on my year in Thailand, flying combat missions over the battlefields of the Plaine des Jarres. Like so many others, I was proud to have volunteered to serve in Southeast Asia and grateful for the opportunity. At the age of 25, I had achieved one of my life goals. I left Southeast Asia with a sense of pride of the positive contribution I had made to the Air Force Mission. It was humbling to have had the opportunity to serve the brave and courageous Hmong warriors of Barrel Roll. It would take years, but eventually, I arrived at the realization the Hmong had given more to me than I could have ever provided to them while serving as Alleycat Intel.

Thoughts about Hilltop were never far from my conscious thought. I couldn't help but think I was abandoning him and his cause. While I was safely ensconced in a World Airways charter plane that was returning me to my homeland, Hilltop was still waging war against the enemy, risking his life every day for the Hmong cause. It was pure fantasy of course, but I wondered if the paths of our lives would ever cross again. For more than four years, he had risked injury and death every day. It was with a sense of foreboding whenever I thought about Hilltop's future. Try as I might, I wasn't optimistic.

The names of the other FAGs with whom I had worked were never far from my conscious thoughts either. For some, we spoke on a regular basis.

They were faceless, but I learned to recognize their voices, which created a more intimate relationship. It hadn't taken long for me to recognize the fear in their voices when reporting TIC and requesting assistance. It was always reassuring to hear relief in their speech when they reported their status after the completion of an air support mission. I feared for their future as well.

At the time, I was too caught up in the excitement of returning home, and reuniting with family and friends, to realize I was leaving something else behind. Later in life, upon reflecting on my year of combat duty, I became more aware of the significant effect the experience had had on me. The many lessons I learned were profound and remained a part of my persona and leadership style. Those life lessons have served me well.

Our "freedom flight" landed at Travis Air Force Base, the base from which I had departed one year earlier. During my time in Southeast Asia, we were aware of student activism back in the States, and we read accounts of the growing anti-war sentiment. However, I was not prepared for the magnitude of the hatred and animosity nor the violent nature of the opposition that greeted us. The loathing for returning veterans was etched on the faces of the demonstrators who greeted us as we passed through the main gate on the way to the rest of our lives.

Our thoughts, feelings, and needs were simple. We mourned the loss of our comrades who made the ultimate sacrifice in their service to one another and our great nation. We were grateful for having returned home safely. We were proud of our service and the sacrifices we had made. All we wanted to do was reconnect with the members of our families, re-assimilate into society, report to our next duty station, and get on with our lives. But for many, that was not to be. The emotional commitment we had made had taken a very deep hold on us, and, sadly for some, one from which they never recovered.

I felt a need to talk about the "world" from which I had just returned, but, to my surprise, no one in my family asked many questions about my year-long experience in Southeast Asia. It was all very confusing and didn't take long to realize and accept the fact I would be alone to process my thoughts and feelings. It was up to me, and me alone, to attach meaning to what I had witnessed and experienced in Southeast Asia.

I know now that I pursued what I thought to be the only logical solution to the ambiguity of the war I was experiencing; I repressed those thoughts and feelings. That strategy seemed to work, at least for a few years. No doubt, my ability to compartmentalize my life and repress any thoughts and feelings regarding my year of supporting the Hmong in Barrel Roll was aided by the necessity of focusing my energy, time, and resources on marriage, graduate school, children, and a new career.

Clearly, it was a different time in America. Active-duty personnel were reluctant to wear their uniforms in public; in fact, during our debriefing before returning to CONUS, we were advised to wear civilian clothing when traveling to our next duty station. The homecoming reception we received was quite different from that which today's veterans are afforded. Many of us were subjected to verbal abuse and harassment, and many suffered the indignity of being publicly mocked and humiliated. Anti-war posters and slogans were prominently displayed, seemingly, everywhere. The media coverage of the Vietnam War reflected Walter Cronkite's narrative that "the war was lost." The prevailing sentiment among demonstrators was that Vietnam veterans were "baby killers." We became the villain in the public debate regarding an unpopular war. A strong feeling of disdain and hatred was assigned to anyone associated with the Vietnam War. For some, the public humiliation was a burden they weren't equipped to endure, and the abuse only served to exacerbate their already fragile emotional well-being.

For those of us who remained on active duty, we had an easier transition than those whose service commitment was ending. For the next two years, I would still be living and working in a military environment, interacting with others, many of whom had also served in Southeast Asia. We shared an understanding of what we had experienced. It was fortuitous that at my next duty station, there were several others with whom I had served at ABCCC. In fact, another junior officer and I worked in the same office. We didn't dwell on our personal experiences, per se; instead, we were comfortable with one another and felt safe to share our feelings. It was reassuring to know we were not being judged.

Aircraft hangar and buildings constructed by the Japanese during WW II when they occupied Udorn Royal Thai Airbase

Control tower constructed by the Japanese during WW II when they occupied Udorn Royal Thai Airbase

Soviet Made 12.7 mm ZPU Anti-Aircraft Gun - A gift from General Vang Pao to ABCCC

Burning "Classified Destruct" documents

Pre-flight completed and C-130 prepared for boarding. Air conditioning unit in the foreground was used to cool the capsule, which got uncomfortably hot during the sun-drenched 100 + degree days.

Take off for a 14-hour mission in Barrel Roll

The author

Typing after-action report during RTB

Final flight shenanigans with Lieutenant Colonel Paul "Shorty" Hartz on St Patrick's Day, 1970. We returned home on the same flight.

More final flight shenanigans.

PART TWO

A LONG, SLOW FAREWELL

— 1 —

HOME AGAIN

After two weeks of leave, enjoying time with family and friends, I reported to my next duty station. I had been assigned to Headquarters Tactical Air Command (TAC), Langley Air Force Base, located in Hampton, Virginia. Technically, I had selected the assignment to Langley AFB. About mid-way through my deployment, the radio operators helped me place a ham radio call to the Air Force Personnel Center located at Randolph Air Force Base in San Antonio, Texas. I was curious about my next assignment and was transferred to the office that handled Intelligence Officer assignments. After speaking with Captain Stein, who had been one of my instructors at the Armed Forces Air Intelligence School at Lowry ABF, Denver, Colorado, I learned my name was already on his "radar," and he had good news to share. I had a choice of assignments. Considering my deployment to and experience in SEA, I was selected to serve as a SERE instructor at the Air Force Survival School at Fairchild Air Force in Spokane, Washington. Or, if I preferred, I could be on the east coast at Langley AFB in Virginia. We agreed to speak again in a week or so.

The SERE assignment appealed to me, but Virginia beaches and proximity to my family won out. I often wondered how my life would have been different if I had accepted the assignment in Washington.

Langley AFB is in the Tidewater Region of Virginia, an area rich in American history. The name refers to the low-lying regions of the mid-Atlantic coast that experience the effects of changing tides on local rivers, and ocean fronts. Numerous military installations and military-related industries are located in the area. Langley was headquarters of the Tactical Air Command (TAC), a major Air Force command that controlled "tactical" assets and operations. At the time, The Air Force organizational chart listed more than fifteen major commands. Among them were:

- Strategic Air Command (SAC)
- Military Airlift Command (MAC)
- Aerospace Defense Command (ADC)
- United States Air Forces Europe (USAFE)
- United States Air Forces Pacific (PACAF)
- Air Training Command (ATC)

I was aware of the other major commands and their general functions, but I didn't know much about TAC's mission and knew nothing regarding the job to which I had been assigned. That was about to change. Following the establishment of the Air Force in the post-WWII era, TAC had been established to serve as a balance between strategic and air defense.

My orders indicated I had been assigned to the Targeting Office. The designation for the office was INT (Intelligence Targeting) and was supervised by Colonel Harold Henschel. Once he learned about the assignment I had just left, he wanted to hear first-hand about the air war in Southeast Asia. Although he had access to all kinds of material regarding the progress of the war, he was interested in the operations conducted by *L'Armee Clandestine*, the CIA's "secret army." At his request, I prepared briefing materials and once a week, I briefed him about various aspects of the war in Barrel Roll. Those briefings continued for several months.

INT was divided into three areas of responsibility: Targeting (INTT), Materials (INTM), and Collections (INTI). INTM prepared targeting materials such as photographs, descriptions, topography, and charts for proposed targets listed in operations plans. INTI was a small section (only one junior officer and one enlisted man), and its work was highly classified. Basically, the office arranged for the collection of needed information about potential targets and took advantage of any available means. Most times it involved government employees (e.g. diplomats and government personnel) who traveled, on official business, to areas of the world in which prospective targets were located. They were "tasked" with a request to obtain certain specified information about the targets while in the official conduct of their travel. INTI's last "resource" was clandestine operatives.

I was assigned to work with another junior officer who introduced and oriented me to the new assignment. Our job was to review, modify, and update several operations plans involving the defense and/or invasion of three Caribbean Island nations. Each operations plan had a targeting document, and working with my colleague, we were responsible for producing, reviewing, and revalidating the Target Intelligence Planning Support (TIPS) document for each of those operations plans. TIPS profiled every target in the operations plan, and each document was under continual review and updating. The assignment required being knowledgeable about all high value targets that had either tactical or strategic value in the defense and/or invasion of a particular nation.

In order to work on those operations plans, my security clearance had to be expanded to include several special access clearances above Top Secret. My previous BI had cleared me through Top Secret, but an expanded background investigation (EBI) was now required. The process did not take long, and within several weeks I had received the necessary clearance. The new clearance resulted in the addition of the prefix "E" to my AFSC (Air Force Specialty Code), which established my security clearance at levels above Top Secret. My new assignment also resulted in changes to my AFSC. My new primary AFSC was changed to E8086 (Air Targets Officer), however, I was assigned a duty AFSC of E8095 (Air Tactical Intelligence Officer).

One of the best sources of intelligence regarding the targets in the countries for which I was responsible was photography, and my assignment to Headquarters TAC provided me with an introduction into the world of satellite imagery. During my deployment in Southeast Asia, I was aware that such technology existed, but the photography with which we worked was almost exclusively obtained from reconnaissance aircraft (RF-4 and RF-101) or Buffalo Hunter drones. The use of satellite images for intelligence purposes had begun with a classified program called Corona, which had its origins during the Eisenhower administration. The next generation of satellite imagery was called Keyhole, and it was Keyhole imagery that I was using at INTT. As of 2008, the military was still using Keyhole satellites for images but with much improved camera technology.

TK imagery was highly classified, and we were not permitted to work with the material in our building. Whenever we needed to review target imagery, we were required to do that work at the Reconnaissance Technical Center (Recce Tech), located in a very large building in an isolated portion of Langley Air Force Base. Not surprisingly, there were no windows in the Recce Tech. With the assistance of photo interpreters, we identified targets of interest, assigned priorities, and prepared target profiles. Once it was agreed that a new target would be included in an operations plan, INTM would then be tasked to prepare the necessary materials for inclusion into the plan. Targets included military installations, transportation facilities (i.e. airfields, port facilities, railroad stations, and yards), POL refinery and storage, bridges and tunnels, power plants, LOCs, and so forth. Major revisions of operations plans were made once every other year. Each ops plan was identified by a four-digit number. As needed changes in targeting materials were made, those changes were distributed as regular document change orders to all units.

Colonel Henschel appointed me briefing officer for INT, and I became a member of a team that provided orientation briefings for visiting VIPs. PowerPoint technology was not available at that time, so we incorporated 35mm color slide graphics into our presentations. As INT's mission and capabilities evolved, the briefing materials had to be updated as well. I enjoyed having that responsibility, and the opportunity to brief general officers provided me valuable public speaking experience, a skill I made good use of in later years and one in which I felt confident.

§

Early in my tour at Langley, the office received word that the Commander of TAC, General William Momyer, would make an inspection tour of our building. General William Momyer was a four-star general and had been a fighter pilot during WWII. He had a reputation of being a brilliant tactician in tactical air warfare. For two years, he had served as the Deputy Commander of the Military Assistance Command (MACV) and had been one of the architects of Operation Rolling Thunder. However, Momyer was not without his critics. As a fighter group commander during WWII, Momyer recommended that the 99th Fighter Squadron, a segregated African American unit (Tuskegee Airmen), be removed from combat operations. The accusation of racism followed him throughout his career. While serving at MACV, General Momyer was an outspoken advocate of an all-jet Air Force, believing jets could outperform propeller driven aircraft. He was proven wrong, of course, as slow-movers assumed critically important roles in the air war.

For several days prior to the date of inspection, our collective efforts were devoted to preparing the office and ourselves for the General's visit. We cleaned every surface and neatly organized our workspaces. We reviewed TAC's mission and the various roles our offices played in support-ing that mission. Finally, the big day arrived, and we were all standing at ease next to our desks. Since the building was three stories high and filled with several Divisions, we felt the odds of the General visiting our office were slim to none. Being one of the junior officers in the office and the most recent arrival, my desk was located at the entrance to the office, near the main corridor. I heard steps in the hallway, and, suddenly, General Momyer, followed by staff members, strode directly into our office! I jumped to and shouted out, "Room, ten hut." I was the first person he encountered upon entering the office. General Momyer stopped directly in front of me and immediately began asking a series of questions regarding our unit's responsibilities. As I stood at attention, all I could see were four bright twinkling shining stars on each shoulder of his uniform. Somehow, I maintained my composure and responded to about four or five questions. The General thanked me, and then he and his entourage turned and left the office. During the entire exchange, I never took my eyes off the stars.

§

The new security clearance I had received permitted me to attend weekly intelligence briefings that were conducted in the Headquarters Building. The briefings were prepared for General Momyer, and his staff.

Several of us from INT attended the weekly briefings, and I rarely missed an opportunity to do so. The briefings were held in a very large vault-like structure, a room within a room. To gain entry, we were required to show our ID cards to armed guards and sign-in next to our names on a roster of those officers cleared to attend the briefings. Briefing information addressed all areas in the intelligence field and had been obtained through all types of interesting sources. Much of the information addressed political and military developments in countries of our Cold War opponents, new weapons technology, US operations throughout the world, Soviet and American space programs, and worldwide current events. While situation reports (SITREP) regarding the Second Indochina War were presented, briefing topics were more of a global and strategic nature. Almost eight weeks had passed since I had ended my official duties at ABCCC, and I was anxiously seeking information regarding the war in Barrel Roll and the fate of my beloved Hmong.

After one of the weekly briefings, I approached one of the briefers and explained my interest and experience in Barrel Roll. He responded positively to my request to visit his Intel Shop and provided me access to the Intelligence resources of his office. I greatly appreciated his consideration and made a conscious effort to limit my visits and not take advantage of the courtesy he had extended. With access to this virtually unlimited source of classified information, I quickly delved into the war in Barrel Roll.

Publications such as the Weekly Air Intelligence Summary (WAIS) proved to be great sources of information regarding air and ground operations in Southeast Asia. I also gained access to a variety of after-action and BDA reports, assessments, analyses, and imagery. Operations in Laos, of course, was my primary area of concern, and I had to sort through the myriad of information I accessed to locate the specific information related to the air and ground war in Barrel Roll. As the war years unfolded, I noted significant events and how the war was trending. I had to be content to observe the war from a distance.

— 2 —

THE WAR FROM A DISTANCE

April 1970

I was pleased to learn that General Vang Pao's forces had regained control of the area surrounding Long Tieng and Sam Thong. However, the successful defense of LS-98 and LS-20 would not have been possible without the assistance of Thai artillery, Thai ground troops, and Thai pilots flying close air support. Under a covert defense agreement, codenamed Operation Unity, Thailand had been providing mercenary soldiers to the Kingdom of Laos. As the war progressed and the situation in Barrel Roll and Steel Tiger deteriorated, the number of Thais fighting on behalf of the Royal Laotian Government increased. At its peak, more than 18,000 Thai volunteers were serving in Laos. Not surprisingly, Operation Unity was funded by the CIA.

The Hmong stood their ground and air strikes pummeled the Communist front lines and interdicted its supply lines. On 25 April 1970, Campaign 139 officially ended, and a large number of Communist forces left the PDJ. The end of Campaign 139 also coincided with the end to the dry season. By the end of June 1970, Hmong soldiers had reoccupied the Vang Pao line and made tentative moves to regain control of various Lima Sites and villages on and around the PDJ.

While I was pleased to note General Vang Pao and his army had regained control of his headquarters at 20 Alternate and had begun to regain control of the PDJ, I wasn't optimistic about the future of the *L'Armee Clandestine*, since General Vang Pao's army continued to sustain casualty rates in excess of 30%. The pool of new Hmong recruits had nearly been exhausted, and the age of new recruits was getting younger and younger. Barrel Roll operations were increasingly dependent on the use of Thai regular and irregular troops. I was not surprised to read that RLA regulars continued to demonstrate an unwillingness to engage in combat and defend their nation, and Barrel Roll operations were totally dependent on air support and air mobility.

"GOMER"

Early in May 1970, while looking at a current issue of WAIS, an article regarding the loss of a Wolf FAC caught my attention. I was familiar with the call sign Wolf and knew it was an F-4D fast FAC out of Ubon Royal Thai Air Base. Wolfs were frequent visitors to Barrel Roll. I was shocked and greatly saddened to read the name of the copilot (back-seater) of Wolf 02, 1st Lieutenant Robert A Gomez of Jacksonville, Florida. Gomer, as he was called, and I had been friends while attending OTS at Lackland AFB after which we were stationed at Reese Air Force Base. I will always remember his big, broad smile and kind words. We drove to Lubbock for some nighttime fun in his beloved blue Corvette and flew his model airplane at the base ballfield. Gomer was the copilot of Wolf 02 on an early evening Fast FAC mission in Laos. As he dove to mark a target, his plane crashed and burned. The body of 1st Lieutenant Robert A. Gomez has never been recovered. Posthumously, he was promoted to the rank of Captain and awarded the Distinguished Flying Cross (DFC).

May - December 1970
As the rainy season began, friendly forces held their own on the PDJ.

The Nam Ou, always an important Communist LOC, was heavily mined to the extent that both the enemy and civilians ceased using the river. During the second quarter of 1970, 7th/13th Air Force continued to frag a large number of strike aircraft to Barrel Roll, and despite marginal weather conditions, gunships reported excellent BDA. Clearly, the NVA were attempting to consolidate and resupply its positions surrounding the PDJ.

Fourteen allied aircraft were shot down in Barrel Roll during those months, an indication of just how active the air war was. Three of the shootdowns involved Ravens, and the remainder were Air Force aircraft. Wolf 02, one of the F-4 Fast FAC out of Ubon, was one of those Air Force losses.

Despite the challenges he faced, the ever-optimistic Vang Pao continued to plan and execute operations against the NVA and PL. I read message traffic that referenced Operation 870. I had to do some digging to learn that Operation 870 was a successful operation that displaced a PL blocking force that had seized control of Phou Khoun, a small village that sits at the important intersection Routes 7 and 13. By controlling that strategically vital intersection, the PL had isolated Luang Prabang to the north from Vientiane to the south. Interestingly, the successful operation was executed by units of the RLA, and it relieved the isolation of the Royal capital and its vulnerability to attack. During Operation 870, the RLA captured large caches of enemy supplies and weapons, which were destroyed. It was a small victory but satisfying, nonetheless.

Scheduled for 3 August 1970, Operation Thanong Kiet (Preserve Honor) was to be a limited operation aimed at recapturing Lima Site 15, Ban Na, an important base located north of the PDJ. Once under Hmong control, Ban Na would be used, as it had in the past, as a jumping-off location for future operations. Not surprisingly, foul weather delayed the start of the operation. While waiting for acceptable weather conditions, the objective was changed to another Lima Site, Moung Soui! The operation launched on 27 August 1970. Troops were airlifted to a position west of the airstrip but failed to recapture the site.

Despite the failure of Preserve Honor, General Vang Pao, ever the optimist, and his military planners prepared a major operation that was launched on 26 September 1970. Called Operation Counterpunch, the operation proved so successful that Operation Counterpunch II and Counterpunch III followed on. Thai artillery supported Vang Pao's troops and elements of the RLG Army participated in the operations.

I read with interest the names of the various Lima Sites and LOCs that were seized during Operation Counterpunch, names with which I was familiar. During the operation, Vang Pao's forces captured 100 tons of rice, tons of munitions, and more than 50 trucks. Operation Counterpunch ended on 7 January 1971, two months into the dry season.

— 3 —

SON TAY PRISON RAID

During the early morning hours of 21 November 1970, a combined force of United States Army and Air Force personnel, participated in a raid on the Son Tay Prison Camp in North Vietnam. Within a day or two of the raid, the operation was publicly acknowledged by the Department of Defense. Once news of the raid had been released, I looked forward to the weekly TAC Headquarters briefing, knowing I would learn specific details about the raid. Codenamed Operation Ivory Coast, 56 Special Forces soldiers and 92 Airmen staged out of Udorn RTAB to conduct a raid on the suspected North Vietnamese POW camp located just 23 miles west of Hanoi. It was hoped the raiding party would rescue 61 Americans being held as POWs. Twenty-eight aircraft participated in the raid, two of which were lost (one helicopter was intentionally destroyed during a crash landing), but only two troops sustained injuries. Technically, the raid was a success. The raiding party surprised the camp's defenders, quickly silenced the opposition, and secured the facility. Unfortunately, no American POWs were being held at Son Tay. It was learned that the prisoners had been moved from the prison camp just a month or two prior to the raid. During the raid, the American forces killed 42 guards, some of whom were thought to have been Russian.

It wasn't until more than six months after the Son Tay Prison Camp Raid that I learned about the peripheral role Alleycat had played in the

Operation Ivory Coast. The DABS for that evening's mission had been given a sealed envelope labeled "Top Secret, Eyes Only" along with instructions to open the envelope only after assuming control of Barrel Roll. The message outlined the details of Operation Ivory Coast. The DABS chose to share the information with the BSOO but didn't share the contents of the message with the battle staff until later in the evening. Just before midnight, College Eye reported MiG activity and numerous SAM alerts were heard on Guard. Once it became obvious that some sort of unusual activity was occurring across the border in North Vietnam, the DABS shared information regarding the prison camp raid with the battle staff.

In the early morning hours, Alleycat monitored a radio call from Firebird 5, one of the F-105 Wild Weasel aircraft that had participated in the raid. He was low on fuel and requested emergency vectoring to a tanker hookup. Alleycat DABS authorized one of the Orange orbit tankers, a KC-135, to cross the "fence," enter Laotian airspace, and rendezvous with Firebird 5. While the two aircraft were about 100 miles apart, the F-105 pilot called a flameout and announced he and his Weapons System Operator (WSO) were going to eject. At the time, Alleycat was less than 20 miles from Firebird 5's location, but there was "no joy" on a visual sighting of the plane's navigation lights. Immediately, members of the battle staff heard the distinctive sound of the emergency beepers. Since the emergency occurred so quickly, and Alleycat was already on the scene, Alleycat became the on-scene SAR commander.

Radio contact with Firebird 5 Alpha (i.e. the pilot) was immediately established. He was safely on the ground, however, he indicated there was ground activity nearby. Firebird 5 Bravo was heard loud and clear, but he was not able to receive the DAB's transmissions. The crewmen were on the ground in Laos about 25 miles east of the PDJ. Alleycat Intel confirmed there were no friendlies in the area. With no gunships available to provide close air support, it was decided to have a Candlestick drop flares over the area, hoping to convince the bad guys that a gunship was working the area. The tactic worked, and the flareship provided battlefield illumination for three hours.

Monitoring the radio traffic, two HH-53 helicopters (Apple 4 and 5) that had participated in the prison raid and its HC-130 tanker (Lime 1) were returning to Udorn and remained in the area to assist in the rescue. As first light approached, Apple 4 picked up Alpha and

Bravo and returned them to Udorn. The following day, Apple 4 Alpha, Major Kilkus visited the Alleycat shack to thank members of the battle staff, personally, for the role they played in his successful rescue.

— 4 —

A LONG, SLOW FAREWELL

I f there was ever any doubt in anyone's mind that Laos would be lost to the Communists, a series of events ensured that 1971 was the beginning of the end for the Royal Laotian Government and its loyal *L'Armee Clandestine*. President Nixon's administration was committed to its policy of Vietnamization. Nixon had reestablished contact with China, and improving diplomatic relations with both China and Russia became his priority. Clearly, the Second Indochina War was of secondary concern, and he was committed to ending America's military presence in Southeast Asia. He called it, "Peace with honor." As the withdrawal of forces was ongoing, Barrel Roll had to compete for its share of tactical air assets. The number of strike aircraft available for missions in Barrel Roll and Steel Tiger had been significantly reduced. In December 1968, over 700 aircraft were being fragged for missions in Laos, and by mid-1971, that number was reduced by half. Part of the reason was that there simply were not enough aircrews and aircraft available.

To make up for the loss of American tactical sorties, the RLAF increased the number of combat missions its pilots flew. In 1969, The RLAF flew approximately 10,000 strike sorties, and by 1971 that number had increased to over 30,000. The one other bright spot in support of ground operations in Barrel Roll was the increase in the number of Arc Light missions.

Operation Lam Son 719 was an offensive campaign conducted by the

South Vietnam Army (ARVN) from 8 February 1971 until 25 March 1971. More than 20,000 ARVN soldiers invaded the southern-most portion of Steel Tiger for the purpose of destroying the NVA command structure, disrupting its supply line, and destroying vehicles and supply caches. With Lam Son 719 established as a priority, American air power that would have normally been fragged to Barrel Roll, was scheduled to support Lam Son 719. That decision further compromised an already reduced level of support for General Vang Pao's army during the first quarter of 1971.

In June 1971, the New York Times published the Pentagon Papers, which disclosed that the Johnson Administration had repeatedly lied to Congress and the American public regarding the extent of America's involvement in the Second Indochina War. The "document" was a comprehensive history of America's involvement in the war from WW II through May 1968. Officially titled, Report of the Office of the Secretary of Defense Vietnam Task Force, the Pentagon Papers consisted of more than 3,000 pages of narrative and almost 4,000 pages of appended documents. While long suspected, the Pentagon Papers confirmed America's air war in Cambodia and Laos and was an indictment of the motives and actions of politicians who had deceived the American public in the way they manipulated and expanded America's role in the Second Indochina War.

Knowing our nation had been involved in peace talks with North Vietnam for several years and was pursuing the policy of Vietnamization was dominating our war effort, it was obvious the Nixon Administration, like the Johnson Administration was unwilling to pursue victory in the war. The outcome of the war was "known." The war had been lost. The only question was "when"? Despite their heroic efforts, the fate of General Vang Pao and the members of *L'Armee Clandestine* was sealed. They were doomed. All that was occurring was a long, slow farewell to freedom.

§

Barrel Roll continued to hold my attention, and I never missed a weekly briefing. My heart remained with the Hmong, and I needed to remain as current as possible with the situation on the ground. I visited the TAC Intelligence shop regularly and continued to pore through ABCCC mission reports to follow the war from a distance. The pace of the war in Barrel Roll never seemed to change. Each side conducted operations to seize "land" to which the opposition counterattacked. In the process, lives were lost and great amounts of war materiel was destroyed. And then, the cycle was repeated.

Despite General Vang Pao's success with Operation Counter Punch at the end of January 1971, the NVA had maintained a presence in the vicinity of the PDJ. During the last week of January, as the dry season began, RWTs and Sycamore reported the NVA were on the move, resupplying its beleaguered forces in Barrel Roll. Analysts predicted a major NVA and PL offensive, and the Communists obliged.

Out of necessity, General Vang Pao was relying more and more on Thais and the RLA to defend strategically important locations surrounding LS-98 and LS-20. On 2 February 1971, the North Vietnamese launched Campaign 74B, its dry season offensive operation. The first objective for the NVA was Moung Soui. A barrage of mortar and artillery fire rained down on Moung Soui, and NVA troops, led by five PT-76 tanks, advanced on the base. Pilots scrambled to get their T-28s safely into the air to avoid the artillery barrage. The planes were flown to Long Tieng to be armed and refueled and returned to Moung Soui to support their comrades. The effort proved to be in vain. In less than three hours, after the assault had begun, Moung Soui was abandoned. Incredibly, but not surprisingly, once again, control of LS-108 changed hands.

After-action reports submitted by Alleycat and Cricket indicated the exact path the NVA and PL followed as they systematically advanced to their ultimate goal, Long Tieng and Sam Thong. One evening, Alleycat reported that every active FAG reported TIC; Blue Moon, Shamrock, Wildcat, Red Arrow, Home Run, Red Hat, Tonto, and Quiet Man.

Leading the attack on Sam Thong and Long Tieng was the NVA's 27th Dac Cong Battalion, an elite unit of the 312th NVA Division. The Dac Cong set up mortar positions and began shelling LS-98. For the first time in Barrel Roll, the NVA introduced 122mm and 140mm rockets. During the early morning hours of 14 February 1971, NVA commandos charged the airstrip, destroying aircraft, and blowing up ammunition bunkers and supply depots. Reports described the confusion and panic among the residents and defenders as the NVA attacked Vang Pao's headquarters. ABCCC requested Phantoms from Udorn that were on runway stand-by. The F-4s responded immediately to provide much needed close air support. One of the elements attacked what they thought were enemy locations. However, in the confusion, an errant CBU struck a friendly position, killing 30 Hmong women and children and wounding 170 more. The tragic friendly fire incident was referred to as the "Valentine's Day Massacre." Unfortunately, it would not be the only short round incident during the campaign.

Adding to the confusion caused by the attack and subsequent counterattack was the fact that General Vang Pao was not present. He had been participating in strategy meetings at Udorn and returned to Long Tieng later in the day, amidst the Communist attack. With him, General Vang Pao brought help, two battalions of Thai mercenaries. They were immediately air lifted to support the Thai artillery units already in place on the ridges overlooking Long Tieng. On 3 March 1971, two more Thai battalions landed at Long Tieng, and twelve days later another two battalions of Thai mercenaries arrived.

The addition of the Thais came with a price. Some desertions occurred, and the soldiers in one of the Thai battalions refused to fight until they received overdue pay. To appease the complaints of another battalion's troops, their commander was replaced. The lack of discipline by some elements of the Thai mercenaries did not bode well for the Hmong cause.

During the attack on Long Tieng, T-28s flew over 1,000 daytime sorties to attack the NVA. At night, Laotian flown AC-47 gunships illuminated the battlefield and provided close air support. By the end of March 1971, with but one month remaining of dry the season, the NVA moved to consolidate its hold on the PDJ. As the NVA moved towards the PDJ, a Thai battalion was ordered to provide assistance to the beleaguered troops occupying Ban Na. It was during this rescue march that a second friendly fire incident occurred. On 3 April 1971 F-4s were, once again, flying close air support missions for the Thais. One of the F-4's dropped an errant 2,000 bomb on the advancing friendly battalion. The short round killed 16 Thai troops, including the Battalion Commander and a Company Commander The rescue mission was aborted, and on 6 April 1971, General Vang Pao ordered the Thai battalion occupying LS-15 to abandon the base. In the aftermath of the second friendly fire incident, from that point forward, a FAG was assigned to each Thai battalion. On 18 April 1971, Hmong warriors retook Skyline Ridge.

One of the benefits I gained through the weekly Headquarters TAC briefings, was that I was able to gain insight into the "thinking," discussions, and planning that were occurring at the highest levels of the civilian and military leaders regarding the Second Indochina War. My primary interest, of course, pertained to the war in Barrel Roll. During my time at ABCCC, we rarely had access to such information regarding the conduct of ground and air operations. Most times, we had little prior information regarding ground operations and just reacted to ground operations as they took place and provided air support as fragged or as needed.

In mid-May 1971, representatives from the Office of the Secretary of Defense visited Long Tieng and were briefed by General Vang Pao regarding his plans for an upcoming wet season offensive operation. His plans were met with skepticism, and he was urged to fight a holding action. The D.C. politicians were anticipating (hoping is a more realistic descriptor) a ceasefire, but General Vang Pao was not fully informed of the rationale. The crafty Hmong leader provided lip-service to the visiting officials, and, instead, sought support from the American Ambassador and Air Attache. They were "experiencing" the war on a daily basis, had an appreciation for the role the Hmong were playing in the defense of Laos and were sympathetic to their cause. To assuage Washington, the Ambassador referred to the General's limited counter-offensive as an "active defense." The reality was that *L'Armee Clandestine* was the Kingdom of Laos' last line of defense.

The General's "active defense" began with a series of decisive actions to remove Communist threats west of the PDJ and restore the "Vang Pao Line". By the end of May, all the territory surrounding Luang Prabang that had been lost to the NVA was recaptured. At the same time, an operation began to clear the NVA platoon's that had remained in the hills overlooking Long Tieng and Sam Thong. By the end of May 1971, the last platoon of the NVA forces that had stubbornly clung to positions on Zebra Ridge were chased from the ridgeline and disappeared into the jungle. Several days later 45 Hmong Commandos parachuted into positions along Route 7 for the purpose of interdicting the NVA supply line. Air America inserted ambush teams at different locations along Route 6 to conduct harassing operations and locate enemy gun positions that were then targeted for air strikes. Eight Hmong battalions conducted sweeping operations from the west onto the PDJ, capturing significant amounts of Communist supplies along the way. It was truly another example of "déjà vu all over again" in the war in Barrel Roll.

By 12 June 1971 several fire support bases were established on the summits of hills overlooking the PDJ from the west. To extend the artillery's range onto the PDJ, 105mm howitzers were airlifted to several fire bases. On 18 June 1971, the NVA conducted small counterattacks against several firebases, destroying two howitzers in the process. After that action, the NVA and PL went silent. They retreated to the PDJ.

General Vang Pao's "active defense" had successfully established a defensive line across the high terrain along the entire western portion of the PDJ, and the General was poised to regain control of the PDJ, once more. His next moves were in hopes of preventing or at least slowing the anticipated Communist dry season offensive. During July 1971, Vang Pao moved his forces from the hills, west of the PDJ, and began a sweeping operation towards the east. The first objective, of course, was LS-108, Moung Soui. During the briefing regarding the efforts to seize control of Moung Soui, I heard a reference to an operation called Golden Mountain. With my interest piqued, I sought information about the operation. Golden Mountain was a successful operation, conducted on 5 August 1971, that resulted in the recapture of LS-108. Throughout the rest of July, General Vang Pao's forces moved steadily across the PDJ. Except for the northern portions of the PDJ and the hills to the north, L'Armee Clandestine was in control of the PDJ.

During one of the weekly briefings, another report caught my attention. On the evening of 25 August 1971, Alleycat was forced to divert to its "fall back" orbit due to MiG activity in Barrel Roll. That was an important development and major shift in NVA tactics. In the past, MiGs had been active at night, occasionally approaching the Laotian border but rarely crossing into Lao air space. Obviously, the NVA were feeling more confident and taking a more aggressive approach. During the third and fourth quarters of 1971, the number of MiG calls in Barrel Roll increased significantly, forcing Alleycat and Cricket to divert to fall back orbits more frequently.

Another first for Barrel Roll and an example of the NVA's renewed commitment to end the war in Laos occurred during the evening of 24 September 1971. The pilot of a Spectre gunship reported receiving three rounds of 57mm AAA. It marked the first time the NVA had made use of such a weapon on the PDJ. By the end of the third quarter of 1971, the AAA order of battle for Barrel Roll indicated the enemy had 329 confirmed guns in place. Clearly, with the dry season looming, the North Vietnamese had begun the preparation phase for its dry season campaign. By the end of the fourth quarter, MiG calls and reports of 57mm AAA firings occurred on a more frequent basis.

The monsoon season ended earlier than usual, and relatively clear weather had arrived by the first week of October 1971. In hopes of staving off the expected Communist campaign, the number of strike sorties fragged to Barrel Roll was increased; however, it fell below the numbers assigned to northern Laos a year ago. General Vang Pao added artillery pieces to the four fire bases he had created around the PDJ and added two additional bases to bring the total of fire bases to six. During the month of November 1971, the NVA were active and conducted probing attacks on the PDJ. Gunships and strike aircraft responded but failed to blunt the NVA advance. RWTs reported the movement of T-34 tanks towards the PDJ, marking the tank's first appearance in Barrel Roll. The T-34 was a Soviet made, WWII era tank that was an upgrade over the PT-76. RWT reports also indicated that 16 130mm field guns were also making its first appearance on the PDJ. While it was a smaller caliber than the 155mm howitzer, the 130mm gun had a far superior range. The number of fresh troops arriving was estimated to be approximately 6,400. The stage was set for events to unfold almost exactly as they had occurred for the past two years.

The annual Hmong New Year celebration began on 16 December 1971, and many SGU officers had found their way home to celebrate the New Year with members of their family. Campaign Z was launched by the North Vietnamese the following day. Newly arrived T-34 tanks and armored personnel carriers led the charge down Route 6 in the Ban Ban Valley and onto the PDJ. Simultaneously, an NVA division attacked the southeastern PDJ. The NVA were prepared, and their objectives were the Thai artillery bases. Long-range guns targeted the fire bases, providing cover for the NVA and PL soldiers to overrun several of the bases. Within the first several days of Campaign Z, most of General Vang Pao's preparations for the defense of the PDJ had been reversed.

Another Communist first occurred on 18 December 1971. To the surprise of everyone, MiG 21s appeared over the PDJ, completely disrupting the air war. Slow mover aircraft hurriedly departed to the west, air strikes were cancelled, and bomb loads were jettisoned. Air Force F-4 fighters engaged the MiGs but lost three fighters to their Communist counterparts that day. The air war in Barrel Roll was preoccupied with SAR efforts the following day, allowing the NVA to easily advance on Thai and Hmong positions with little to fear from the air.

By 20 December 1971 all six fire bases, manned by Thai mercenaries, were lost. RLA and Hmong forces were being overwhelmed by superior fire-power and numbers. On the following day, long range artillery continued shelling the important base at Ban Na until it had to be evacuated, leaving a clear path for the NVA to attack Long Tieng and Sam Thong, once again.

In just four days of combat, the RLG forces (RLA and Hmong) suffered 286 KIA, 418 WIA, and over 1,500 MIA, a staggering loss. In addition, 24 howitzers were lost to the enemy. Once again, the Communists controlled the PDJ, and the situation was critical. Desperate times called for desperate measures. To stiffen its defense of Barrel Roll, six RLA battalions from Steel Tiger were airlifted to Barrel Roll and the number of Arc Light missions was increased. During the month of December 1971, B-52s flew 111 missions in support of RLG units in Barrel Roll.

Efforts to stiffen resistance to the Communist onslaught only slowed the NVA and PL advance. Within several weeks, Long Tieng and Sam Thong would, once again, be the target of Communist artillery.

— 5 —
CIVILIAN LIFE

As Vietnamization was unfolding, units from all branches of the military were being recalled from Southeast Asia and returning to home bases in CONUS. As a result of the drawdown, the Air Force, and presumably the other branches of the military as well, found itself well above its newly authorized manpower requirements. Junior Officers was a category of personnel the Air Force was interested in reducing. Technically, it is called a Reduction in Force (RIF), and for years, the various branches of the military have used RIFs on both an involuntary and voluntary basis. Voluntary RIFs are referred to as an Early Out and for valid reasons, they were awarded on a routine basis.

My five-year Air Force active-duty commitment was scheduled to end on 17 November 1972. However, I had been accepted into a graduate assistantship program at Syracuse University, the start date of which necessitated a three month early out. I made an appointment with the Office of Special Actions and completed paperwork to request an early out for mid-August. I was assured it would be a routine matter. By the time I had returned to the INTT office, a message was waiting for me from the Sergeant with whom I had just met. Less than thirty minutes had elapsed since our meeting. I returned the call, and he told me that as soon as I had left his office, they had received a TWIX from Air Force Headquarters. The Air Force announced its intention to down-size its officer corps due to the draw-down of American forces in Southeast Asia. To reach its manpower requirement, junior officers could be discharged up to a year prior to their normal discharge date. I returned to the Office of Special Actions and completed a new early out request form, requesting a separation date of 29 February 1972. My plan was to visit family before embarking on a three-month cross-country road trip. Suddenly, I was a short timer.*

LONG TIENG AND SAM THONG STILL IN THE CROSS HAIRS

With my separation date fast approaching, my ability to follow the war in Barrel Roll in relatively real time would coincide with the end of my Air Force career. During my last two months of active duty, I made frequent trips to the Headquarters Intel shop. Incredibly, events during the first two months of 1972 mirrored the events in Barrel Roll I had followed in the first quarter of 1970.

As the NVA advanced toward LS-98 and LS-20, the PL was also following its battle plan from previous campaigns. Their assignment was to attack the RLA forces controlling the strategically important intersection of Routes 7 and 13 at Phou Khoun. In anticipation of such an attack, the RLA planned for its defense. It was called Operation Maharat (King), and it was intended to prevent the PL from seizing control of the intersection while maintaining governmental control of Route 13, hoping to preclude attacks on Luang Prabang and Vientiane.

During the two previous Communist dry season campaigns, the PL had seized control of the intersection, threatening the Royal Capitol. Phou Khoun was being defended by two battalions of RLA and a Lao artillery battery. On 30 December 1971, the PL began its attack on the strategically important intersection. After two weeks of intense fighting, momentum shifted in favor of the PL. On 21 January 1972, on the very day a relief brigade of RLA soldiers arrived, the Communists overran the position. The Royalists scattered into the hills, leaving their artillery behind. The PL wasted no time in taking advantage of its victory. They extended its force more than 40 miles to the north, toward Luang Prabang and 27 miles toward Vientiane to the south. Once again, the PL had cut off the Royal Capitol of Luang Prabang from the political Capitol of Vientiane.

---

* Military jargon for one who is approaching the end of their deployment.

Reconnaissance photography and Raven reports indicated NVA construction crews were keeping busy. Working at night, they made improvements to Route 5, a trail running southwest from Xieng Khouangville toward the hills surrounding Sam Thong. The obvious intent of the road improvement project was to provide a means for the NVA to quickly move men and materiel into position from which they could launch attacks on Sam Thong and Long Tieng. Road improvement efforts by the North Vietnamese were on-going throughout the Second Indochina War.

Following its battle plans from previous dry season campaigns, the NVA advanced toward the high ground surrounding Long Tieng and Sam Thong. Radio intercepts indicated the NVA force was comprised of 24 battalions. In anticipation of the attack, air operations were shifted Long Tieng to Ban Xon (LS-272), the TACAN navigation system was moved from Skyline Ridge to a more secure hill to the south, and Hmong family members were evacuated from both Long Tieng and Sam Thong.

On 31 December 1971, NVA 130mm artillery rounds began falling on LS-98. The artillery barrage destroyed the primary ammunition dump as well as the RLAF facilities. Fortunately, the fix-winged aircraft had been dispersed, however, CIA helicopters remained at Long Tieng. Ban Xon, located several miles to the west of 20 Alpha, became the temporary forward operating base for redeployment, resupply, and SAR operations.

On the morning of 1 January 1972, several sappers penetrated the base perimeter, and for a short period of time, elements of the NVA controlled the south end of the runway. After a fierce exchange of gunfire, Hmong defenders regained control of the base. Shockingly, while Long Tieng was under attack and his troops were fighting for control of the south end of the main runway, General Vang Pao left Long Tieng. An Air America chopper flew him to Ban Song, LS-29, located about 15 miles southwest of his headquarters at LS-98. His CIA advisors followed and convinced the Hmong leader to return to Long Tieng and direct the defense of the base, which he did. Four days later, General Vang Pao was admitted to the Base Hospital at Udorn and treated for "pneumonia."

§

It took more than 30 years for me to learn more about what had occurred during those fateful days and the General's sudden departure from his headquarters. While the charismatic leader might well have been suffering from pneumonia, he was also suffering from physical and emotional exhaustion. When his advisors entered the hut, they found the General weeping and cursing the "lack of air support." Obviously, the many years of shouldering the major responsibility of fighting the North Vietnamese and Pathet Lao attempts to seize control of Laos had caused a brief lapse of emotional control for General Vang Pao. It was no secret that the *L'Armee Clandestine* was, by far, the most effective fighting force in support of the Royal Laotian Government. In fact, in the opinion of many, it was the only military force that achieved any measure of success in resisting the Communists. It was a testament to General Vang Pao's enormous mental and physical strength, stamina, and courage that enabled him to return to full duty in just a few days. His return lifted the morale and spirits of his troops who valiantly fought off repeated NVA assaults, eventually regaining the ground on the base perimeter they had lost.

By 5 January 1972 more than 600 artillery rounds had landed on Long Tieng. In the following days, sappers continued to attempt to penetrate the base perimeter, causing significant damage, before being killed. The NVA battalions that were scattered in the hills overlooking Long Tieng began to systematically attack the Thai artillery batteries located at the top of Skyline Ridge, Zebra Ridge, and other locations. The Hmong guerillas positioned along the base perimeter were also subjected to daily assaults. NVA attacks against the base pushed some defenders from their hardened bunkers, but the Communists couldn't achieve a lasting hold. RLA and Thai reinforcements were hurriedly flown in to support the Hmong. Laotian flown T-28s and AC-47 gunships flew air support missions around the clock. By 24 January 1972, the NVA were pushed from Skyline Ridge, however, control of Long Tieng was still very much in question.

§

The time had arrived for my separation from the Air Force. I was leaving at a time when General Vang Pao and the Hmong faced, yet once again, an uncertain future. The Communists had come perilously close to defeating the sole military power that kept the RLG in power. The fate of the *L'Armee Clandestine* was yet to be decided, but in the minds of many, including me, it had already been determined.

I was about to lose my final direct "connection" to Barrel Roll. My departure came at a critical point in the war, and with the loss of my access to classified information, I would have to rely upon open-source information. Years would pass before I learned the specifics regarding the final war years in Barrel Roll.

One of my out-processing responsibilities was to attend a security briefing conducted by two men in civilian clothing. I don't recall them introducing themselves to me or identifying the organization they represented. I had the impression they were FBI, but they could have been Air Force security personnel. I was reminded of the non-disclosure statements I had signed when I received the two security clearances and my legal obligation not to disclose any classified information to which I had access. I was asked to sign another non-disclosure statement, again, attesting to the fact I fully understood my legal obligations regarding the disclosure of classified information. To conclude the briefing, I was given a telephone number and instructed to keep it in a safe place. In the event I was ever approached by anyone inquiring about or seeking classified information, I was instructed to call the phone number to report the incident. I never had any reason to call that phone number, and in time, the number was lost. On 29 February 1972, I became a civilian, once again.

Without the benefit of accessing classified information regarding the Second Indochina War, I had to rely on newspapers and news magazines to follow events in Barrel Roll. The information, of course, was outdated by the time it reached the public domain, and the demands of graduate studies precluded me from remaining current. In fact, it would be several years before I could piece together the details of the last year of the war in Barrel Roll, up until the time of the United States' withdrawal from Laos in 1975.

— 6 —

THE LAST DOMINO FALLS

At the time of my separation from the Air Force, the Communists had launched Campaign Z and were threatening to seize control of Long Tieng, the Headquarters of Vang Pao's Hmong Army. The NVA and PL came up short, once more, and the RLG and General Vang Pao retained control of LS-98. A major factor prompting the NVA withdrawal were two Commando Vault missions, similar to what the Air Force had done in the defense of Long Tieng in 1970. By the end of January 1972, T-28s returned to 20 Alpha, and air operations resumed from the base. The beleaguered *L'Armee Clandestine,* with considerable assistance from Thai mercenaries and RLAF air power managed to push enemy forces back toward the PDJ, thus, ending the Communist Campaign Z.

In February 1972, General Vang Pao launched a 5,000-man task force to attack the NVA in the area of Xieng Khouangville to disrupt its supply line. The friendlies met stiff resistance and by 24 February 1972, the unproductive operation ended.

In early March, FACs reported several significant sightings of vehicles north of the PDJ, evidently waiting for the opportunity to make a dash across the area whenever lulls in air traffic occurred. Clearly, with another month or two left in the dry season, further NVA operations could be expected. Incredibly, the NVA launched yet another attack on Long Tieng and Sam Thong on 11 March 1972, using the newly improved

Route 5 to infiltrate the area. While the NVA seized several key locations, a major assault on either of the important bases never materialized.

Even though I was no longer actively part of the Air Force, my desire to keep up with what was happening in Barrel Roll remained strong. I continued to research all that I could; however, not all of the information came easily. As a result, I continued to research well after the war ended, fitting crucial pieces into the puzzle as I learned about what happened.

For instance, during the first quarter of 1972, I learned MiG calls continued to occur on a regular basis in Barrel Roll and Steel Tiger, necessitating movement to fall-back orbits for ABCCC aircraft. As the year progressed, the number of MiG alerts in Barrel Roll increased dramatically. The NVA were clearly planning its end game in Laos and Vietnam. In addition to the introduction of larger caliber AAA guns into portions of Barrel Roll and Steel Tiger, the NVA also installed SAM sites in the northern regions of Barrel Roll. Knowing the United States would soon be withdrawing its forces from Laos and South Vietnam, the NVA and PL were positioning themselves to seize control of General Vang Pao's and the CIA's center of operations at Long Tieng. By doing so, the war in Laos would be, essentially, over, with Communists the victors.

The build-up of enemy troops, supplies, and materiel along the DMZ in Vietnam and movement along the Ho Chi Minh Trail indicated a large-scale invasion of South Vietnam was imminent. In light of the massive build-up and a lack of progress at the Paris peace talks, the United States walked away from the table on 23 March 1972. Six days later, on 29 March 1972, NVA forces streamed through the passes into Laos and across the DMZ in Vietnam. The so-called Easter or Spring Offensive had begun.

Approximately two weeks later, the United States launched a series of special air operations, striking targets in North Vietnam, South Vietnam, and Laos.

Ever the optimist, General Vang Pao met with CIA advisors at Udorn RTAB on 26 July 1972 to begin planning a wet season offensive. Joining them was the Thai general in charge of furnishing mercenary troops to Laos. It was called Operation Phou Phiang II.[1] From its outset, the operation was plagued with challenges and destined to fail, which it did. The year ended with the NVA occupying locations in the hills overlooking Long Tieng and Sam Thong and launching intermittent attacks against the bases. The strategically located and vital Lima Site,

Moung Soui, remained under Communist control as did portions of the PDJ and road intersections in the vicinity of Luang Prabang.

§

On 27 January 1973, the Paris Peace Accords were signed, and the demise of Laos, as well as Cambodia, was all but assured. It was a huge leap of faith to believe North Vietnam and the Pathet Lao would honor the agreement and abandon its ambitions of the past thirty years. A month later, Prince Souvanna Phouma and the Pathet Lao negotiated a settlement. Called the Vientiane Treaty, it called for an equal sharing of government positions between the Royal Laotian government and the PL. Each side was assigned five of the ten cabinet positions. The Red Prince, Prince Souphanouvong headed the National Assembly, and, not surprisingly, the PL assumed greater influence and power in the government. In a matter of months, the Communist PL assumed absolute control of Laos.

The last regularly fragged Air Force missions in Laos were flown on 10 March 1973. Officially, Air Force participation in Barrel Roll was over. Financial assistance from the United States to Laos was reduced from $360 million in the previous year to just $100 million in 1973 and reduced even further the following year.

For the next two years, the respective combatants, the PL and the RLA and *L'Armee Clandestine*, essentially, remained in place, controlling the territory they had occupied when the Vientiane Treaty was signed.

On 17 April 1975, Cambodia fell to the Khmer Rouge and the fall of South Vietnam less than two weeks later. The last Domino in President Eisenhower's Domino Theory was barely standing.

A representative of Souvanna Phouma flew to Long Tieng on 10 May 1975, and ordered General Vang Pao to meet with a representative of the Pathet Lao, Khammouane Boupha, and the Prime Minister the following day. The General refused to attend the meeting and accepted the Prime Minister's request for his resignation.[2]

The brilliant military career of the compelling and courageous Hmong leader, who had devoted his life fighting for a free Laos and its people, was over. Launching his military career as a teenager, Vang Pao had defended his homeland, non-stop, for almost thirty years. Instead of military honors and an expression of national gratitude, General Vang

Pao was forced into exile. Nonetheless, ever the warrior, General Vang Pao continued to fight for the freedom of Laotians for another 30 years.

Incredibly, no organized plan had been established for the evacuation of the more than 50,000 Hmong soldiers and family members who lived in and around Long Tieng. General Vang Pao had been assured by the CIA that the United States would always support his secret army, and in the event an evacuation was required, his soldiers and family members would be evacuated.

A hastily organized evacuation plan was put together.[3] Over the next three days, more than 3,500 Hmong, mostly high-ranking officers and their families, were flown to Nam Phong Air Base in Thailand. The evacuation ended on 14 May 1975, when General Vang Pao and his CIA advisor boarded a helicopter for a flight to Udorn RTAB. General Vang Pao and a few others were quickly permitted to relocate to the United States.

Left behind on the runway and in the hills at Long Tieng, anxiously awaiting the return of more aircraft that would take them into exile, were over 40,000 Hmong refugees. Sadly, there would be no more flights. Instead, with no other option to escape the Communist onslaught, they were forced to embark on a dangerous overland journey seeking freedom and safety in Thailand. For many, that journey took almost three years to complete. Sadly, many lost their lives at the hands of the PL, who relentlessly pursued the fleeing Hmong. Others died due to starvation, exposure, or illness. For those who made it to the safety of Thailand, they were forced to endure the hardship conditions of Thai refugee camps.

On the afternoon of 14 May 1975, the shelling of Long Tieng began, and the following day, the PL marched into LS-98, unopposed.[4] *L'Armee Clandestine* ceased to exist.

— 7 —

THE BETRAYAL OF THE HMONG

Depending upon the source, the numbers differ, however, the undeniable conclusion is that once the Laotian monarchy was overthrown and the Communist Pathet Lao seized control of Laos, the Hmong suffered. And they suffered mightily. In what was a further disgrace in America's involvement in the Second Indochina War, thousands of Hmong, who chose to follow their charismatic leader, General Vang Pao, were abandoned by the United States. We betrayed their loyal service and left tens of thousands to fend for themselves as a hostile government launched an aggressive campaign to track them down, capture, and kill them. Those courageous Hmong warriors comprised the most effective fighting ground force in all of Laos during the war. Their loyalty to their leader, General Vang Pao, and to the United States was never in question. They were at the forefront of defending Laos.

At its height of operations, *L'Armee Clandestine* numbered approximately 40,000 soldiers. As the years passed and casualties mounted, the number declined, and the recruitment of new soldiers to fill the ranks was an on-going challenge. In the latter stages of the war, some of those volunteers entered the service at the age of 12 or 13. According to General

Vang Pao, more than 20,000 of his soldiers had been killed and another 2,000 or so were declared Missing in Action (MIA). After having evacuated General Vang Pao and his family, as well as 3,500 other Hmong advisors, high-ranking officers, and members of their families, America's evacuation of the Hmong ended. The date was 14 May 1975. Left behind were more than 35,000 (some place the number closer to 50,000) Hmong soldiers and members of their families. Those left behind were no less important than the "high priority" evacuees who were afforded safe passage to the United States, away from the impending Communist retribution. Surely, our government was well aware of the fate that awaited those we left behind. It was either gross ineptitude or callous disregard that left the Hmong on the tarmac at Long Tieng that day in May.

Immediately, the Communist regime began to systematically hunt down the Hmong who had fought with General Vang Pao, chasing them through the mountains of Laos on their march to freedom. The Lao Communist regime pursued a policy of genocide against the Hmong. If captured, the fleeing Hmong were killed as were family members who were left behind. The cruelty to which the Hmong were subjected was the terrible price they paid for allying themselves with the Americans. Taking circuitous routes through the mountains of Laos, between 1975 and 1992 approximately 215,000 Laotians (a large percentage of which were Hmong) sought freedom in neighboring Thailand. On that hazardous journey, which for some took up to three years, more than 100,000 Laotians lost their lives to the pursuing Pathet Lao, starvation, exposure, and disease.

For those who reached the border with Thailand, one final deadly obstacle remained, the Mekong River. The river symbolized hope for their future and once crossed, freedom from the Communist Pathet Lao. Incredibly, nearly half of the 100,000 deaths of Laotians seeking to escape their homeland were due to drowning in the waters of the Mekong River. It is a fast-moving river and ranges from between four to five hundred yards in width. The lucky ones were safely ferried across the river by friendly Laotians and Thais. Others, few of whom knew how to swim, attempted to float across the river on handmade bamboo rafts. Poorly constructed boats capsized, and adults and children were swept away by the fast-moving current. For Hmong survivors and their descendants, the watery tomb of the Mekong River is viewed as a shrine to the memory of those who were denied their freedom.

It is thought that some Hmong refugees were encouraged to remain in Thailand by associates of General Vang Pao. Purportedly, the "left behinds" would be called upon to provide support and assistance to the Hmong warriors who had remained in Laos to continue the war against the PL. It is an intriguing story.

— 8 —

CHAO FA

The original group of Hmong who fled into the mountains were veterans of the *L'Armee Clandestine*. They were joined by other Hmong, who opted to remain in Laos instead of fleeing their homeland and successfully eluded the pursuing Pathet Lao. That led to one of the more interesting facets of the Second Indochina War, one about which not much is known in the public sector. Those courageous Hmong, who chose to remain in their homeland, sought the safety of the one place in which they felt secure, the mountains of Laos. They also resorted to a life in which they excelled and to which they were committed, being an anti-Communist warrior. The Hmong warriors who took to the mountains were called Chao Fa or freedom fighters.

§

Including family members, the Chao Fa numbered about 10,000 and, perhaps, as many as 15,000. They took refuge in the rugged mountains of the Phou Bia region, located at the edge of the PDJ, not far from Long Tieng. It was an area in which they had conducted numerous operations and with which they were quite familiar.

The Chao Fa were dispersed into several groups, perhaps as many as ten, possibly more. Initially, they were armed with only the weapons they carried following the evacuation of Long Tieng. However, in the inter-vening years, after 1975, the Chao Fa were supplied with satellite radios, AK-47 rifles, M-79 grenade launchers, 60 mm mortars, and non-guided anti-tank rockets. With its weaponry, the Chao Fa conducted raids against the Communist controlled Laos People's Democratic Republic (LPDR) armed forces. Reports of armed freedom fighters in possession of sophisticated weapons conducting attacks on LPDR troops begs the questions, who and how were the Hmong supplied with such weaponry? Interestingly, for years, the LPDR had denied both the existence of any freedom fighters living in the mountains and raids against its forces.

In desperate need of assistance, the Chao Fa turned to the refugee camps in Thailand. In March 1978, Chao Fa leaders crossed the Mekong River and entered Thailand. They remained in Thailand for several months, and during that time, they traveled to several Hmong refugee camps, meeting with Hmong leaders as well as Thai security forces. Apparently, it was during those months in Thailand, when the Chao Fa established a vital link to the outside world and a channel through which much needed supplies and weaponry could be sent to the Chao Fa in the mountains of Barrel Roll.[5]

They were called Blackbirds. A network of Hmong volunteers was established, and it was they who transported supplies to the Chao Fa, enduring long and dangerous journeys across the Mekong River and into the mountains of their homeland. In time, the Blackbirds left the refugee camps and operated out of covert locations within Thailand.[6] Conditions for the Chao Fa were harsh and difficult. Relying only on the food they were able to hunt and gather or collect from sympathetic Laotians, reports indicate they were malnourished, susceptible to disease, and lacked medical care. Over the years, their condition deteriorated, and the non-stop pursuits and attacks by the Laotian military took its toll on the freedom fighters.[7]

— 9 —
THE LEGACY OF
GENERAL VANG PAO

The Federal government called it Operation Tarnished Eagle. Others referred to it as a sting operation and set-up. On the morning of 4 June 2007, warrants were issued for the arrest of General Vang Pao and nine others, all but one of whom were Hmong. A task force of some 250 federal agents, representing a variety of federal agencies, conducted raids on the homes and offices of those nine individuals. They were charged with a violation of the Neutrality Act, and General Vang Pao was accused of leading a conspiracy to "overthrow the existing government of Laos by violent means, including murder, assaults on both military and civilian officials of Laos and destruction of buildings and property."

The federal charges alleged that General Vang Pao, and his co-conspirators had agreed to purchase $9.8 million worth of military weapons. They were accused of inspecting weapons that included AK-47 and M-16 rifles, Stinger surface-to-air missiles, anti-tank rockets, C-4 explosives, Claymore mines, and rocket propelled grenades with the intent of purchasing them and smuggling them into Thailand where they would be shipped to resistance fighters in Laos. Judged to be flight risks, Vang Pao and his associates were denied bail and imprisoned. They would remain in prison until 12 July 2007 when a federal judge granted a bail request.

The one non-Hmong in the group was Lt. Colonel Harrison Ulrich Jack, a retired California National Guard officer who had been an Army

Ranger and served in Southeast Asia during the Second Indochina War. After retiring from the Army in 2005, Colonel Jack worked as an ombudsman for Yolo County employees who experienced workplace issues. In time, after working with Hmong in his community, he developed an interest in their plight and lobbied politicians on their behalf. He became passionate regarding the Hmong refugees and those left behind, either living in refugee camps in Thailand or remaining behind in Laos. Jack established a non-profit organization, the Hmong Emergency Relief Organization and underwrote the cost of producing a documentary about the plight of the Hmong. In time, Colonel Jack met General Vang Pao and his trusted assistants, from which a friendship ensued.

The "conspiracy" was initiated by an undercover agent of the Federal Bureau of Alcohol, Tobacco, and Firearms who made a call to Colonel Jack at his home in Woodland, California. Posing as an arms dealer, the federal agent said his name was Steve Hoffmaster and had received a tip that Jack was in the market for assault rifles. The agent recorded the telephone conversation as well as all future meetings with Colonel Jack. Following the phone call, the two met at a local restaurant, the first of several meetings that took place. The agent claimed he was a former Special Forces soldier, had served in Iraq, and sold military-grade weapons.

On 7 February 2007, Jack brought several Hmong leaders, including General Vang Pao, back to the restaurant to meet the undercover agent.[8] The agent indicated he had a surprise for the group. He led them outside to his RV in the parking lot. Inside was an arsenal of AK-47 and M-16 rifles, grenade launchers, C-4 explosives, Claymore mines, and RPG grenade launchers. General Vang Pao's only comment was "Good selection." That was the only time the undercover agent met with the General and his only recorded conversation with him.

Following that meeting, Hoffmaster provided a list of weapons he could provide at a cost of $9.8 million. No money was ever exchanged. Once Colonel Jack indicated, "It doesn't look like the Hmong community is going to be in a position to continue with their activities," the undercover agent continued his efforts to lure the Hmong further into the trap. He indicated he "just got my hands on three Stingers." In a later phone call, Hoffmaster indicated, "I'm willing to bet, Harrison, that the CIA is aware of what's going on. They don't want to get into another Vietnam but if Vang Pao goes in there and takes over the frickin' country and gets things squared away and then wants to have democratic elections it's going to be like that. I have no doubt in my mind."[9] He went on to indicate it was a different CIA and the Hmong would have the backing of the United States government.

Vang Pao's hatred of the Communist regime in Laos was no secret, and his statements regarding his desire to see the Lao government overthrown, was used as "evidence" of Vang Pao's involvement in and support of the conspiracy. Indictments were obtained and arrest warrants issued.

With his reputation tarnished, General Vang Pao had to wait two years for his day in court. On 18 September 2009, the Federal Government dropped all of the charges against the General as well as those against his associates.

One has to wonder who it was in the Federal Government that authorized the sting operation, and why the operation was permitted to continue. In light of his loyal service to America and the leadership position he assumed in our nation's efforts to defeat the Communist incursion in Laos, General Vang Pao had earned and deserved to have been treated as the hero he was during the Second Indochina War. Instead, there were those in the United States Department of Justice who, for unknown reasons, sought to humiliate, dishonor, and punish General Vang Pao. First, it was the Hmong who were betrayed by the United States and then the beloved leader of the international Hmong refugee community, General Vang Pao, was betrayed.

§

General Vang Pao's vision, leadership, and life-long commitment to his beloved Hmong, greatly improved the quality of their lives. Incredibly, within two generations, Vang Pao's leadership had transformed the Hmong from a male-dominated culture, with limited educational opportunities into a vibrant and economically prosperous community in the United States. Vang Pao was proud of what his people had achieved.[10]

During the war years, in addition to being their military leader, General Vang Pao was also the inspirational and civic leader of the Hmong community. In addition to making regular visits to his soldiers on the front lines, he made a point to visit the wounded, always presenting them with gifts of money. His stamina and strength were legendary.

The General also made time to visit Hmong communities and enjoyed the time with "his people." It was Vang Pao who was responsible for the construction of roads to remote communities as well as the establishment of schools and health clinics in the villages. His compassion earned the endearing and enduring respect and admiration of the Hmong. It was General Vang Pao who broke down barriers for Hmong women and provided them with opportunities to assume roles in their male dominated culture. He insisted that female students be recruited to become members of the Nurse Corps. Using funds provided by the United States for the war effort, Vang Pao established the first-ever teacher education program for Hmong, almost all of whom were female. Those teachers were then dispersed throughout the mountain villages to establish schools for the Hmong children. This was the first time the Hmong had access to a formal education. Despite the demands of his war against the Communists, General Vang Pao never lost his passion to improve the quality of life of his people.[11]

While General Vang Pao's military career might have ended when he arrived in the United States, his devotion and service to the Hmong never ended. His new mission in life was to assist the Hmong in their transition into American culture and society. Knowing no other way to approach his responsibilities other than devoting himself fully to the mission, Vang Pao embarked on a second career of community service. Through his leadership, he established a network of community leaders within the Hmong communities. In 1978, he founded Lao Family Community, a non-profit organization that helped Hmong and Laotians adjust to life in their new country. Lao Family Community quickly expanded and opened numerous branches across the United States.

§

In the early 1980's, working with others, General Vang Pao created the Lao Human Rights Council and the United Hmong International Council. The purpose of the Lao Human Rights Council was to educate the United Nations, elected officials, the media, and the public regarding the unfolding humanitarian crisis in Laos and the refugee camps in Thailand. The Lao Human Rights Council's efforts to advocate on behalf of the Hmong produced some positive results. The United Nations took a more active role in the Thai refugee camps, and conditions improved somewhat. In time, several journalists, with assistance from Blackbirds, made the arduous and dangerous trip to the mountains of Laos, established contact with members of the Chao Fa, and reported their findings. While the plight of the freedom fighters never attained any significant public interest, the limited publicity did manage to keep the LPDR on the defensive. Unfortunately, due to an apathetic America, the plight of the Hmong never attained a level of national interest that might have created significant public support.[12]

§

General Vang Pao was also credited with the creation of the 18 Clan Council in Minnesota. The council worked with the Hmong clans in Minnesota to promote Hmong culture and resolve conflicts within and between the clans. The council provides legal and social services to assist with the transition of newly arrived Lao and Hmong immigrants.

One of General Vang Pao's proudest accomplishments was the creation of Lao Veterans of America, a non-profit, non-partisan, and non-governmental organization that represents the interests and needs of the Hmong-American veteran-refugees who served in the *L'Armee Clandestine*. From its inception in 1990, the organization and General Vang Pao advocated and lobbied on behalf of the Hmong veterans and was instrumental in helping to pass the Hmong Veterans Naturalization Act of 2000. The legislation waived the English language barrier and portions of the civics requirements, easing their path to citizenship. Finally, the United States recognized the sacrifices made by the thousands of Hmong who fought on behalf of the United States during the Second Indochina War. Though long overdue, a pathway for citizenship had been created for the Hmong veterans.

General Vang Pao and the Lao Veterans of America also successfully lobbied for the official recognition of *L'Armee Clandestine* veterans and those Hmong who lost their lives during the war. On 14 May 1997, 22 years after the end of the Second Indochina War, the Lao Veterans of America Monument was dedicated at Arlington National Cemetery. The Hmong were recognized for their covert service, the first time the United States officially acknowledged its covert role in Laos.

During the years he lived in America, General Vang Pao traveled extensively, visiting Hmong communities and meeting with his fellow countrymen. He consistently encouraged the Hmong to pursue the "American Dream" and become productive American citizens.

Vang Pao urged them to embrace the American ideals of freedom and democracy and emphasized the importance of education. Vang Pao's love of the Hmong, his sacrifices and service on their behalf will, no doubt, continue to be an inspiration for generations of Hmong.

§

After attending a Hmong New Year celebration in Fresno, California on 26 December 2010, General Vang Pao was admitted to the hospital, complaining of chest pains. The General had battled heart disease and diabetes for years. He remained in the hospital for ten days, surrounded by family and friends who maintained a vigil for the Hmong father-figure. On 6 January 2011, after having developed pneumonia and cardiac complications, General Vang Pao passed away. He was 81.

As news of Vang Pao's death spread within the Hmong community, thousands of mourners gathered outside the hospital to grieve the loss of their beloved father-figure and spiritual leader. A dignified and grand procession among members of the Hmong community began an elaborate six-day funeral service to honor the life and memory of their beloved leader. The funeral ceremony was conducted at the Fresno Convention Center. More than 10,000 Hmong attended the first day's events.

Vang Pao's family and members of the Hmong community petitioned to have the General buried at Arlington National Cemetery, a request that was denied. General Vang Pao is buried at the Forest Lawn Cemetery in Glendale, California.

— 10 —

LEADERSHIP LESSONS

It took many years, but I gradually realized my year in Southeast Asia had had a far greater impact on my life than I had thought. Similarly, it took that time to fully understand the ambiguity in my life I had been harboring since my return to the "real world" in 1970.

As life unfolded, following my separation from the Air Force, my focus was consumed by family and professional responsibilities. Initially, my Vietnam War experience was relegated to the deep recesses of my mind and conscious thought. It took time, but gradually those repressed memories, thoughts, and feelings began to resurface. There was never an "Ah Ha" moment, nor was I aware of the emergence of those thoughts and feelings. Events and experiences led me to the realization that the part of me that survived "that place" remained in "that place" and always would remain. This notion was not unlike the experiences of other combat veterans throughout the ages.

After teaching and coaching for several years and becoming an athletic administrator, I became more and more aware of the impact the Air Force experience had had on my life, and those experiences began playing increasingly more important roles in my life. The Air Force years taught me many valuable life lessons and leadership skills that have served me well in both my personal and professional lives. The crucible of combat had reinforced my core values and given me the wonderful gift of recognizing the important of establishing priorities in my life and the discipline to focus energy and time on those priorities.

§

The importance of mission was not lost on me. From the outset of my Air Force experience, the concept and importance of mission was continually reinforced. Each unit within the Air Force (similar to other branches of the military) has its mission, which collectively, support the Air Force mission. Depending upon the type of unit to which one was assigned, the area of operation (AO), and changing tactical and strategic situations and conditions, one's mission also changes. However, while a squadron's mission might change, one's commitment to the mission never wavers.

Throughout my career as an educational administrator, it was my responsibility to ensure every member of our team had a common understanding of and commitment to our shared mission. My job was my job to establish a climate in which team members trusted one another, understood what was expected of them, felt a sense of ownership, and took pride in their contributions to the attainment of our department's mission. The military called it unit cohesion; in the world of education, we called it team building. It's the same thing.

Working, living, and surviving in a combat zone, required an incredible amount of hard work, personal sacrifice, an ability to focus and concentrate on one's task, and adjust to less than desirable living and working conditions. Unit cohesion is simply a shared commitment to achieving your mission. When engaged in combat, that shared commitment grew into an emotional attachment and closeness that were heightened to the point where seemingly ordinary individuals became capable of performing extraordinary acts of self-less bravery for the sake of others. Many knowingly sacrificed their lives so others might live. It was an awesome privilege, a wonderful gift, and humbling experience to have been given the opportunity to serve with such courageous warriors.

In the context of military service, unit cohesion became a matter of life and death, and that reality provided me with another valuable leadership lesson, perspective. For those who served in Southeast Asia, it was inevitable that death was a part of our daily lives. One quickly learned how precious the gift of life was and how fleeting it could be.

Having the ability to employ perspective made the decision-making process much easier for me and helped me to distinguish between the significant and the less important matters I faced each day.

A common refrain among my Air Force instructors was KISS; "keep is simple, stupid." Over the years, that "simple" message made more and more sense to me; a concept that was infused into my personal and professional lives. Regardless of the task in which I was involved, the concepts of "authentic" and "real" dominated my thinking and action. It was important to focus energy on tasks and programs that would have a positive impact on our department mission. Initiatives were broken down into easy to understand and accomplish sub-tasks. We sought the simplest solutions and to eliminate extraneous tasks and complicated strategies.

One of the more commonly quoted maxims in the Air Force was, "Keep up your airspeed and sense of humor." Being able to see the humor in events, particularly self-deprecating humor, goes a long way towards enhancing a leader's effectiveness as well as preserving one's sanity. Humor is vital for team building, lightens the mood, disarms opposition, relieves tension, motivates team members, and softens the impact of negative messages.

DOGWOOD 2

No one epitomized the Air Force wisdom regarding the need to maintain air speed and a sense of humor as did Major Joe Crecca. I met Joe when he was a guest of our VFW Post and spoke to us about his experience as a POW at the infamous Hoa Lo prison (Hanoi Hilton) in downtown Hanoi.

Joe described a feeling of foreboding on the morning of 22 November 1966 when he awoke. He was scheduled to fly his 87th combat mission against targets in North Vietnam. He was the command pilot of an F-4C and his call sign was Dogwood 2. While flying in the vicinity of Thud Ridge, just north of Hanoi, his plane was struck by a SAM. He successfully ejected from his stricken aircraft and immediately captured upon landing. For the next 2,280 days, Major Joe Crecca was a POW.

Joe described, in detail, the beatings and torture he experienced at the hands of his North Vietnamese captors. Eventually, the beatings ceased, and Joe and his comrades were forced to live in harsh conditions and forced to subsist on meager rations, which, often, were spoiled and infested with insects. When asked to describe the source of the inner strength that helped him endure his brutal captivity, Joe indicated that a strong belief in God, Country, Family and Self helped him survive. He added that a sense of humor was also important to him and his fellow POW's.

I was dumbstruck that while being subjected to the evil and depravity of their Communist captors, Major Crecca and his comrades could possess a sense of humor and could laugh. A sense of humor can help overcome any challenge faced by the human spirit.

During my Air Force years, I was exposed to a variety of leadership styles, which, during my nascent administrative career provided me with valuable insight. Those commanders whom I respected and from whom I learned the most had several character traits in common. A leader's ability to perform with confidence, passion, and intensity was inspiring. I also witnessed, first-hand, leaders who displayed enormous courage and loyalty in taking initiative against overwhelming odds in order to come to the assistance of others. They were the leaders who led by example, and it was from them I learned about compassion, humility, and character. Once we knew a commander was competent, caring, and supportive, our loyalty followed.

— 11 —

WELCOME HOME

As the years passed, memories of my Air Force years and combat experience became more prevalent in my conscious thought. Three particular events led me to the realization that the year of combat had shaped and defined me as a person. While combat Vietnam veteran became my private identity, it never became a part of my public persona. Those three events were transformative and led me on an incredible, once in a lifetime journey.

§

Officially, it is called the Vietnam Veterans Memorial, but to those who care and understand, it is simply, the Wall. To date, I have visited the Wall four times. My first and most profound visit occurred in 1989, seven years after the memorial had been dedicated on Veterans Day, 1982. The impact of that first visit to the Wall was powerful. As I approached the memorial, I immediately stopped in my tracks. Ahead of me stood two huge black walls that met at an angle. The pathway led slightly downhill. It was a sight of magnificent beauty, but I hesitated moving forward, not sure if I was prepared to "experience" the Wall. I immediately felt an overwhelming sense of grief, sorrow, and guilt. I cried.

When I reached the bottom of the memorial, I looked at the Wall and saw my reflection among the names. It was a powerful connection to the past. With my left hand on the smooth black granite surface, I dropped to my knees, sobbing uncontrollably. Years of silence and repressed thoughts gave way to a flood of memories. I was overcome with grief and sorrow for those who never returned and those who were broken by the personal hell of their combat experience. There was also anger and resentment towards those who vilified Vietnam Veterans. It was a mix of emotions but one I embraced.

In a beautiful and understated manner, the memories of the more than 58,000 men and women, whose names are etched in stone, are honored. The Wall is a sacred, stunning, simple, and magnificent tribute to the ultimate sacrifice those courageous warriors made in service to our nation, the defense of liberty and freedom, and to save the lives of others.

§

Another significant event that led to my awakening occurred in November 2003. The Town of Huntington unveiled and dedicated its newest addition to the Town's Veterans Plaza. The new monument honors those town residents who served during the Vietnam War. The new addition features several bronze plaques that list the names of those who served in Southeast Asia during the Second Indochina War.

The usual roster of elected officials participated in the ceremony. The most moving portion of the program was the reading of the names of those Huntington residents who were killed in action and the introduction of those Gold Star families. They are individuals to whom our nation owes so much for the sacrifices they made.

The keynote speaker for the ceremony was Lt. General Frank Libutti (USMC, Ret.), who at the time was an Under Secretary in the Department of Homeland Security. Much of General Lubutti's message has been lost to the passage of time, but I vividly recall several principal elements regarding those who wore the uniform and served during those tumultuous times: they served with honor and courage in the best military tradition of our great nation; our nation will be forever grateful for the sacrifices they made; they should be justifiably proud of their service; and the nation owes them a debt of gratitude that can never be fully repaid. The most memorable of his remarks, however, was when General Libutti spoke directly to the Vietnam Veterans. His message was, "Welcome Home."

Like my first visit to the Wall, that simple phrase was transformative; it was cathartic, liberating, and greatly appreciated. No one had ever said those words to me. That simple greeting expresses so much that is important to a generation of service men and women who never received a public expression of thanks or appreciation for their service. Those two words mean there are others who understand and who care. They are the simple words I use whenever I meet a fellow Vietnam veteran. Those who had served in "that place" and left a little bit of themselves in "that place", understand.

§

I had become a member-at-large of the Veterans of Foreign Wars (VFW) several years before I retired from my career in education in 2007. Upon retirement, I moved to Mill Creek, Washington, a small city about 20 miles north of Seattle. Once retired, and for the first time in many years, I had the time to become an active member of VFW. I became a member of VFW Post #8870, Edmonds, Washington and immediately became immersed in its various programs. I was surrounded by others who had served and done so in a theatre of war. I was particularly pleased to become friends with those whom I have idolized since my youth, veterans of WW II and the Korean War. It was an honor to be considered a comrade and friend of those heroes.

§

On the morning of 4 July 2008, I gathered with my comrades to prepare and line up for what would be my first parade. Others had told me it would be a positive experience, but I had no comprehension of the depth and meaning of what I was about to experience. The impact was immediate. Once the fire trucks had preceded us to officially start the parade, our VFW unit stepped-off. To my amazement, with hundreds of American flags waving, spectators stood up, clapping their hands and cheering. And then I heard the words, "Thank you for your service." That was the first time anyone ever directed that simple message to me. Those gestures of respect continued along the mile-long parade route. That wonderful reception was totally unexpected and very humbling, and like General Libutti's message, very much appreciated. It proved to be, yet, another precious moment in my life. I was overcome with emotion by the wonderful gift I was given by those patriotic Americans who had gathered in Edmonds, Washington to celebrate America. The sunglasses I wore hid my tears.

I was more than happy to become involved in various leadership positions in the VFW Post, but I was particularly honored to be able to provide support and assistance to the aging veterans of our Post who, unfortunately, we were losing at a rate of almost a half dozen every year. In time, our ranks were being replaced with other Vietnam veterans with whom I had so much in common. Finally, I found myself in an environment with friends who were comfortable with the mutual sharing of experiences, thoughts, and feelings about where we had been and what we had experienced.

I was being led on a journey. It should have been obvious to me years before, but it made complete sense. I needed to return to the battlefields of the Plaine des Jarres of Laos and search for that part of me I had left behind.

PART THREE

THE INCREDIBLE JOURNEY

— 1 —

REVELATIONS AND PREPARATIONS

I had allowed myself to become one of those Vietnam veterans who had fallen into the trap of harboring resentment and animosity toward those who, in expressing their anti-war sentiment had, in our opinion, "crossed the line." Some seemed to care more about the NVA, Viet Cong, and PL than those Americans who wore the uniform and made untold sacrifices. In military jargon, this behavior was referred to as "giving aid and comfort to the enemy," and in the view of many veterans, it fell just short of treasonous behavior. Others chose to slander those who served in Southeast Asia, painting them with the broad brush of claims of atrocities, rampant drug abuse, and insubordination. Many of the dissidents participated in hostile receptions for returning veterans, organized on-going efforts to denigrate our service, and some of the resisters went so far as to organize vile protests at the funerals of Vietnam veterans.

The enmity of many Americans was directed toward two Americans, in particular, Jane Fonda and John Kerry. In my view, the way they chose to demonstrate their opposition to the Second Indochina War went beyond the tenets of free speech. Their hatred of America was directed toward those who had served, which I greatly resented. I knew my feelings were a betrayal of my Christian beliefs regarding forgiveness, but, somehow, I just couldn't let go of my feelings of anger and bitterness. Those feelings of contempt resurfaced during the months in which I was planning my journey. While I don't think I became obsessed with that negativity, it did detract, somewhat, from what should have been a totally positive experience. That was about to change.

In the fall of 2014, I had found myself, once again, in search of a new church, and on 2 November 2014, I attended Evergreen Church (Bothell, WA) for the first time. Leading the service for that day was a guest pastor. The sermon was the third and last in a three-part series titled "Overcoming Offenses." Matthew 18:21-22 served as the underpinnings for the sermon. In the scripture, Peter asked Jesus, "Lord, how many times must I forgive my brother when he sins against me. Up to seven times?" Jesus answered, "Not seven times, but seventy times seven." I was familiar with that scripture, of course and understood its meaning and significance, which caused me a sense of guilt regarding my inability to forgive the actions of anti-war protestors like John Kerry and Jane Fonda. I had stubbornly held onto what I considered righteous anger. I knew, in my heart, I should just let it go, but I never seemed able to do so.

Towards the end of the sermon, on that fateful day, the pastor quoted another biblical passage, Philippians 3:13, "I am focusing all my energies on this one thing: Forgetting the past and looking forward to what lies ahead." It made all the sense in the world. Immediately, the anger and resentment I had harbored for so many years disappeared. It vanished. It was gone. An overwhelming sense of peace and calm came over me. God had whispered in my ear. Several weeks later, I would come to realize how He had prepared me for my return to Southeast Asia, where I would be taught lessons in forgiveness and redemption from totally unexpected sources.

§

Although I didn't realize it at the time, planning for my return to the Battlefields of the Plaine des Jarres began almost ten years before the journey. Two events, seemingly unrelated, nudged me. It had started in 2005 when I made the decision to write a journal regarding my family heritage and the "life and times" of a small-town boy. The project produced more than 750 pages of written words and 800 pages of family history in the form of documents and images. I'm not sure why, but the writing project started with a chapter titled "The Military Years." Amazingly, as thoughts were put to paper, a flood of memories was released.

In many ways, the journey began then as the details regarding my year in Southeast Asia emerged. Suddenly, I recalled the names of villages, roads, rivers, and caves, details I thought had been long forgotten. Once again, Barrel Roll and the PDJ assumed a place of importance in my life.

The second event had occurred in 2008 when I was contacted by a former ABCCC colleague, Ray Roddy. Ray was nearing the final stages of publishing a book, *Circles in the Sky* (Infinity Publishing Company, 2009), and his request for information triggered more memories. Somehow, Ray had gained access to personnel records and after-action reports of ABCCC from the Air Force and written a history of the squadron. His book provided me with a chronological compendium of day-to-day events that told the "story" of the air war in Laos. Some of what I read was from mission reports I had written.

§

While the decision to return to the Battlefields of the Plaine des Jarres had been made, the journey became a matter of when and where. I wanted to be in Laos during the dry season and decided on a December visit. The "where" portion of the journey began in early 2014 with a visit to a local bookstore. I bought a map of Vietnam, Laos, and Cambodia and planning began in earnest. There were several goals I needed to achieve. I hoped to:

• make a connection with the Lao people, visit their villages, and interact with those who were impacted by the war;
• visit long-ago abandoned Lima Sites where battles were fought and many brave warriors lost their lives;
• travel along the same LOC's that played such vital roles during the war;
• explore cave systems used by the PL and NVA as field hospitals, command and control, and for sanctuary from air strikes;
• meet former combatants and allies of the war; and
• walk on the hallowed ground where the Hmong warriors lived, fought, suffered, and died.

With chart in hand, I began reacquainting myself with Barrel Roll, the PDJ and surrounding environs. While some of the names had been forgotten, I remembered dozens of villages, roads, rivers, and caves, locations with which I had been so familiar. Highly motivated, I devoted lots of thought and time to establish my itinerary.

After a one-day visit to Hanoi and another two days in Vientiane, my Barrel Roll adventure would begin in Phonsavan, a city in the heart of the Plaine des Jarres. The PDJ, of course, was the crossroads for all traffic in Barrel Roll and a shifting battleground as opposing forces moved back and forth in the ebb and flow that was the war in Barrel Roll. In the months leading up to my departure, I was focused, solely, on the geography of Northern Laos that had, at one time, been my "life." As the planning process unfolded and the departure date approached, I became consumed by my time in Southeast Asia and memories of that deployment were never far from my conscious thoughts. At the end of the journey, I discovered that those memories had new meaning.

By March 2014, I agreed to terms with a travel agency that would serve all of my travel needs. They arranged for all travel within and between the countries I visited, coordinated transfers, and made all hotel accommodations. It was my responsibility to provide them with a timeline for the cities/towns/locations I wanted to visit. The 18-day journey began with two days in Hanoi and ended with three days in Siem Reap, Cambodia.

For those "special" friends I knew I would be meeting, I purchased 75 Air Force challenge coins. They were heavy colorful coins with the Air Force logo on one side and the Vietnam War ribbons on the other. For others, whom I would be meeting, I purchased flag pins; 50 Cambodia/American flag pins, 100 Laos/American flag pins, and 30 Vietnam/American flag pins. Excitement began to build as the departure date approached. Emotionally, I was prepared to return to Southeast Asia and the battlefields of the Plaine des Jarres.

I set my alarm clock for 2:45 AM. It was the morning of 3 December 2014, and my plan was to be out of the house by 3:30 AM for the drive to SEA-TAC Airport. I had a 6:00 AM Air Alaska flight to Los Angeles. I needn't have bothered with the alarm clock, because, in eager anticipation of the trip, I was wide awake well before 2:00 AM. The drive to SEA-TAC was uneventful, and I quickly passed through TSA security. I arrived at the gate more than an hour and a half prior to departure, which is how I like to travel. The flight arrived at LAX at 8:45 AM, which gave me plenty of time to walk to the International Terminal, pass through security, and arrive at the gate in time for the 11:00 AM departure. The first leg of the flight was twelve hours in duration. I had a two-hour layover in Inchon/Seoul before boarding the connecting flight to Hanoi, Vietnam. A wonderful life journey, perhaps my best, was about to begin.

— 2 —

SOUTHEAST ASIA AGAIN

4 December 2014 – Day #1

With passport and requisite visa in hand, my processing through immigration was uneventful. Waiting for me was Le Bhuong Duong, who was my guide during my two-day visit to Hanoi. His nickname was Sonny. Sonny explained that in Vietnam, an individual's last name appears first, followed by a middle name, and lastly, the first name. Like all of the guides with whom I travelled during my Southeast Asia adventure, Sonny was outstanding. His English was terrific, he was proud of his country, and he extended himself to address all my needs. Thanks to the wonderful guides with whom I traveled, I enjoyed a wonderful learning experience regarding the history and culture of the three countries I visited. In turn, and in response to their inquiries, I provided the guides and drivers with a Vietnam War veteran's perspective regarding the war, a topic about which they expressed great interest but knew very little. In fact, there seemed to be a general lack of knowledge regarding their nation's involvement in the Second Indochina War. They, like me, were eager to learn.

Before leaving the terminal, Sonny helped me with withdraw Dong, the Vietnam currency, from an ATM. In addition to having currency to purchase small items, I always like to take home foreign currency for my grandchildren. Outside the terminal, our driver, Niem, was waiting. In each country I visited, I traveled with an English-speaking guide and driver. To a person, they were courteous and conducted themselves in a professional manner.

On our drive to the hotel, I had lots of questions for Sonny. He patiently responded to my inquiries and volunteered information regarding life in Hanoi, under Communist rule. During our time together, Sonny was quite outspoken about the government and indicated that the younger generations in Vietnam were restless about the lack of certain freedoms but were very careful not to express their criticisms publicly. However, Sonny indicated progress was being made, and a form of capitalism was emerging. Citizens are permitted to own their own business and farmers are allowed to keep whatever profits they make from the sale of their crops. In Sonny's view, the spirit of emerging capitalism was a significant motivating factor among the Vietnamese.

Sonny helped me register at the Anise Hotel, and I was pleased to be informed I had been upgraded to a suite. Before Sonny left the hotel, we reviewed the sites I wanted to visit during my brief stay in his country. Sonny and I had agreed to meet at 8:00 AM the next morning, and I was eager to sleep after a long journey. Other than a slightly firm mattress, the room was just fine. I closed my eyes, but sleep evaded me. How could I sleep knowing I was about to reunite with the part of me that I had left in Barrel Roll so many years ago?

— 3 —

HANOI

5 December 2014 – Day #2

I didn't sleep particularly well and was up early. My morning shower had plenty of heat and hot water, but during the journey, that was not always the case. I walked up one flight of stairs to the 11th floor to the restaurant where I found an abundant breakfast buffet. I enjoyed hot black tea and toast which became my morning breakfast ritual throughout the trip.

A little after 7:00 AM, a woman's voice began speaking to the citizens of Hanoi over loudspeakers on the street. When I inquired about the broadcast, Sonny simply replied, "Communist propaganda." Evidently, most cities and villages in Vietnam have loudspeakers and the citizens receive daily messages regarding their duty and obligation to the government, the evils of western nations, and the compassion of the government toward its citizens.

Well before my meeting time with Sonny, I stood on the street in front of the hotel and was totally amazed at what I saw. The volume of traffic moving along the street was incredible; it defied description. Mostly, they were motorbikes with a sprinkling of cars and taxis. Some of the motorbikes were stacked high with boxes and packages that seemed to defy gravity and, certainly, all common-sense safety procedures. Many of the motorbikes had but a single driver, but others were loaded down with two, three, or more passengers. Some parents were holding infants and toddlers in their laps as they drove along the streets. No one wore a helmet.

I learned from Sonny that due to the high volume of street traffic, trucks are not permitted on the streets during daytime hours; they are restricted to making deliveries and travelling on the streets of Hanoi at night. Crossing a street was a huge challenge, and with the help of a kind elderly woman, I learned how to navigate the streets of Hanoi. The Vietnamese made it look easy. They simply walked out into the traffic, motioning with an arm to "ward" off the motorbikes, and strolled across the road. Somehow, the oncoming traffic anticipates pedestrian movement and makes needed adjustments. By the end of the day, I was crossing streets just like the locals. One of the secrets, I learned, is that once you start walking across the street, keep moving.

One of the great frustrations of the war was the Rules of Engagement and the restrictions those rules placed on combat operations. Officially, the ROE was established by the Department of Defense, however, it was common knowledge it had been written by the Secretaries of Defense and State with the input and approval of Presidents Kennedy and Johnson. The ROE dictated the conditions and manner in which the use of force was to be employed and was intended to reduce the likelihood of collateral damage to civilian targets. A major portion of the ROE identified and defined areas in which military operations were not to be conducted. No bomb lines (NBL) were placed around a variety of what were considered to be areas of historical, religious, and humanitarian importance. When Sonny and Niem arrived promptly at 8:00 AM, we set out to explore the city of Hanoi and visit several very special places to which I had attached significant meaning. By the end of the day, my views regarding the ROE changed somewhat.

§

The city of Hanoi had many areas and structures that were strictly off-limits, according to the ROE. One of those sites was Van Mieu. To better understand why those restrictions had been imposed, I visited Van Mieu, the Temple of Literature. The temple was built in 1069 and was one of several temples in Vietnam dedicated to Confucius. Vietnam's first university, Quoc Tu Giam or the Imperial Academy, was established within the temple grounds and educated Vietnam's bureaucrats, nobles, royalty, and elites.

The entire complex is surrounded by a brick wall, containing five courtyards that are ornately decorated, beautifully landscaped, and designed for quiet reflection. Large turtle steles, carved from blue stone, line the interior of one of the courtyards. Turtle depictions symbolize longevity and appear all over Hanoi. The steles contain the names and birthplaces of graduates who successfully passed the royal exams. In addition to the names of the graduates, the steles cite reasons for holding the exams and names of teachers who prepared the exams.

Everything about ancient Van Mieu is breathtakingly beautiful. After experiencing The Temple of Literature, I was grateful the complex had been spared from air strikes, and I began to view the ROE differently.

§

I wanted to visit Ba Dinh Square because of its historical importance to the Vietnamese. Originally built by the French, it was where, on 2 September 1945, Ho Chi Minh read the Proclamation of Independence of the Democratic Republic of Vietnam. Interestingly, the declaration quoted portions of the U.S Declaration of Independence; "All men are created equal and that everyone has the right to life, liberty, and pursuit of happiness." Twenty-four years later, in 1969, many of those same citizens returned to Ba Dinh Square to attend the funeral of their beloved leader, "Uncle Ho." His body was preserved and lies in a mausoleum in Ba Dinh Square.

To the north of Ba Dinh Square, surrounded by a wrought iron fence, is the Presidential Palace. Constructed in the early 1900's, it was designed to reflect the glory of France and be the home of French Governor General of French Indochina (Vietnam, Laos, and Cambodia). According to French custom, it is painted bright yellow to reflect royalty.

When Vietnam won its independence from France in 1954, newly elected Chairman of the Communist Party, Ho Chi Minh refused to live in the house. Instead, he had built and lived in a traditional Vietnamese stilt house on the palace grounds. He lived in the simple house from 1958 until his death in 1969. The house has but two rooms, each measuring approximately 100 square feet. Meetings with his military and political leaders were conducted on the open deck under the living quarters. Nearby is an underground bunker that served as a bomb shelter in the event the palace grounds were attacked.

Ho need not to have worried since Ba Dinh Square, the Presidential Palace, and its surrounding grounds were off-limits to air strikes.

Hoa Lo Prison (Hanoi Hilton)

The first on my priority list of sites to experience in Hanoi, was the infamous Hoa Lo prison in which nearly 600 American Prisoners of War (POWs) were held captive, tortured, and subjected to ghastly physical and emotional abuse during the war. Referred to as the Hanoi Hilton, it was one of several prisons in North Vietnam in which Americans were held as POWs. Hoa Lo was built by the French in the late 1800's when Vietnam was part of French Indochina. The name of the prison is Maison Centrale (Central House). A renovation in 1913 expanded the prison's capacity to 600 prisoners; however, by 1954, the prison held over 2000 political prisoners. Prisoners were held under brutal, sub-human conditions, and the physical abuse at the hands of the French has been documented in graphic detail. Some of those prisoners were even beheaded by guillotine, which is on display. As I walked from room to room and peeked into each of the cells, I was overwhelmed by the level of cruelty that had been heaped on the Vietnamese by the French. Almost all of those incarcerated by the French were political prisoners, members of Viet Minh, a nationalistic movement organized to gain independence for the Vietnamese. Many of the future leaders of the Communist movement in North Vietnam were, at one time, held captive at Maison Centrale. Those former prisoners, are held in high regard, and their contributions to the Communist movement are honored and well documented in prison exhibits.

Today, only the front portion of the prison remains; a reception area, several large cells that held groups of prisoners, a dozen or more solitary confinement cells, interrogation rooms, the guillotine room, and several other rooms, the original purposes of which could not be determined. The rear portion of the prison complex, which housed the American POWs was demolished in the late 1990's to accommodate a new high-rise luxury apartment house. More than half of the displays in the Hanoi Hilton are devoted to the struggles of the Viet Minh during the First Indochina War. On the second floor, several rooms are devoted to the American POW experience. The first American to be held at Hoa Lo was Navy pilot Lt. J.G. Everett Alvarez, Jr. who was shot down on 5 August 1963. He was released on 12 February 1973 along with 575 of his prison mates.

The exhibits devoted to the Second Indochina War focuses attention on the assistance provided to North Vietnam by other nations. There are photos of various anti-war demonstrations that took place in the United States, as well as the public anti-American sentiment being expressed in other nations.

Two of the second-floor rooms display flight suits, helmets, survival equipment, and personal effects taken from captured air crewmen. A large sign explained the pictures and objects displayed in the rooms:

> "United States government carried out a sabotage warfare by Air Force, and Naval force against the North of Vietnam from 05 August 1964 to 15 January 1973.
>
> Thousands of planes were shot down, hundreds of United States pilots were arrested by the North Army and people. Some of them were imprisoned here.
>
> During the war, the national economy was difficult but Vietnamese government had created the best living conditions to US pilots for they had a stable life during the temporary detention period.
>
> Upon agreement on war termination was concluded in March 1973 in Paris. All the arrested US pilots were released to US government by Vietnam government.
>
> Some of the pictures and objects on these two exhibition hall show details of US pilots' life when they were temporary imprisoned at Hoa Lo Prison."

As "proof" that American POWs were being held under humane conditions, there were photographs of American prisoners engaged in a variety of recreational activities (e.g. volleyball, checkers and chess tournaments, soccer, and gardening), receiving mail and Red Cross packages, and singing in a choir. Further, "proof" of the captors' leniency, caring, and compassion was provided in a list of "Camp Regulations":

"American servicemen participating in the war of aggression by U.S. administration in Vietnam and caught in the act of while perpetrating barbarous crimes against the Vietnamese land and people, should have been duly punished according to their criminal acts; but the Government and people of Viet-Nam, endowed with noble and humanitarian traditions, have given the captured American servicemen the opportunity to benefit a lenient and generous policy by affording them a normal life in the detention camps as practical conditions of Viet-Nam permit it and conforming to the situation in which the war is still on."

Of course, all of the activities in which our POW's were purported to have been engaged had been staged for propaganda purposes. No mention was ever made or alluded to the brutal torture and beatings to which American POWs were routinely subjected. It wasn't until the release of our POWs that the American people were made fully aware of the widespread brutal conditions under which our service men suffered. Once it was determined the end of the war was approaching, only then did conditions at the Hanoi Hilton improve.

My time walking among the ghosts of Hoa Lo Prison was a solemn and moving experience. For decades, warriors had been held within the walls of the infamous prison and were subjected to untold misery, first at the hands of the French and later by the North Vietnamese. During my days as an Air Force Intelligence Officer, I read all of the classified documents I could get my hands on and attended regular briefings regarding American POWs. I read first-hand accounts of the beatings and torture to which our POWs were subjected. I could only marvel at their courage, faith in country, will to live, and strength. I am in awe of the resilience of those men who survived their terrible ordeal and returned, with honor, to their homeland. Our great nation will always owe those courageous Americans a debt of gratitude that can never be repaid. I left tears at Hoa Lo Prison and took with me a handful of soil from the courtyard. Our POWs, the living and dead, are forever in my prayers.

— 4 —

THE BRIDGE AND SENIOR
LT. NGO THOI BINH

5 December 2014 – Day #2 Continued

My final stop on my Hanoi itinerary was the Long Bien Bridge. During the war, the bridge, which spans the Red River, was one of the most important strategic targets in Hanoi. The city was also the most heavily defended area in the history of warfare with many SAM sites and a heavy concentration of radar controlled 57 mm and 85 mm AAA as well as smaller caliber weapons surrounding Hanoi. Throughout the war, the Long Bien Bridge was continually targeted for airstrikes at the cost of the loss of many air crewmen and aircraft. Pilots who flew the combat missions against the bridge, as well as other targets in the vicinity of the Red River, qualified for membership in the Red River Pilots Association. They referred to themselves as River Rats.

The bridge was built by the French and completed in 1902. It was officially opened in 1903. At the time, it was the longest bridge in Asia and the 4th longest bridge in the world. It was viewed as a symbol of technological innovation in Indochina as well as a demonstration of the supposed benefit of colonialism. At the time of its completion, Paul Doumer was the Governor General of Indochina, and, often times, we referred to it as the Paul Doumer Bridge.

During the war, the bridge was the only continuous rail and road transport between Hanoi and the important port of Haiphong. Most of the war materiel supplied to North Vietnam by Russia and China arrived by ship at Haiphong. In an effort to stop the flow of the materiel, the Paul Doumer Bridge was an important strategic target. The first successful attack on the bridge occurred on 11 August 1967 when three of the 19 bridge spans were destroyed. Repairs to the bridge began immediately, but within days of the successful attack, the ever-industrious North Vietnamese were moving supplies and materiel across the Red River by using ferry boats that towed huge barges. Makeshift support columns were constructed and bridge spans were fabricated from salvaged steel. Within several months, the bridge was carrying rail and vehicular traffic once again. With the introduction of laser guided munitions in the early 1970's, a May 1972 attack rendered the bridge unusable for more than a year.

In many ways, the Long Bien Bridge became a metaphor of the Vietnam War. Despite the relentless attacks on the bridge, the will of the North Vietnamese to fight for unification and defeating the enemy could not be broken by the technologically superior enemy. I had a compelling desire to cross the Red River by walking across the legendary Long Bien Bridge.

Today, the bridge serves as a railroad bridge and accommodates motorbikes, bicycles, and pedestrians. All other vehicular traffic use any of the other five bridges that now span the Red River. As we started our walk across the bridge, below us were the dikes that hold back the waters of the Red River during periodic flooding. During the war, it was the opinion of some policy makers to destroy what were at the time, earthen dikes. The Johnson Administration, however, rejected such action and placed the dikes on the NBL list. Today, the dikes are constructed of concrete.

From the bridge, we had a great view of the Hanoi Fruit Market where all of the nearby grown produce is brought to market every day for sale to distributors and vendors. The market is huge and bustles with the activity of people negotiating prices and loading up motorbikes with unbelievably large and seemingly impossible loads. At the rear of the market and in perfect view from the bridge lies a shantytown of tin roofed makeshift structures where some of the poorest and downtrodden of Vietnam live. A huge dump with burning debris lies along a polluted canal. Numerous people, adults and children, could be seen sifting through the debris, seeking to eke out an existence.

As we walked further across the bridge, I noted numerous farms and small villages that were located on the flood plain below. Produce was being grown in neat rows, and farmers could be seen working in the fields, cultivating and watering their crops. On the bridge deck, we passed numerous women selling produce. Others had set out small stools and were cooking food over small charcoal fires. One of the most popular items seemed to be roasted sweet corn. We bought a bunch of small bananas, and as we walked across the bride, we snacked on those delicious treats.

A little beyond halfway across the bridge, we came to Centre Island, which as its name suggests, is an island lying in the approximate middle of the Red River. Stairways lead from the bridge deck to the island below, which supports more farms. Centre Island is also the location of the darker side of life in Hanoi. It is here where drug addicted youth and orphaned boys live their homeless lives, trying desperately to survive. As we walked under the bridge, we saw numerous used syringes scattered on the ground.

However, the primary reason for walking under the bridge was to examine the support columns and newly constructed bridge spans that had been fabricated in 1967. The newly fabricated columns had been placed next to the original support columns built by the French that are still standing. One of the support columns is nothing more than a box of rocks with a span placed on top. The newly constructed spans are easily identifiable by the gray appearance that stands in stark contrast to the brown rusted appearance of the original spans. Also, when the new bridge spans were constructed, in the interest of time, the supporting super structure was omitted. As I stood at the center of the Long Bien Bridge, I looked up and did my best to imagine the flights of American aircraft popping up over Thud Ridge to begin their bombing runs on the bridge.

As we left the Long Bien Bridge, I experienced a flood of emotions. Those many years ago, the bridge had been a major focus of the intelligence community and the air war. The Red River and Long Bien Bridge had invoked a sense of dread, danger, fear, and hatred. But now, after experiencing the bridge and river firsthand, what once had been a prime military target was now a tired and rusty means of crossing the Red River and facilitating commerce. My thoughts were with those air crewmen who had lost their lives or had been captured while flying missions to attack the Red River Bridge. What had been viewed as a "barrier" between two nations so many years ago, was now a "bridge" to understanding between two cultures. It was with a sense of fulfillment and exhilaration that I walked off the bridge. It had been a day of learning and enlightenment for me, one in which I gained insight, understanding, and appreciation for the history and culture of Vietnam. Amazingly, I felt a connection to Vietnam, something I never expected or thought possible. Emotionally, I was drained and felt a sense of total satisfaction with what I had experienced on my first day in Southeast Asia. However, my day was not yet over. I was about to engage in an astonishing chance encounter.

§

Shortly after leaving the Long Bien Bridge, we walked to the train station, located at the east end of the bridge. I was curious to see where many of those passengers who crossed the Red River during the war years began and ended their journeys. Surprisingly, the station was quite small and like many facilities in Southeast Asia, open-air. I don't think it has changed much during the intervening years. The tracks continued beyond the station, leading into residential areas and presented an incredible sight. On both sides of the tracks were two- and three-story homes. The dwellings were located within several feet of the tracks, and there were no safety barriers. Trains moved through the area while life went on. Children were playing less than two feet from the moving trains, and men and women cooked over charcoal fires. Train traffic was just a normal part of their lives, and there seemed to be little concern for safety. It was an amazing sight to behold, totally foreign to life in overly safety conscious America.

Since we were just a few blocks from the hotel, we decided to walk through the streets of the Old Quarter. We had walked, perhaps a hundred yards, when something that was pure serendipity occurred. It was the first of several wonderful encounters I experienced during my return to Southeast Asia.

Ahead of us, we saw an older man who was standing in the street, talking with several other men. He was wearing a military uniform that fit him perfectly. As we got closer, I noticed more than 18 medals, ribbons, and pins adorned his uniform. The name on his metal name tag read Ngo Thoi Binh. In response to my question, he indicated that, yes, he had served in the Peoples' Army of Vietnam during the war.

Ngo Thoi Binh had just returned from a military ceremony honoring veterans of the PAVN (NVA). It was pure happenstance that had brought us together on a street in Hanoi. I was elated to have the opportunity to meet this man, a comrade in arms and former enemy combatant. He was surprised to meet an American walking down his street. We shook hands, and without thought, immediately embraced. We clung to one another. I felt an instant bonding with this total stranger, and I was sure the feeling was mutual. We felt the bonds of brotherhood. There was no doubt in my mind it had been meant for us to meet.

Ngo Thoi Binh shared his story with us. In 1965, at the age of 19, he joined the Ground Forces (Army) and began a six-month training program in North Vietnam. He remained in the Ground Forces until the end of hostilities in 1974, having risen to the rank of Senior Lieutenant, an officer's rank equivalent to an Air Force Captain. He had served in the PAVN for over nine years.

It took Ngo Thoi Binh more than three months to traverse the Ho Chi Minh Trail system to reach South Vietnam. Since attacking the infamous Ho Chi Minh Trail was one of ABCCC's major responsibilities, I was curious about life on the trail and conditions he encountered along the way. They traveled at night, of course, and almost always had to walk. He indicated that the soldiers remained well spread out in the event of an airstrike and made sure to arrive at the security of one of the numerous truck parks before sunrise. He laughed and smiled when he told us that for the nine years in which he served, he was always tired, hungry, and sore.

Their biggest fear was of our gunships, because of its accuracy, huge weapons load, and ability to remain on station for extended periods of time. It was during one of those gunship attacks, along the trail, when he sustained his first wound. Ngo Thoi Binh said the second most feared weapons system of ours was the B-52. Those missions were devastating since the bombs caused such a wide swath of destruction and the explosive concussions caused as much devastation as the exploding ordnance. During daylight hours, they hunkered down under the tree canopy or in underground bunkers and did their best to rest and sleep, distracted by the constant presence and threat of enemy aircraft overhead.

Upon his arrival in the south, Ngo Thoi Binh told us he was engaged in combat operations, practically non-stop. During the war years, he never had the opportunity to return to his home, near Hanoi, to visit his family. He confided he never really expected to survive the war, a foreboding feeling we had in common.

Ngo Thoi Binh told us that most of his nine years of service was in South Vietnam, but he had also engaged in several combat operations in Lao. He had been wounded a total of four times, none of which had been life threatening and from which he had fully recovered. However, he indicated that disease also posed a serious challenge for all soldiers. In addition to his wounds, he had suffered from intestinal parasites, and what was an astounding coincidence, like me, Ngo Thoi Binh had contracted dengue fever. Usually, it wasn't until lulls in the fighting occurred that NVA soldiers were able to be "evacuated" to a field hospital, which were located in caves or underground bunkers.

He was in Saigon when the war ended, and despite the jubilation of having defeated South Vietnamese and American forces, he was emotionally and physically drained. He, like his comrades, were overjoyed the fighting was over and wanted nothing more than to return home. His return home was a much easier journey since they rode in trucks along paved roads and avoided the harsh conditions of the Ho Chi Minh Trail. Upon his return, he learned that two of his brothers had been killed in the war.

A bright smile lit up his face when I told him about my service in the Air Force. In an instant, we felt a strong emotional connection to one another. As we smiled at each other, we held hands and repeatedly embraced. At one point in time, we had been enemy combatants, each fulfilling our duty to serve our respective nations. It was as if we had been long-time friends who had been separated and were now being reunited. When I inquired if he might have any feelings of anger or hatred toward the United States or those against whom he fought, he seemed surprised by my question as if such thoughts or feelings had never occurred to him.

"Absolutely not," he replied.

There was no hostility, anger, or resentment over the fact we had, at one time, been adversaries. Ngo Thoi Binh had left the past in the past. He smiled and extended his arms upward when he talked about his children and grandchildren. Like all grandparents, Ngo Thoi Binh took great joy in being a grandfather, and he told me how much he looked forward to enjoying a long life with his family. I will never forget his words, "I only look to the future."

I was stunned by what I was experiencing and what I was hearing. Within 24 hours of arriving in Southeast Asia, I had met a former adversary, an officer in the North Vietnamese Army. I felt the wonderful embrace of brotherhood. He explained that while our countries may have been at war, the two of us were never enemies; we were simply soldiers following orders in the discharge of our duties to the best of our ability. We were brothers, he assured me.

As an expression of friendship, I gave Ngo Thoi Binh an Air Force challenge coin. He fingered the coin, feeling its heft. His eyes widened, and he asked what the words and symbols meant. He was clearly moved by the gift, an expression of friendship and brotherhood. Immediately, he disappeared. When Ngo Thoi Binh returned, he presented me with a very special gift, one I will forever cherish. He gave me one of his metal uniform name tags. It was a wonderful gift, one of significant importance and value to him and me. I was honored and humbled by his extraordinary gift, and once again, we embraced and held hands. In addition to the gift of his name tag, Ngo Thoi Binh had given me the gift of brotherhood. As we parted, we embraced one final time, and he kissed me. After walking about ten yards, I turned to see Senior Lieutenant Ngo Thoi Binh looking at me. Smiling and with tears in our eyes, we saluted one another. I was overwhelmed with emotion, wonderment, grateful appreciation, and a knowledge that God was walking along that street in Hanoi with me. I offer thanks to Him for having brought us together.

— 5 —
RETURN TO LAOS

6 December 2014 - Day # 3

With my brief stay in Hanoi over, I boarded a plane, looking forward with eager anticipation to a 12-day adventure in Laos. I arrived at Wattay Airport in Vientiane, a facility that played a crucial and central role during the Second Indochina War. It was through Wattay that personnel and materiel passed to support the "secret war." The CIA had a presence at the airport, and it was in Vientiane that the U.S. Ambassador to Laos and the Air Attache were located. Except for the aircrews that flew directly to their assigned targets in Laos, everyone else who was involved in hostilities in Laos flew into Wattay.

The name Wattay still appears on the sign welcoming travelers, however, the arrivals building and adjacent buildings supporting air operations all looked new. On the opposite side of the main runway, I was able to see a number of older structures. Unfortunately, security personnel and chain link fences precluded me from investigating further what I thought to be the hangars and administration buildings utilized by the CIA during the Second Indochina War.

I stood in line to obtain a visa for my 12-day stay in Laos. Vietnam had required a visa prior to my arrival, but visas for Lao and Cambodia could be obtained upon arrival in the countries. Varason, who would be my guide during my two days in Vientiane, was there to meet me. We stopped at an ATM so I could obtain some Kip, the Lao currency. At the time, one US dollar equaled approximately 8400 Kip. Our driver, whose name was Some, drove us to the hotel in which I would be staying during my time in Vientiane. It was called the Mandala Boutique Hotel, and it was located just a block from Settatharat Road, one of the main roads in the capitol city of Laos.

Varason took us to a local restaurant for a late lunch. The cold drink was refreshing, and I enjoyed a bowl of noodle soup. Varason and Some were interested to know more about me and my reasons for visiting their country. I explained my "connection" to their country, and we discussed the sites in Vientiane I wanted to visit. I was interested to note that, just like Sonny in Hanoi, Varason was critical of the Communist government and felt that most of the Lao shared that view. However, just as in Vietnam, people were reluctant to express those views publicly.

After lunch, we walked along the Mekong River, passing some impressive statues that honored past kings, before returning to the hotel by walking down Settatharat Road. We agreed upon our itinerary for the following day.

At 5:00 PM, we drove to the home of a woman named Nook. Her business is called Lao Experiences, and it provides visitors with hands on experience in Lao culture and cooking. That evening, I was her only guest, and with her capable assistance, I prepared several traditional Lao dishes. While I knew I would never prepare those recipes again, it was fun and the food was absolutely delightful. We prepared Loop Gai (chicken salad with banana flowers), Mok Pa (fish steamed in banana leaves), sticky rice with Jeow Mak Len (tomato dip), Tam Mak (spicy papaya salad), and for dessert, Khoo Nioow Mak Moong (mango and sticky rice sweetened in coconut milk). When all was in readiness, we sat down to enjoy great food and conversation.

It was fitting that my journey to Laos began at fabled Wattay Airport, the port of entry for the warriors who fought in the "secret war." With thoughts of returning to the battlefield of the Plaine des Jarres dominating my thoughts, sleep was difficult.

— 6 —

VIENTIANE

7 December 2014 – Day #4

Varason had been a monk for seven years and was quite knowledgeable regarding Buddhism and life in the monasteries. Our first destination was Wat Si Saket, which, fortunately, was built in the early Bangkok style. I say fortunately because this was the only temple left untouched by the Siamese (Thais) when they destroyed the city in the invasion of 1828. It is the oldest temple in Vientiane. The temple was built by Chao Anuvong, the last king of the Lan Xang Kingdom. The interior wall of the cloister is filled with small niches containing thousands of tiny Buddha images and rows of hundreds of seated Buddhas. The images date from the 16th to 19th centuries, come in all sizes, and are made of stone, wood, and bronze. I learned that stone images are the oldest. In total, there are more than 6,800 Buddhas in the temple. The temple has beautiful surrounding verandas, a five-tiered roof, a drum tower, and a small library building.

Our next stop was the Wat Ho Phra Keo, also referred to as the Temple of Emerald Buddha. The temple was originally built in 1565 as the Lao royal family's personal temple and as the home for the Emerald Buddha. During my visit, I learned some interesting history about the Emerald Buddha. When I was stationed in Thailand in 1969-1970,

I made a couple of visits to Bangkok. During one of those visits, I participated in a temple tour and visited Wat Phra Kaew, which was home to the Emerald Buddha. My recollection was that the Emerald Buddha had been taken from the Lao Kingdom, and the Laotians are the rightful owners of the Buddha image. That was my understanding, then. Now, I learned that Laos came into possession of the Emerald Buddha when King Chao Anuvong invaded northern Thailand and stole it from the Siamese. The sacred Emerald Buddha was reclaimed by the Siamese when they invaded the Lao Kingdom in 1778.

The temple is the only surviving portion of the old royal palace, however, its use now is as a museum. It houses many Lao treasures such as Khmer stone and wooden carvings, bronze frog drums of the royal family, manuscripts, a gilded throne, Buddha images, and Buddhist stone tablets. The only remains of the original temple are the magnificent 16th century lacquered front doors. The wooden doors are adorned with carved images of Buddha in nature settings. The structure is the result of a 1937-1940 restoration, directed by Prince Souvanna Phouma, an engineer and future prime minister of Laos. A nearby garden provides a peaceful retreat from the bustle of Vientiane and contains lush green lawns, colorful plants and flowers, and a small jar from the Plaine de Jarres.

The third temple we visited was Wat That Luang, or the Great Stupa. It is the most sacred location in the country, is the national symbol, and its image appears on the nation's currency. It looks like a fortress with a gold leaf tower that stretches 148 feet into the air. It is thought that the original structure was built as early in the 3rd century to house a breastbone of Buddha. The relic had been brought to Laos by five Laotian monks who had been studying in India. It is believed that That Luang was built over the original stupa containing the sacred relic. The current structure was built by King Setthathirat in 1566. It was King Setthathirat who moved the royal capitol from Vientiane to Luang Prabang in the mid 1500's. A statue of the king stands at the entrance to That Luang.

Originally, the Great Stupa had four temples, of which only two remain: Wat That Luang Neua to the north and Wat That Luang Tai to the south. Burmese and Chinese invasions of the 18th and 19th centuries left That Luang in ruins, and it was the French, in 1930, who undertook the restoration of the sacred site.

We headed north on one of Vientiane's main arteries, Lane Xang Avenue (Avenue of France). Our destination was Laos' version of France's Arc de Triomphe. It is called Patuxia, which translates to Victory Gate. However, the structure's original name was Anousavali (Memory), and it was built to honor the memory of Lao soldiers who had died during WWII and the war of independence from France. When the Communist Pathet Lao seized power in 1975 and ended the monarchy, the monument was renamed Patuxia.

The monument is also referred to as the "vertical runway" because it was built by funds and cement provided by the United States for the construction of a new airport in Vientiane. The monument has gateways facing in each of the four cardinal directions, and ponds are located in front of each gate. The ponds represent the open section of the lotus flower. The corners of the gateways are decorated with statues of a Naga King (great snake, usually a king cobra) that protects the gateways and spray water into the ponds. The water represents nature, fertility, welfare, and happiness. The monument has two concrete staircases that climb through the five towers, leading to the top floor that offers a spectacular panoramic view of Vientiane.

§

During the Second Indochina War, it is estimated that from 1964 to 1973, the United States flew more than 580,000 bombing missions in the skies of Laos, dropping over two and a half million tons of ordnance.[13] Of the ordnance that was dropped, it is further estimated that approximately one third of the munitions failed to detonate. All 17 provinces in Laos have been contaminated by unexploded ordnance (UXO). Since the end of hostilities, over 25,000 civilians, many of whom were children, have been killed or injured as a result. Cluster Bomb Unit (CBU) munitions pose the greatest threat because each unit contains hundreds of bomblets, grenades, or mines that were dispersed over wide areas. UXO impede the development of land, and villagers in rural areas whose numbers are growing and who seek to expand cultivation are particularly susceptible to those threats. The value of UXO scrap metal exacerbates the problem.

I visited the Cooperative Orthotic and Prosthetic Enterprise (COPE) to learn about its work. COPE, in a partnership with the Lao governmental agency Center for Medical Rehabilitation, provides services to those Lao who, as a result of contact with UXO, have sustained injuries and suffered physical disabilities. Those victims are provided with free access to a nationally managed rehabilitation service as well as prosthetic devices. Counselors are also helpful in placing their clients in jobs.

While visiting COPE, I was pleased to learn the United States has been working closely with the government of Laos to support its efforts to address the problem by providing both technical services and financial assistance. In fact, the United States has been the largest contributor to this work.

I returned to the hotel a little after 4:00 PM and immediately set off for a walk along the Mekong River. On the opposite side of the river was Thailand, and approximately 30 miles due south was Udon Thani (Udorn). Several miles south of my location, the Friendship Bridge had been built, which now provides direct access between the two countries. In 1969, the only means of crossing the Mekong was by boat. As I looked down on the river below, there were several fishermen in long boats plying their trade. The houseboats on which they lived were tied up on the nearby shore. As I stood there looking out over the wide river, my thoughts were with the thousands of Hmong who had drowned in the river, desperately trying to flee their homeland while Communist Pathet Lao were in pursuit.

I was treated to a beautiful sunset. My two-day stay in Vientiane was over. In the morning, I would head north to the PDJ.

— 7 —

FINALLY, MUONG SOUI

8 December 2014 - Day # 5

The flight time to Phonsavan was only 30 minutes. We landed at one of the old airfields in Xieng Khoang Province, located just 5 miles from Phonsavan. I had arrived in the heart of Barrel Roll. As we decelerated and approached the old terminal, we passed approximately a half dozen MIGs lined up on the tarmac. Clearly, in addition to commercial traffic, the airfield was also being used for military purposes. When I was flying missions over northern Laos, we referred to the old city as Xieng Khoangville, and it was at the center of many skirmishes and battles. For long stretches of time, Xieng Khoangville was under control of the Royal Lao Government (RLG). Ultimately, the city was almost destroyed during the war, and Phonsavan was built in the late 1970's and established as the new capital of the province. What remains of Xieng Khoangville is now called Muang Khoun.

Xieng Khoang Province and its neighboring province, Houa Phan, were of strategic importance considering its proximity to North Vietnam. Houa Phan, in particular, was a stronghold of the Pathet Lao. Due to its common border with North Vietnam, the NVA could easily supply its allies and move troops into the PDJ through Houa Phan.

During the war, there were three major routes on which the

combatants traveled; Routes 7, 6, and 13. At the time, Routes 6 and 13 were dirt roads and as they led into the mountain regions beyond the PDJ, they became narrow trails. Major portions of Route 7 was a hard surface, but continual combat operations resulted in a road that had many potholes, bomb craters, and crumbling pavement. Today, all three routes are paved but still narrow. It would be on those important lines of communication I would be traveling during my time in Barrel Roll.

§

Boun Lieng, my guide for my remaining time in Laos, met me at the airport, along with our driver, Nou. We drove directly to the hotel, the Phouviengkham Resort, which sat on a hill over-looking Phonsavan. It was an attractive setting and the room was large. However, it wasn't until my second day that I learned I had to turn on a circuit breaker in order to get heat in the room. On that first night, I slept with a heavy sweater, long running pants, and cap to stay warm. On a positive note, there was plenty of hot water. The last two nights were more comfortable, in fact, the room was quite warm!

Upon our arrival at the hotel, Boun Lieng and I sat down and reviewed the areas I wanted to visit over the next three days. My first priority was to visit Long Tieng, which was the headquarters for CIA operations in MR II and General Vang Pao's headquarters. At its peak, *L'Armee Clandestine*, numbered about 40,000[14], all of whom were volunteers who called Long Tieng home. Today, most of the Hmong survive by farming and hunting and often have chickens, pigs, cows, and water buffalo grazing in their villages. Rice, peppers, and corn are staples and are among the most frequently grown crops.

In addition to Long Tieng, I was anxious to visit Sam Thong, located about 25 miles north of Long Tieng. However, it was not to be. Numerous calls were made to local authorities, seeking permission to visit the sites, but since they were active military installations, we were denied access.

After reviewing our itinerary for the next several days, we headed out for our first destination, LS-108, Muong Soui. The village is located on the western edge of the PDJ. We followed Rt. 7, which led us directly to Muong Soui, the name of which is Nong Tang, today. Muong Soui had been the site of numerous battles during the war, and control of the battle-weary

Lima Site and village changed hands numerous times. Typically, the North Vietnamese Army (NVA) and Pathet Lao (PL) made sweeps westward across the PDJ from its strongholds in the north and east during the dry season, only to be driven back by Vang Pao and his forces during the rainy season.

Muong Soui was the location of a forward operating base, Lima Site 108, from which many ground operations were launched. In addition to the abandoned airstrip, I wanted to visit a large cave complex in the mountains on the outskirts of town. The caves were called the Buddha Caves. During periods when the NVA used the cave complex as a field hospital and to bivouac troops, the Buddha Caves were targeted for air strikes.

As we approached the village of Muong Soui, we stopped at a restaurant, located at the end of a picturesque lake. We needed directions to the old airstrip and Buddha Caves. The proprietor, Phayvanh Asang, greeted us and provided the information we needed. Later, we would return to the restaurant for lunch where Phayvanh Asang would share her amazing story with us.

§

Moung Soui had been an important base from which many ground operations were launched. Troops were ferried to this forward location, into the heart of PL and NVA controlled territory. The old runway was clearly visible, but I wasn't able to locate the ruins of any support buildings that had been present back in the 60's and 70's. The name of the site was, almost always, mentioned whenever PDJ operations were discussed. It figured prominently in the war, and many warriors died while trying to either attack or defend the airstrip. On numerous occasions, ABCCC directed air assets to LS-108 to support the friendlies.

I walked up and down the length of the old runway, trying to imagine life at Moung Soui during the war; calm and peaceful days interspersed with the frenetic pace of combat. I climbed the small hill that lined the west side of the old runway and looked out over what once had been a bustling military outpost but had now been forgotten by time. This was one of the compelling reasons I had traveled to Laos, to walk, for the first time, on hallowed ground. In silence, I walked among the ghosts of Moung Soui, anonymous and courageous warriors all. I kneeled on the runway in prayer, left tears on the red soil, and scooped up a handful of dirt from LS-108.

The solemnity of the moment quickly changed to joy as I approached the entrance to a school that had been built adjacent to the old airstrip. It was a large school, having over 900 students. I learned that schools in Laos are organized similarly to schools in America. Children start school at the age of five and if they graduate, they will have attended school for 12 years. There was a new building on one end that housed the equivalent of a high school. At the other end of the campus were a series of older buildings, which were classrooms for elementary and middle school students. The simple buildings were constructed of wood, had but one door, and several large windows that were propped open. The classrooms had dirt floors. None of the rooms had electricity, and they were quite dark. I visited several classrooms and noted the typical class size was well above 30 students. I was impressed by how serious the students were; they listened carefully to their teachers and made meticulous notes in their paper notebooks (similar to what we might refer to as exam booklets, the infamous blue books we used for college exams).

It was lunch time when we walked onto the campus, and students were scattered all over the large field that separated the two classroom complexes. For lunch, many students went home to eat while others had brought bag lunches from home. Throughout my time in Laos, we saw many children walking along the roads, either going to or from home to school. Most students walked, but some rode bikes. Many of the older boys and girls rode motorbikes, a very common and practical means of transportation.

Upon entering the school grounds, I approached two older girls who were seated on the ground. We talked a bit about their school and the subjects they studied. All High School students are taught English, and the girls and I were able to exchange a few words in English. Like most Laotians I met during the trip, the girls were curious about America and me. I thanked them for their time and gave them each an American/Laos flag pin. As I walked past other groups of students, I realized I had become the center of their attention, somewhat of an oddity. Obviously, I looked different, and later after having spoken with several teachers, I learned that the presence of foreigners at the school was a very rare occurrence. As I passed by, children laughed and giggled and some held their hands to their mouths in shocked surprise at seeing a foreigner. I was a curiosity. Some even ran away.

Initially, I didn't see any adults in the huge courtyard. I walked into an empty classroom, followed by curious students. Others looked into the classroom through the open windows. With Boun Lieng translating, I wrote my name on the chalkboard and started to "teach" an English lesson. Evidently, word spread rapidly among the students that an American was visiting their school, because soon, the classroom and windows were overflowing with inquisitive children.

In my comments, I stressed the importance of getting an education and how it will help to obtain a job and improve the quality of their lives. I urged the students to study hard and remain in school until they graduated and consider continuing their education in college. We had a wonderful time together, sharing smiles and lots of laughter. The students were attentive, respectful, and very well behaved. I was delighted to respond to their questions about America and myself.

After "entertaining" the students for almost thirty minutes, we left the classroom and met a small group of teachers. Just like their students, they were curious about the American who was visiting their school. They all spoke English, and except for a few, the group of teachers looked very young. They were interested in the fact I had been a teacher, and they asked questions about schools in America. We took pictures together and exchanged e-mail addresses. I promised I would send copies of the pictures we had taken, which I did upon my return home.

We exchanged farewells, and the teachers and students returned to their classrooms. As Boun Lieng and I were leaving the school grounds, a thought occurred to me. There were several small stores on the campus, and, in addition to food, candy, and drinks, they also sold school supplies. As a gesture of friendship and a way to express my thanks for welcoming me into their school, I purchased notebooks for the students. I bought 20 bundles, each of which contained 20 notebooks. I returned to the classrooms to present one bundle to each teacher. When I walked into each classroom, the students all rose and gave me the traditional Lao greeting by placing their hands together in front of their faces and bowing slightly. Clearly, from my brief visit, disruptive behavior in Lao schools didn't appear to be a problem. The teachers were appreciative of my gifts, and the kids practiced their English by saying, "Thank you." The visit to the Moung Soui School was the first of four visits to Lao schools. Two days later, I discovered that my gifts did not go unnoticed by local officials.

During my two-hour visit, I experienced very powerful emotions on opposite ends of the spectrum. I had walked onto the abandoned airstrip at LS-108 and grieved for those who had died while either defending or attacking this small piece of real estate. And then, I enjoyed the pure joy, innocence, enthusiasm, and inquisitiveness of youth.

— 8 —
LOOKING TO THE FUTURE

"Brothers and sisters, I do not consider myself yet to have taken hold of it. But one thing I do: Forgetting what is behind and straining toward what is ahead..." **Phillipians 3:13**

We left LS-108 and drove to the Buddha Caves of Muong Soui, several miles away. The cave complex is huge, and we were told that several of the caves meandered deep into the rock-solid hillside. We climbed up and down some very steep steps to reach the entrance of the first cave called the Buddha Cave, so named for the giant Golden Buddha located inside the cave's entrance. There were numerous small Buddha images that, over the years, had been left by those who had made pilgrimages to the cave to pray to Buddha.

The second cave was larger than the first. The North Vietnamese had used this cave as a field hospital; scattered around the floor were medicine bottles, broken syringes, and remnants of medical equipment. I was shocked that those artifacts still remained, which indicated to me the caves were not well known nor were they a popular tourist attraction. After descending the hill from the cave entrances, we walked through a wooded area that had many bomb craters, which would become a common sight throughout my time in Laos. I also noticed a series of trenches scattered among the bomb craters in front of the caves. Those trenches, I learned, were the former graves of North Vietnamese soldiers who had been killed during the war. Their bodies had been buried in shallow graves near the field hospital where they had been treated. Following the war, the bodies had been retrieved and reinterred in cemeteries in Vietnam. More ghosts.

We left the Buddha Caves and returned to the restaurant for lunch.

Over noodle soup and chicken, Phayvanh Asang spoke about her childhood. In 1970, she was three years old and has vivid memories of the war. Her father was a rice farmer, and she recalled how her family's life was uprooted from time to time when the NVA and PL emerged from the hills and invaded their village. Knowing the American planes would be dropping bombs on the enemy, at such times, the family moved to the safety of the Buddha Caves, just like many other villagers. Her father risked injury and death by remaining behind to tend to his animals and crops. She vividly remembered the fighting that took place in February 1970. As she recalled from later discussions with her parents, the fighting was more ferocious than in the past and the destruction caused by the bombing raids was devastating to village residents. While this three-year-old girl was seeking shelter in a cave with her family, I was flying overhead, communicating with the FAG at LS-108. Air assets were diverted to support the friendly forces who were defending the outpost. Phayvanh Asang noted that while friendly forces successfully regained control of the base, the enemy remained in control of much of the surrounding area. She and all members of her family feared the Communists who treated the villagers brutally. Thankfully, all members of her family survived the war.

As I listened to her story, I was stunned to discover the incredible connection that linked our lives. While I had gone about discharging my duties as an Air Intelligence officer in 1970, Phayvanh Asang was huddled in the relative safety of the Buddha Caves with her family. Just twenty thousand feet of altitude had separated us. As my journey in Laos unfolded, this would be the first of several remarkable connections with Laotians revealed to me.

As we sat in her restaurant, discussing the violence that had, at one time, consumed her life, I focused on one of the overriding purposes of my journey. I asked Phayvanh Asang if she held any resentment, anger, or hatred towards the United States for the destruction we had brought to her country during the war years. Clearly, she was a victim. I was astounded by her response. Without hesitation, Phayvanh Asang indicated she rarely thinks about past events and, instead, focuses on the well-being of her family and their future. Despite the hardships the war caused, there was no bitterness or hatred in her heart. I was speechless, having expected an entirely different response. I thought, for certain, the United States would be identified as the cause for the misery and suffering inflicted upon the civilian population of her country. I interpreted her response as forgiveness, a remarkable gift.

Unbeknownst to her, Phayvanh Asang had quoted, almost verbatim, the Biblical verse that had changed my life just a month before I visited her country; Philippians 3:13. I thanked this incredible woman for her time and presented her with an Air Force challenge coin and some Kip.

§

Boun Lieng and I discussed the strategy we would use to meet villagers who would might have knowledge about the war years and how their village might have been impacted. We decided that once we had arrived at a village, we would seek out a village elder and engage him in conversation about the war years.

Khong Khai, a small village located in the heart of Barrel Roll, was another high priority destination on my itinerary. During my deployment in Southeast Asia, the village was, for the most part, free from major combat operations, however some skirmishes and fighting did occur in and around the village. Due to the presence of a Chinese Cultural Center, the village was off-limits to American aircraft. However, that all changed in March 1970, just before I left SEA. That was when a major battle for control of Khong Khai took place. We closely monitored the battle as it unfolded and kept busy providing air support for our ground forces. During the three days of fighting, the village sustained considerable damage, and the cultural center was destroyed.

Upon our arrival in Khong Khai, we immediately went in search of the oldest man we could locate, a village elder. He directed us to a small home just a block off the main road running through the center of town. We found a man sitting next to a small fire, with several others gathered around. They were doing their best to stay warm on a chilly day. As we approached, the owner of the home rose to greet us and invited us to sit down with him. In addition to the homeowner and his wife, a friend of his was visiting, accompanied by his wife as well. The conversation that unfolded during the totally chance encounter was incredible and revealed another connection.

The men did almost all of the talking, with the wives offering nods of agreement and lots of smiles. Several of the homeowner's 11 children and 14 grandchildren were present, but they remained in the background except when serving snacks and water. The men explained they have been lifelong friends, having both been born and raised in Khong Khai and living in the village their entire lives. As 12-year-old boys, they were walking to school one morning in March 1970. It was during the major NVA and PL offensive against Vang Pao's forces on the PDJ, and Khong Khai became the site of a major battle that resulted in the destruction of the Chinese Cultural Center and much of the village.

With the unmistakable sound of American fighter-bombers in the air, the boys sought refuge in the nearby woods. Within minutes, the bombs started to fall, creating a frightening and noisy scene of destruction. While the boys had experienced such attacks before, and up until that fateful day, they had remained free from harm. Their run of good luck ended that day. As they huddled amongst the trees, a bomb exploded perilously close to them. They were both rendered unconscious, and when they regained consciousness, they knew they had been seriously injured. The concussive force of the blast caused bleeding from their ears and partial hearing loss, and they were bleeding from injuries from the flying shrapnel and debris. When the man finished describing the attack, he raised a pant leg to reveal a prosthetic leg. He then said something to his friend who also raised a pant leg. He also revealed a prosthetic leg. They had each lost a leg in the attack on their village by American planes in March 1970.

They had been victims of the battle for Khong Khai and suffered life-altering injuries by the resources we had diverted to support the friendly forces. During the battle, I closely monitored the ebb and flow of the battle, providing support to the Hmong warriors as needed. We were deeply disappointed when the NVA and PL assumed complete control of the village. While I was busy preparing for my return to the states, those 12-year-old boys were fighting to recover from their injuries.

An errant American-made 500-pound bomb delivered by an Air Force fighter had almost killed those two men, with whom I was now visiting. After learning about their recovery and subsequent fitting of the prosthetic devices, I asked each of them if they held any anger or bitterness toward the United States. They both indicated that any anger they may have had so many years ago, was long gone. Their focus, instead, was on the well-being of their children and grandchildren and living happy lives. Once again, clear victims of the Second Indochina War, held no animosity toward the United States and the planes that brought destruction to their village. The homeowner confided he and his family were grateful to the United States for its efforts to bring freedom to Laos. He also told me that life under Communist rule was difficult.

Both of my new friends received a challenge coin and 100,000 Kip. Judging by the expressions on their faces, they were honored and pleased to receive those gifts. As I left, we embraced one another and departed as friends.

My first day on the PDJ had been exhilarating and filled with powerful and meaningful experiences, all of which had a profound effect on me. The day had far exceeded my expectations, and in eager anticipation, I looked forward to another momentous day.

— 9 —

PLAINE DES JARRES

9 December 2014 - Day # 6
Thong Hai Hin (Plaine des Jarres Site #1)

Our first destination was Thong Hai Hin, identified on maps as Plaine des Jarres Site #1. Of the sites open to the public, this is the most spectacular of the three. The PDJ, of course, got its name from the presence of stone "jars" that are located throughout the Xieng Khoang Province. Archeologists believe they were used as funeral jars.

The first area we visited was in a low-lying area of slightly surrounded on two sides with rolling hummocks. The hills were used for military purposes since they provided clear views of the surrounding valleys and were easily defensible from ground attack. Just a few trees dot the landscape. I was thrilled to be able to, finally, walk among the Jars, an archeological marvel about which I had heard so much during my year in SEA. I touched the stone, peered into the jars, and wondered about the people who had created those wonderful artifacts so many centuries ago. I followed a path that ran to the base of a hill and discovered another of the multitude of caves that define the ubiquitous karst mountains and hills of Laos. No doubt, the PL and NVA soldiers sought the protection of the caves when they occupied the area and for our allies when they controlled the PDJ. It was humbling to walk among the ghosts of the PDJ.

As I walked along the paths at Thong Hai Hin, I noticed white markers lying flat to the ground that littered the way. Each marker had the letters MAG, which identified that spot as an area from which an UXO had been safely removed or destroyed.

I climbed a path to what our SGU forces referred to as the Hill of Big Jars. Big Jars indeed, as well as bomb craters and other surprises. My memory is that the jar sites were, generally, off limits to bombing raids. However, the bomb craters at both the bases and tops of the hills were proof there were occasions when the ROE was ignored in attempts to dislodge the enemy. Some of the jars on the hill were huge and one stood at the very edge of a bomb crater. At the top of one of the hills, I was surprised to find a series of fighting trenches that had been dug by the PL and NVA when they occupied the terrain. Typical of such trenches, they zigzagged across the top of the hill, providing a field of fire in all directions. Connected to the trenches was a larger and deeper fox hole that was, no doubt, a command structure that afforded a more secure location for personnel and equipment during bombing raids and strafing runs. Judging by the evidence of the bombing to which this location had been subjected, this hill was, clearly, a prime target during the war where men had lived, fought, and died on the Hill of Big Jars.

As I stood on the hill and looked over the valley below and the mountains beyond, it was easy to visualize and understand the tactical and strategic importance of the PDJ. Thong Hai Hin was a special place. As I did on numerous occasions during my trip to Laos, I knew I was standing on hallowed ground, ground on which many lives had been lost. And for what purpose?

§

During the war, Route 7 was barely a hard surface road, nevertheless, it was one of the most important lines of communication in Barrel Roll. Route 7 runs east to west, and the eastern terminus of the road leads into North Vietnam through the Barthelemy Pass. The western end of the road intersects with Route 13, one of the main north/south routes in northern Laos. Whether it was the PL, NVA, RLA, or Vang Pao's Special Guerilla Units (SGU), they all advanced or retreated along these strategically vital roadways. When the PL and NVA were moving men and materiel, they were continually subjected to interdiction by American air power. Inevitably, as opposing forces moved back and forth along Route 7 skirmishes occurred as well as major encounters. As we traveled eastward along Route 7, we passed through villages, the names of which appear in the history books regarding the "secret war" in Laos. In our bomb damage assessment (BDA) and after-action reports, we dutifully recorded the names of villages such as Ban Lao, Tai Dam, Nam Mot, Gnum Chong, Nam Men, Nong Pet, and Ban Napa. There was a time in my former life when those small villages were the primary focus of discussions, plans, and operations. Now, they were peaceful villages, and I smiled as we saw people scurrying about, getting on with their lives. Little children played while older children worked alongside their parents. Farm animals grazed and moved about as they pleased. It gave me great joy to observe them living in peace. Unlike the ghosts from 50 years in the past, the present-day villagers don't have to be continually on the alert and worry about their safety.

§

Nong Het is the easternmost town in Laos on Route 7, lying just a few miles from the border with Vietnam. The town has the distinction of being the birthplace and childhood home of General Vang Pao. During the war, the area was, mostly, under the control of Communist forces; however, SGU conducted regular operations in the area. The border crossing was one of several used by the North Vietnamese to infiltrate men and materiel through Barthelemy Pass (called Bart Pass) into Laos.

As was our routine, Bien Lieng and I walked along the streets of the village, in search of an elder. On a dirt road a block or two north of Route 7, the main street of the village, we observed an elderly man standing along the road. We learned later he was curious about a vehicle driving down his road; scooters and motorcycles were common, but vans were not that common. We approached the man and greeted him, and as was so typical of the Lao we met, we were warmly received and immediately invited into his home. With his huge smile and hospitality, we felt an immediate bond of friendship. We were offered small wooden stools to sit on, and the four of us sat in a circle on a dirt floor in the middle of a room that served as kitchen, dining room, living room, storage, and bedroom. Also present in the small house was the man's wife who was caring for a granddaughter who clung to her grandmother. They stood off to the side at a back door and did not participate in our conversation. In fact, during our entire hour-long visit, neither of them spoke a word. On reflection, more than likely I was the only Caucasian who had ever visited their home. I was a rare and curious oddity.

His name was Seng Keu, and he was 80 years old. He was Hmong and more comfortable in speaking his native language rather than Lao. Luckily, our driver, Nou, was also Hmong and fluent in the language. He played a vital role in the amazing discussion that ensued. Our conversation proved to be interesting challenge inasmuch as Boun Lieng translated my questions and comments into Lao for Nou who then translated my questions and comments into Hmong. Then, whenever Seng Keu spoke, the process was reversed.

Seng Keu and his wife had raised 14 children, five of whom had died. Two of his sons were killed during the war while, like their father, were Hmong warriors, serving in the *L'Armee Clandestine* and fighting against the PL and NVA. Seng Keu told us he and his wife had many grandchildren and great grandchildren, but didn't know exactly how many, assuring us it was well over 30.

Seng Keu was overjoyed to learn I had served in the Air Force. He jumped up, grabbed my arms, embraced me, and told me we had been comrades. Seng Keu was curious about my role in the Air Force and was delighted to learn our squadron had been involved in supporting General Vang Pao and his Hmong comrades. When I told him our call sign was Alleycat, he jumped up again, approached me with open arms, and we embraced once more. He knew of Alleycat, and with tears in his eyes, he held my hands and thanked me for the many nights when Alleycat had sent Spooky (gunships) to his team when they were engaged with the enemy. The strength of our bonding and emotional connection became overwhelming as we marveled at how the paths of our lives had crossed so many years ago. Similar to my reaction when I had met Ngo Thoi Binh in Hanoi, I immediately felt a bond of brotherhood with Seng Keu.

As we sat on the dirt floor in his modest home, Seng Keu shared his story with us. Feeling a sense of loyalty to his hometown leader, General Vang Pao, he volunteered to serve in the *L'Armee Clandestine*. He couldn't recall the exact year, but it was in the early 1960's. After hiking more than 40 miles, he and several other recruits, including two of his sons, arrived at a small airstrip (presumably, one of the numerous Lima Sites in Barrel Roll). For the first time in his life, Seng Keu boarded an airplane and was flown to a large "camp" (his word). More than likely, that "large camp" was Long Tieng (LS 98). After being formally inducted into Vang Pao's secret army, Seng Keu was then flown to Thailand (he didn't know where in Thailand) for more than two months of training. He told us the instructors were supervised by Americans, most likely CIA para-military. Once training was completed, they returned to Northern Laos, and that was where his ten plus year combat experience began. For the next ten years, Seng Keu was assigned to and fought in an SGU.

Seng Keu had fought almost exclusively in Barrel Roll, moving from Lima Site to Lima Site as the ebb and flow of operations dictated. Initially, his unit, like most of the newly formed SGU, engaged in guerrilla operations, ambushing enemy units and then just as quickly retreating into the relative safety of the jungle from which they had emerged. In time, however, American strategy changed, and Vang Pao's forces began to be used in more of a conventional warfare role, conducting well planned operations, with air support, against NVA and PL forces.

I was mesmerized as Seng Keu ticked off the names of the locations at which he had engaged NVA and PL forces in skirmishes and battles, places, all of which, I was familiar; Muang Kham, Ban Muang, Khong Khai, Xieng Khoang, Ban Ban, Moung Soui, Nong Pet, and Muang Pang. As I listened, my mind was drawn to those many nights when Alleycat supported reports of TIC at those locations, and I marveled at the likelihood that the paths of our lives had intersected so many years ago.

Seng Keu, and his fellow Hmong, were dispatched as needed and as events dictated. Early in his enlistment, they trekked over jungle paths, and were grateful whenever trucks could transport them, even if it was just for short distances. Eventually, SGUs were routinely transported by helicopter, which, initially, created fear and suspicion among the Hmong, many of whom had never seen a helicopter before. That fear had been exacerbated by the fact that some soldiers had been killed after walking into the turning rotors. My new friend, Seng Keu, also described two occasions when he participated in the rescue of downed pilots, one American and one Lao.

§

Following the end of hostilities in 1975, the victorious Communist government systematically rounded up civil servants and RLA and SGU officers and sent them to re-education camps; many of whom were never heard from again. The Communists were determined to "wipe out" those who had aligned themselves with the RLG. Fearful for his safety, Seng Keu, and thousands of other SGU troops, were reluctant to return home. Eventually, he became a member of a group of four soldiers who lived in the mountains outside of Nong Het. Relying on the villagers for food and needed supplies, they survived together, in the mountains, for almost four years. On occasion, under the cover of darkness, Seng Keu visited his home and family, returning to the safety of his mountain home well before first light. Finally, tired of mountain living and judging it safe to return home, he was reunited with his family. During subsequent years, he led a quiet life.

There was a spirit about Seng Keu, one of optimism and positivity. Despite the fact he had lost two sons in the war, suffered multiple injuries, and had to endure living in the mountains of Laos for several years, Seng Keu considered himself one of the lucky ones. He had survived the war, recovered from his wounds, overcome bouts of malaria, and endured the hardship of mountain living. During our time together, a smile remained firmly in place, and he exuded peace, happiness, and an appreciation for life. I was happy for my new friend.

After about 45 minutes of talking and sharing information regarding our lives, Seng Keu suddenly stood up and disappeared into a back room. He emerged with a huge smile on his face, holding a bottle of homemade whiskey. A shot glass appeared, and he poured the first of many shots that were consumed. As the host, he drank the first shot, and then it was my turn. While I am not a drinker, there was never a thought that I would do anything except honor his hospitality and Lao custom. I toasted my new friend and drank my shot of whiskey. Thankfully, it didn't seem too strong, and I managed the homemade brew with little discomfort. Then, in succession, Boun and Nou drank their rounds. We each drank a second shot when Seng Keu disappeared once more. He then returned with another, larger, bottle of homemade brew. I had no idea what we were drinking, but we drank several more rounds to celebrate our newfound friendship. As we sat on the dirt floor, I marveled at the providence that had brought us together and thanked God for having arranged to have the path of Seng Keu's life intersect with mine, once again.

During our time together, Seng Keu mentioned that his village had been subjected to intense bombing during the war, and his house had sustained damage. More than likely, the bombing raids were conducted by American forces, and I asked if he felt any anger about the raids that had threatened his family and damaged his property. Not at all, he told us. He believed in defending his nation against the Communists and was thankful for America's support of the country he loved. Seng Keu became philosophical when he went on to say that many Americans gave up their lives for the Lao people for which he was thankful. In the pursuit of being able to live free, Seng Keu told us Laos, also had to make sacrifices. It was Seng Keu's desire to not look back on what happened in the past. He was thankful he had survived the war and only wanted to enjoy his family and continue farming crops.

We walked into his back yard, and there, 20 feet from the rear of his house, was a huge bomb crater. Without access to soil to fill the crater, crops were simply planted in the crater. As I scanned the yards of his neighbors, I saw several more bomb craters. In fact, it was a familiar scene in just about all of the Barrel Roll villages we visited.

We talked a bit more about Seng Keu's life during the war years, and soon, it was time to say goodbye. I gave my new friend an Air Force coin and 100,000 Kip. He was very expressive in his thanks, and we, again, felt that strong sense of bonding, friendship, and brotherhood. We hugged, and Seng Keu kissed me goodbye. On our ride back to Phonsavan, I reflected on another miraculous encounter. I was privileged to have met a person with whom we shared a wonderful moment of bonding, mutual respect, and brotherhood. More than 50 years later we had been reconnected. It was another thrilling and humbling day.

—10—
DETAINED FOR QUESTIONING

10 December 2014 - Day # 7

We headed west on Rt. 7, with the intention of locating LS-22 near the village of Muong Om. But our search was in vain. No one seemed to know the whereabouts of the abandoned airfield. Instead, we headed north toward the Phou Kout District that had been a stronghold of the Pathet Lao during the war and the target of frequent air strikes.

As we drove slowly through the village of Muong Paek, we saw an older man who was seated alongside the road. We stopped and approached the man, who was just sitting in a chair with little expression on his face and, seemingly, in deep thought. We introduced ourselves, and he seemed genuinely pleased that we had stopped to talk with him. He greeted us warmly and immediately invited us into his sparely furnished home. Unlike other Laotian homes we had visited, we sat in chairs. It soon became obvious why he needed a chair; his home was in what had been a store front. A small cooking area was on one side of the rather large room, but there was no visible sleeping area. His wife sat on a bench during our visit, and as in our other visits, other than greeting us and smiling, she never spoke a word.

His name was Somdy Khantavoung. When I asked if he had fought in the war, he smiled and said that, yes, he had. I was stunned to learn he had fought with the Pathet Lao and was even more incredulous when he told us he was Hmong. For all the years since my deployment to Southeast Asia, I had erroneously assumed that Hmong only fought in support of the RLG.

The war had taken its toll on his body and my new friend had not aged well. He was only 60 years old. Over the next hour and a half, prodded by my questions, Somdy Khantavoung told us about his war-time service fighting with the Pathet Lao. I was excited about the good fortune of having the opportunity to meet a man who, all those years ago, had been considered the enemy. My mind was flooded with thoughts and questions; there was so much I wanted to know.

His family was poor, and his father, like most others in their small village of Muong Paek, barely eked out a living for his family, growing rice, vegetables, and raising pigs. His father had little interest in the politics of the day, however, Somdy Khantavoung recalled that all village residents were subjected to lectures by village leaders. Since Muong Paek was located in an area controlled by and sympathetic to the Pathet Lao, the village leaders to which Somdy Khantavoung referred, were, no doubt, Communist cadre.

As a young boy, with no formal education, Somdy Khantavoung, also, had no understanding of the rival factions that were fighting for control of Laos, but reminders of the war were a daily occurrence. Planes were regularly seen in the skies over their village, and the sounds of war, off in the distance, were reminders of the danger that had come to his world. On some days, the sounds of war were close to home, and Somdy Khantavoung recalled, there were times when bombs dropped on his village and near his home. He described how his family and villagers were forced to flee their homes and seek shelter in the nearby jungle. Danger was an everyday fact of life for the villagers of Muong Paek.

Another fact of life for Somdy Khantavoung was the knowledge that when he reached the age of 15 he would be forced into service, joining and fighting for the Land of the Lao (Pathet Lao), a peasant army fighting those who had "invaded" his country, the United States. In 1968, Somdy Khantavoung was 14 years old at the time, two soldiers visited his village and told the village chief they needed three young men to join the Land of the Lao. That very same day, when the soldiers appeared, Somdy Khantavoung said goodbye to his family and was taken away. Willingly or not, at the age of 14, he had become a member of the Pathet Lao. Like almost all the young recruits, Somdy Khantavoung had no education, no political views, and certainly no military training. With meager rations, Somdy and his fellow villagers walked for days through mountainous terrain until reaching what proved to be a training base. His training included three parts: basic education, cultural studies and military training. Illiteracy was wide-spread in Laos, and recruits received basic instruction in how to read and write. The literacy training Somdy Khantavoung received by the Pathet Lao was the only formal education he ever received.

As he described it, cultural studies was nothing more than political indoctrination. They received hours of lectures regarding the evil of capitalism and how United States imperialism made the Lao people poor. The virtues of Communism were continually being reinforced. He was told it was his duty to fight oppression and to fight for the liberation of their country. The Pathet Lao, they were told, sought independence. Somdy Khantavoung did as he was told.

The training period lasted for more than two months, and the greatest portion of the time was devoted to the military training phase. His memory was amazing, and I marveled as he quickly ticked off what was referred to as, the Five Great Techniques: creeping and crawling; firing a rifle; fighting with a bayonet; digging fortifications; and using grenades. They learned how to plan ambushes and engage in hand-to-hand combat. Since the use of air power was so prevalent, methods of firing against aircraft were also stressed. Somdy Khantavoung must have excelled at that portion of his training, because his assignment was that of an anti-aircraft gunner, a role in which he served for his entire time as a PL soldier.

Somdy Khantavoung fought for the PL, almost non-stop, for five years, engaging in hostilities all over the PDJ and beyond. Whenever his unit was not engaged in skirmishes, they were hiking to its next objective, always traveling by foot. To the best of his ability, he could remember only one or two times when he ever traveled by truck, and that was for short distances only. They avoided hiking along roadways, opting, instead, for ancient game trails that meandered through the dense foliage. They lived in primitive conditions, being sustained by meager rations of rice, sugar, and salt. When operating in areas controlled by the PL, the villagers provided shelter and rations of food that included poultry, vegetables, and beef. Tobacco was a luxury, a highly sought after item. The PL soldiers were paid 8 Kip a day, which equated to about 5 cents a day. The meager pay was sent home to each soldier's family.

I asked about the North Vietnamese, and Somdy Khantavoung indicated they rarely saw NVA troops. At the battalion level, North Vietnamese soldiers served as advisors. The NVA forces did not trust PL and looked upon them with scorn and a feeling of superiority. The NVA never considered PL fighters to be their equals. Evidently, the NVA and PL were allies but not friends.

Somdy Khantavoung's responsibility was to man an anti-aircraft gun. He described the incredible hardships he and his comrades endured, having to lug around a 12.7 mm Russian-made anti-aircraft gun, tripod, and ammunition. The gun, alone, weighed over 70 pounds. Nevertheless, his squad of 10 to 12 soldiers carried their personal rifle and gear and shared the added burden of the 12.7 mm machine gun. Protective gear was non-existent. As a result of five years of firing his weapon, Somdy Khantavoung suffered a loss of hearing. He was also wounded on several occasions; gunshot wounds suffered during skirmishes and shrapnel injuries from bombs and CBUs. The physical hardships he had endured and the years of malnutrition and sleep deprivation, wreaked havoc on his body resulting in chronic back pain and severely limited mobility and flexibility. In 1973, at the age of 19, Somdy was disabled to the extent that he was discharged from the PL. It took him weeks to hobble home and be reunited with members of his family, whom he had seen only twice during the previous five years.

Somdy Khantavoung was curious about the airplane in which I flew. He wanted to know if our plane dropped bombs. I assured him that we did not drop bombs on or shoot guns at the PL. I did my best to explain our role in the war. Somdy Khantavoung indicated they were particularly afraid of the gunships and described the fear they experienced when being attacked by those planes. Flareships also caused problems, because they disrupted their night-time movements and attacks on SGU positions. As we talked, I realized the paths of our lives had crossed all those years ago, when Alleycat overflew the PDJ while Somdy, and the members of his squad, moved about either in pursuit of or retreat from the SGU.

I was particularly interested in Somdy Khantavoung's feelings toward the United States, in light of the suffering the Lao endured during the war years. He told me he had no feelings of anger or resentment. He was at peace, and he and his wife take great joy in being with their family. As we talked, he held my hands, and the gentle man said we were brothers. During the war years, we had been adversaries, but now we shared a strong emotional attachment. I told him I was honored to have met him and considered him now a friend and brother. I expressed my admiration of him for the courage he exhibited during the war and for the sacrifices he and his family had made during that extremely difficult period of time. As we parted, I presented him my usual gifts. I expressed my wishes for good health and peace to Somdy Khantavoung and the members of his family. We left him standing alongside the road with a sad smile on his face as we drove away. I marveled at and thanked God for having brought us together.

§

We continued to drive in a northerly direction to an area that had once been one of the PL headquarters and a frequent target for bombing and strafing sorties. Our destination was the tiny village of Phou Kouk. Except for several houses, a few shops, and numerous bomb craters, there wasn't much to the village of Phou Kouk. However, the village did have a schoolyard full of little kids, which drew my attention. I spoke with one of the teachers and learned the school housed the equivalent of Kindergarten through second grade and had a student population of approximately 90 students. With her permission, I bought pieces of candy for the students and entered the school yard.

It was apparent the school drew children from families of varying levels of income. Many of the children were dressed appropriately for the slightly chilly weather while others were barefoot in thread-bare clothing. However, they did have something in common. Children are children wherever one travels. They were all smiling as they played on the dirt playground. The shouts of happiness brought a smile to my face as I watched them interact and take joy with one another. Some were oblivious to my presence, but others stopped their play, looked at me, and overcome by curiosity, approached me. A few shy ones sought refuge behind their teachers and cautiously sought glimpses of the stranger who had entered the schoolyard. However, once I started to hand out the candy, all play stopped and the children lined up to receive their treats, which were quickly consumed. Once the candy had been distributed, the teachers organized the kids for a group picture, one of my fond memories of the trip. As I left the school yard and those beautiful children and their dedicated teachers, I felt slightly guilty, because I noticed the playground was littered with candy wrappers.

We left the smiling children of Phou Kouk, returned to Rt. 7, and headed west to the village of Xieng Gna. An airstrip was located in the nearby hills several miles to the south of the village. The airstrip was called Nam Son, and it had been used extensively by SGU forces to launch offensive operations in the PDJ. At the time, the area was a loyal stronghold of the RLG, loyal to General Vang Pao and the *L'Armee Clandestine*.

Seeking more information regarding the location of the airstrip, we stopped at the village to make some inquiries. We were greeted warmly by the very first woman we met, and like all of the Lao we met, she graciously invited us into her home. Within several minutes of arriving in the village, our shoes were off, and I was given a cushion to sit on. Everyone else sat on the bare floor. Word spread quickly about the American who had arrived in their village. Several local men joined us, while others gathered outside, curious about the visitor. I answered a lot of questions about myself and the reasons why we had stopped at their village. Several men knew of the abandoned airstrip and were familiar about its use during the war years. We were told it was located about ten miles outside of town, but it was a challenge to get there. The road was heavily rutted and had numerous steep hills. A special, off-road vehicle would be needed. Clearly, our van would not be able to make the trek. One of the men, who was a schoolteacher, volunteered his son to take us. However, it would cost the equivalent of $50 to make the trip. I consented to the arrangement.

As the man left the room to call his son, a woman placed a huge platter of food before us. I was interested to note I was the only one to receive a bowl. Thankfully, I was warned about one of the dishes; it looked like fried onions, and I was told it was extremely spicy. I didn't realize it at the time, but, wisely, I quickly scooped up several items into the bowl I had been given. The women moved to the kitchen area of the house, leaving the men to eat together. Among the beautifully arrayed food items was a huge bowl of sticky rice and a bowl of noodle soup. It was then that I received a lesson in Lao eating etiquette. The bowl of soup was a common bowl for all. They merely dipped their spoons into the bowl and ate the soup. The other dishes were eaten by using their fingers. I watched as one man used his finger to move the pieces of beef around in the dish until he found a piece to his liking. And that was the manner in which the other dishes were eaten, with their fingers. I chose not to return for seconds. For dessert, the woman of the house brought out rice cakes. They were quite large, generally flat and very light. They had been fried and were absolutely delicious. I ate more than my share of rice cakes.

Finally, our ride arrived, and Boun Lieng, Nou, and I sat in the SUV for our trip to the abandoned airfield. The road had once been a trail on which Vang Pao's troops and those of the enemy used to move about the country. We went up and down very steep hills, drove over and through huge ruts, and slowly progressed along the very narrow road. On several occasions, we passed cargo trucks that were carrying huge loads of corn, which made for some interesting maneuvering. As we approached the old airstrip, the driver received a call that seemed to unnerve him. He advised us that he had been told we were not permitted to take any pictures or get out of the truck. What had once been a landing strip was now the main street of this small and very isolated village. I had to be content with looking up and down the old landing strip and the houses that had been built on both sides. The village was surrounded by hills, which must have made it challenging for the pilots to fly into and out of the area. Even though I couldn't leave the vehicle, I was thrilled to be at another location that had played such a prominent role in the war. When we returned to Xieng Gna, we found out why we were told to remain in our vehicles.

Upon our return to Xieng Gna, we were greeted by a local police-man, the village leader, and the village security officer. Boun Lieng told me we were being detained by the authorities for questioning. Evidently, we had entered a restricted zone and had done so without having had received permission to do so. I was told to bring my passport. We followed the officials to the house of the village leader. We climbed a flight of stairs to a large room in which we sat in a circle on the floor.

Boun Lieng did all of the talking with the officials, answering their seemingly non-ending questions. For a few moments, I could focus only on the fact I was in a Communist controlled country and being held by the authorities for questioning. The thought did occur to me that the possibility existed I might just disappear, never to be heard from again. As the officials asked questions and Boun Lieng answered, a policeman was writing furiously in an official looking journal. The questioning continued for almost an hour. In time, there was some laughter among the officials, and a huge wave of relief swept over me. Boun Lieng told me there was no problem, just a misunderstanding.

The officials explained that the area was the location of resistance fighters who were living in the mountains, and for their safety, visitors were not permitted into the area without a police escort. I was invited to return the next day, and the policeman would personally escort us into the area and permit me to take photos of the abandoned airstrip.

Suddenly, it all made sense. I was aware that thousands of Hmong resistance fighters had remained behind and were living in the mountains in remote regions of the country. Nam Son was located in one of those remote areas, and inadvertently, we had entered a region in which Chao Fa was active. It was no accident that the Hmong who "took to the jungle" would settle in an area where the local population would be sympathetic to their cause. The authorities wanted to be sure I was not attempting to establish contact with the rebels to provide support.

I noticed Boun Lieng giving some Kip to one of the men, and the next thing I knew, a case of Beer Lao appeared. Someone handed me a glass, and I knew the official "hearing" was over. We were now friends. Sensing it was a tradition among Lao to celebrate with round after round of toasting one another, I joined in once my beer was poured, toasting my new friends. Several inquisitive villagers heard the antics and joined in.

It was then when providence interceded, once again. Yet again, I met another person with whom I had a connection during the war.

An older man sat down next to me. His name was Kong and he was 85 years old. When he learned I had been in the Air Force and had flown missions over Laos, he beamed and hugged me. Living in an area allied with the RLG, Kong had volunteered to be a truck driver for Vang Pao's army and had fought along-side American forces. Like all combatants, he had been separated from his family for long periods of time, and during his more than six years of service, he had been wounded several times. Once hostilities ended, he had been a prisoner for over a year before being permitted to return home. Similar to what had occurred previously with the people I had met; we immediately bonded. It was if we had been friends for all our lives, and I was overcome with joy and elation. Like the other friends with whom I had been "reunited," Kong and I felt a connection, for which we were most grateful. With our arms around each other, we toasted one other for the next two hours. As soon as our glasses approached half way filled, we promptly refilled each other's glass. For being a non-drinker, I drank a lot of beer that evening. Finally, and, thankfully, after we had consumed a second case of beer, it was time to leave and say goodbye to my new friends. Before leaving, I presented Kong with gifts. I told him how honored I was to meet him and become his friend. Like the others I met on the journey, I will never forget the brief time we shared together. In what was becoming the norm for saying goodbye to my newfound comrades, Kong and I embraced, and he kissed me.

It had been another incredible day. I was fortunate to have met two more combatants from the past, one an adversary and one an ally. Our bonding was immediate, and we expressed our respect and esteem we held for one another.

However, there was one more surprise. About 30 minutes after leaving Xieng Gna, while driving east on Route 7 on our return to Phonsavan, Boun Lieng's phone rang. The village security guard, who attended the interrogation, was calling. He was excited. It seems that when he arrived at his home, he told his family about the American who had been detained and questioned. His daughter spoke up indicating that the American her father was describing sounded like the same man who had visited her school and given notebooks to all of the students. He was calling to express his appreciation for my act of kindness to his daughter and her school mates and to invite us to have dinner with him and his family. Reluctantly and regrettably, we declined the invitation. It was approaching 9:00 PM, it was dark, we had consumed a lot of beer, and we still had a long drive back to the hotel. If the timing had only been different, we would have been honored to accept the invitation and accept his hospitality. One of the few regrets I have in life is not having accepted the dinner invitation.

—11—
BAN BAN AND THE CAVES OF THAM PIU

11 December 2014 - Day # 8

It was another early departure for the long drive awaiting us. We headed north on Route 6, another vitally important LOC during the war. The route runs north/south, connecting the PDJ with the northern Houa Phan province and its capital, Sam Neua, one of the least visited cities in Laos. It lies in a beautiful setting, a valley almost 4,000' in elevation and is surrounded by mountains on all sides. In the 1950's, following France's departure from Indochina, Sam Neua was a stronghold of the RLA, however its proximity to North Vietnam virtually assured its eventual control by the NVA and PL. With the assistance of the NVA, the PL seized control of Sam Neua in 1960, and from that point forward, the city and the surrounding territory was under the firm control of the PL and remained so for the duration of the Second Indochina War. We knew, with a high degree of certainty, the headquarters of the PL was located in Sam Neua but were unsure of its exact location. It didn't matter, since the ROE precluded airstrikes against the city, another reality of the war that made no sense. However, we were aware of the caves of Vieng Xai, located on the outskirts of Sam Neua and knew the caves played a major role in NVA and PL operations. The caves were heavily defended and regularly fragged for bombing missions.

At the intersection of Routes 7 and 6 lies a village called Muang Kham. During the war, the area was referred to as Ban Ban, a name that will not be found on any of today's charts or maps. In Lao, Ban means village and most Laotian villages begin with Ban and then followed by another name; for example, Ban Naxa, Ban Khong, and so forth. Due to its strategically important location, Ban Ban, or Muang Kham, and the surrounding area were subjected to continued combat operations and air strikes. Control of the area changed hands throughout the war.

Since Communist forces could be easily ambushed as they came down Route 6, they often dispersed into the surrounding valley, to the east, and approached Route 7 from different locations. We called that valley, which lies to the northeast of Routes 7 and 6 intersection, Ban Ban Valley. Again, that name will not appear on maps, and locals did not know what I was talking about when I inquired about Ban Ban or the Ban Ban Valley.

It was at Muang Kham where we made the first of several stops at Hmong villages that sit astride Rt. 6. Our reception in the village was just like those we received in other Laotian villages; the residents greeted us with smiles and welcomed us to their village. As usual, the children were curious. Some stared in curious fascination while others ran away or laughed and squealed with delight when I acknowledged their presence. I took pictures of many of the children, and huge smiles adorned their faces when I showed them their image on the camera. Many squealed with delight.

During our visit to Muang Kham, I made it a point to stop at the local school and met a teacher named Tuavang. When he learned I had also been a teacher, he offered me a job as an English teacher at his school. He invited me into a classroom, and the students promptly greeted me by standing, bowing their heads as they clasped their hands in front of their chests and said, in unison, "Sabaidee" (hello). Outside, students were playing, some jumping rope. With the exception of the school uniforms the children were wearing, the scene looked just like any school playground in America. As we moved on, we stopped to watch two women grinding corn with a hand turned stone. As one woman moved the stone around in a circle, another woman dropped kernels of corn onto the grinding surface. They seemed happy to have their picture taken and invited me to take a turn. I turned the stone for only a few minutes. It proved to be hard work and another reminder of how the Lao are such a hard-working and industrious people.

During my return trip to Southeast Asia, thoughts and remembrances of Hilltop were continually on my mind; Ban Ban Valley was a must-see. I thought of the watch he had given me as well as the story of how he had obtained the Soviet-made souvenir of the war. On a whim, I asked Boun Lieng to have us turn onto a dirt road that led into a valley lying between the mountains on both sides of Route 6. We were driving through fabled Ban Ban. I had often wondered if the relic of the tank Hilltop has sat upon so many years ago was still there. It was a quixotic and whimsical notion. Hilltop said his squad had ambushed an NVA unit and destroyed two tanks in Ban Ban near the village of Muang Kham. For all those years, the image of Hilltop sitting on top of the captured tank had been ingrained in my mind.

The road meandered a bit, and we had traveled about a mile or two. We passed several houses but saw no people. I didn't see it. I was looking out the right side of the van when I heard Boun Lieng tell Nou to stop. There, sitting just a few feet off the road was a vestige of the Second Indochina War; the rusted remains of a PT-76 tank. I have always loved examining military artifacts and was thrilled with the discovery.

PT-76 TANK

The PT-76 tank was introduced in the early 1950's and became the primary reconnaissance tank for the Soviet Army and other Warsaw Pact nations. One of the tank's features that made it well-suited for reconnaissance was that it was amphibious. The tank was exported to nations allied with the Soviet Union such as Syria, Iraq, North Korea, and North Vietnam. It was one of the primary fighting vehicles for the NVA during the Second Indochina War, one with which I was quite familiar. The PT-76 had a three-man crew; the commander, who also served as the radio operator and gunner, a driver, and a loader. The commander and loader stations are located in the turret, and the driver sits in the center and very front of the vehicle.

I now had the opportunity to clamber aboard the rusted and broken remains of a PT-76 tank. While the hatch covers were gone, the gun turret was still in place as were the seats for the three-man crew. I was interested in the driver's seat because I knew that an escape hatch was located directly below it. Sure enough, just as the briefing materials I had read so many years ago had indicated, I located the emergency exit. I climbed all over the relic, examining what was left of the interior and the drive train. I stood on top of the tank, just as Hilltop had done so many years ago. I felt connected to Hilltop and felt the presence of the ghosts of the men who had fought and died in Ban Ban. Of course, I will never know if the tank I found was the very same tank that Hilltop had stood upon in 1969. I like to think it was.

We returned to Route 6 and headed north. At the village of Kang Kao, a young mother, who was carrying her baby on her back, greeted us and invited me into her home. The house was like so many others I had visited in Laos. The kitchen area was located in one corner of the house, where a charcoal fire was burning. The house had a dirt floor, and it was quite dark inside. Like all Buddhist homes, there was a small alter to the spirits on one wall. Various items were stacked in the other three corners. The room in the rear was where the family slept, and it served as a storage area for various items including bags of rice and corn, staples for the Lao. I thanked her for her kindness and gave her a flag pin and kip. Another woman, who was spinning thread, invited us into her home. This family had two looms, one inside and one under the house. Her 15-year-old daughter demonstrated the weaving process, and I was impressed by what was a most intricate design. Even more remarkable was that the beautiful fabrics were created without the use of patterns.

As I walked further through the village, a young man approached me, and in perfectly clear English welcomed me to his village and asked where I was from. He was proud of his ability to speak English and happy to have the opportunity to practice his language skills. I asked him about life in the village and his plans for the future. He indicated he wanted to attend college, and I reinforced the concept of furthering one's education. After several minutes, a friend of his joined us and he also had terrific command of the English language. They were remarkable young men, and I have thought about them often. I hope they will find a way to leave their small village, attend college, and improve their standard of living. Ironically, as we were leaving the village to return to the van, another young man spoke to me in English. He was older than the other two boys with whom I had previously interacted. This young man had graduated from college in Vientiane, but being unable to find a job, he had been forced to return to his Hmong village of Kang Kao.

§

Distinctive features of central and northern Laos are the limestone mountains or karst. Over millions of years, the dissolving of soluble rock and underground drainage have produced a landscape of a multitude of complex cave systems and grottos. The caves of Laos have long played important social, cultural, and religious roles in the lives of the Lao. A resurgence of cave occupation occurred during the Vietnam War, and because of the tactical and strategic value they held for the enemy, known cave complexes were routinely targeted for air strikes.

During my return to Laos, one of the several cave complexes I wanted to visit were the caves of Tham Piu. In Laotian history of the war, the caves of Tham Piu hold a special place because of an incident that occurred on 24 November 1968. Intelligence sources indicated the Caves of Tham Piu were being used by the PL as a field hospital, and it became an important military target. On that fateful morning, during an attack by American and Laotian strike aircraft, either a bomb, missile, or rocket entered the mouth of the cave causing horrific damage. What is not known, however, is the exact number of Lao who lost their lives on that day, were they civilians or military, or who had fired the weapon? The PL claimed 374 civilians were killed in the attack, but we knew, with a high degree of certainty, the cave was being used by the PL as a field hospital. More than likely, it was a mix of civilian and military personnel who lost their lives in the attack. As a result of that incident an Annual Day of Remembrance is conducted at the caves every year. The Day of Remembrance at Tham Piu is the equivalent of a Laotian national holiday.

Prior to climbing the hill to the caves, I visited a small museum located at the base of the mountain. The museum contains many pictures of the incident and describes the efforts of the PL to defeat the Americans. According to the museum, "wave upon wave of American fighter bombers targeted the wooded hillside every day for three months until all the vegetation had been destroyed, leaving the cave entrance exposed". It is also asserted that bones of the victims still lie among the ruins. The Lao government refers to the bombing as a war crime. The following is a description and explanation by the Lao government regarding Tham Piu:

"Following their massive and humiliated defeat in each operation, the U.S. Government decided to increase their Air Force strikes to a full scale air bombing, moving from military targets to civilian targets which included habitations, schools, hospitals, temples, citizens, and all civilian properties. From these numerous air raids, the Tham Piu is and will be for ever remembered since 374 lives were annihilated by U.S. fighters in a few seconds. The air raids took place on 24th of November 1968. Many of those who died were farmers living in different villages surrounding the site, they had come to live there with the hope that the cave was the last refuge under the constant U.S. bombing."

We started our ascent to the cave. Along the pathway, there are memorials, dedicated to those who lost their lives during the attack. It is at that location where the annual ceremony is conducted followed by a visit to the caves. Nearby stands a very large Buddha image. I climbed the steep steps to the cave entrance and walked inside. Although the cave runs for more than 300 yards into the mountain, visitors are not permitted beyond a short distance from the entrance. I stood quietly in the huge room amid the stone rubble. On the dirt floor were many small Buddha images, memorials dedicated to the memory of loved ones whose lives were lost in the 1968 attack. I stood in silent reflection of the horror that occurred in the caves of Tham Piu and felt remorse. The ghosts of Tham Piu were reaching out to me.

I closed my eyes, trying to imagine the chaos, confusion, and horror of 28 November 1968 and the overwhelming grief caused by the incident. I thought of Somdy, the PL warrior who might well have stayed in Tham Piu during a period of convalescence and the tens of thousands of other warriors and Laotians who had sought protection in the caves of Laos. The Second Indochina War made victims of so many.

On our return to the parking lot, we stopped at one of the small refreshment stands to enjoy a cold drink. The woman who served us indicated that another stand in the parking lot was owned and operated by a survivor of the attack on Tham Piu Cave.

Her name was Nang Boua, and she greeted us with a smile. I introduced myself and expressed condolences for her loss, and asked if she would share her story with us. Without hesitation she began to tell us her painful story. She was a 13-year-old when the incident occurred.

Nang Boua lived in the village with her mother, five siblings, and a grandmother. Her father lived in another village and had not been a part of her family since her early childhood years. Due to the frequent air attacks in the area, she and the members of her family were living in the caves of Tham Pieu as were many other villagers. On that fateful day, Nang Boua had left the cave in the morning with an aunt. They were headed out to visit her grandfather who was recovering from wounds he had received from a previous bombing of their village. When they reached the base of the mountain, planes appeared in the sky. They sought safety in a trench in the nearby woods, clinging to the earth as the attack began.

She recalled the overwhelming sounds of war; explosions, the roar of aircraft, and the rhythmic sound of anti-aircraft fire. And then, she heard the screaming, wailing, and shouts of the survivors of the deadly attack as the debris of the attack began reigning down on them.

Once the aircraft had left the area, frightened and with a sense of foreboding, Nang Boua and her aunt returned to the cave to search for the members of their family. The search was in vain. They found total devastation. She was overwhelmed with grief to learn that her mother, five siblings, and grandmother had all been killed in the attack. Following the tragedy of 28 November 1968, Nang Boua lived with and was raised by her aunt.

Nang Boua wanted to know if the plane in which I flew dropped bombs, to which I did my best to explain our role in the war. I asked if she knew if the PL had a hospital in the cave, and she indicated there had been. She added it was common to have civilians seek refuge in caves and share the space with the PL whose soldiers were being treated for their wounds or recovering from illness.

I was fascinated with her remarkable story and thought, surely, if there was a Lao who was embittered toward America for our role in the war, Nang Boua would be the one. Incredibly, that was not the case. I asked her if she had any hatred for Americans in light of her horrible loss. She smiled sadly and indicated that what had occurred was all in the past and she had long ago forgiven those who caused the tragedy in her life. She indicated that when she looks at the mountain and the cave, she feels sadness, but her focus is on the future. She is married, has three children, lots of grandchildren, and works hard to support her family. Like the others who had suffered during the war years, Nang Boua kept talking about the future and her grandchildren. Once again, I was amazed by the resiliency of those gentle people I had been honored to meet. I was impressed by their ability to be so forgiving, to maintain such a positive attitude, and to focus their energies on the future. As I said goodbye to Nang Boua, I was reminded, once again how God had prepared me for this journey when He shared with me the scripture in Philippians 3:13, a verse Nang Boua had recited to me, almost word for word.

§

The road to Sam Neua, Route 6, is a narrow, winding, steep, and treacherous road. Today, it is paved, but during the war years, it was, essentially, a mountain trail. Other than the Nam Ou River, which lies to the west, there was no other north/south LOC by which the NVA and PL could move troops and materiel to and from the PDJ. Due to its strategic importance, Route 6 was under constant surveillance and attack. As a result of the geography of the region and the steep hillsides through which the trail had to pass, it was highly vulnerable to interdiction. That was particularly true during the rainy season. As the ground on the steep slopes of the mountains became saturated, landslides were a common occurrence. In fact, as we drove north on Route 6, on our way to Sam Neua, traffic was slowed or stopped at several locations as construction workers were using heavy equipment to clear debris from recent slides. Crews were also reinforcing hillsides to preclude future slides, and erecting barriers to protect the road surface. As I looked across the valleys, there were numerous red soil tell-tale scars of past landslides on the sides of other mountains. Route 6 was one of the frequent targets for Motor Pool missions.

As we continued north to Sam Neua, we were treated to spectacular views of the mountains and valleys of northeast Laos. My mind drifted back to those nights so many years ago when sources reported moving traffic along this very same road. Under cover of darkness, thousands of young warriors traversed the difficult terrain to support the ideology of their cause. They moved with a sense of urgency, knowing they must reach the safety of truck parks and rest areas before first light, all the while, planes flew overhead, searching for their presence. Ambushes, skirmishes, and battles occurred all along Route 6. On those nights when landslides successfully interdicted the road, convoys were often trapped on the treacherous trail, and the back-up of vehicles provided lucrative targets for gunships and slow-movers. I marveled at my journey along Route 6 that had been, essentially, a 50-mile-long battlefield.

§

Sam Neua had always been an enigma to me. The United States made Sam Neua a sanctuary for the enemy, and I never understood why. Since the early 1960's, Houa Phan Province had been firmly under the control of the PL and NVA, and the PL were headquartered in Sam Neua. For reasons unknown to me, an NBL had been placed around the city. Vang Pao's forces and air power would chase enemy forces northward, but once they entered city limits, they could be targeted no longer. In time, Sam Neua became a significant military depot for the transshipment of fighting forces and materiel, but those men and supplies did not become military targets until they left Sam Neua and headed south on Route 6 toward the PDJ. Such were the nuances and illogic of the ROE.

It was dark by the time we rounded a bend in the road and looked down to see the lights of Sam Neua. We crossed the Nam Xam River, a major LOC in the Second Indochina War, and entered the city. The Nam Xam was a part of a complex of connecting rivers and trails used by NVA and PL to infiltrate the PDJ and supply its forces in Barrel Roll. In the days ahead I followed the general path of that river complex (Nam Xam, Nam Neun, Nam Et, and Nam Ou), visit villages on the banks of the rivers, and travel on two of the rivers in long boats.

—12—
CAVES OF VIENG XAI

12 December 2014 - Day # 9

After breakfast, we headed east on Route 6B. Our destination was a small town about 20 miles from Sam Neua. The town was Vieng Xai, which lies in a narrow valley among limestone mountains and three lakes. It is quite picturesque, quiet, and quaint. As we drove into town, we passed Victory Statue, a monument to both celebrate victory in the Second Indochina War and honor the memory of those who died during the war. The monument provided a clue to the historical importance of the village.

The statue has a bright gold finish, similar to Buddha statues and images in Southeast Asia. It depicts three individuals, two of whom, a man and a woman, represent the peasants who supported their military comrades. The Communist symbol, a hammer and sickle, are prominently displayed. The figure in the middle is a soldier who is holding an AK-47 aloft in a stance symbolizing victory. Hand grenades hang from his belt. The peasant woman is holding bundles of corn and has a rifle strapped to her back. The peasant man is holding a hammer on his shoulder and has an arm raised in victory, like his soldier comrade. However, for me, the most expressive and revealing feature of the statue is the peasant's left foot. It is placed squarely on the top of a bomb on which the letters USA are written.

The Communists earned the right to boast. They endured nine years of the heaviest bombing campaign in history and emerged victorious. It was from the picturesque, quiet, and quaint village of Vieng Xai that the PL's war effort was directed. We were in Vieng Xai to visit the famous cave complex that was home to the PL Politburo, its military leaders and soldiers, as well as thousands of civilians.

We knew the cave complex played an important role in the PL's war efforts, but I don't think we ever fully understood the enormity and overall importance of the Caves at Vieng Xai to the Communist cause. The massive network of more than 500 caves was used as the headquarters of the Communist PL.

§

The leadership of the PL was based on the Communist model and had been influenced, greatly, by the leaders in Communist North Vietnam. In some respects, the PL Central Committee was a puppet organization of their ally to the east. There were seven members of the Politburo, each of whom had his own cave in which they and the members of their families lived. While considered "luxurious" when compared to the living conditions under which others lived, those private quarters were small. In addition to rooms in which they slept, there were primitive bathrooms, areas in which personal bodyguards stayed, and an office/library. Each of the seven leaders also had an "emergency room," a small room that could be sealed with steel doors. The rooms had a hand cranked pump that supplied the rooms with fresh air. The emergency rooms were constructed in the event of a chemical attack. Amazingly, the cranks can still be turned, and one can feel the flow of fresh outside air.

Kaysone Phomvihane was the undisputed leader of the PL. At the First Party Congress on 22 March 1955, the clandestine Lao Peoples Party was officially created. The meeting was attended by 25 delegates who were purported to represent a party membership of 300-400. Other elected leaders, all of whom had been active in resisting French colonialism, included Souphanouvong, the Red Prince, Sisavath Keibounphanh, Sisomphon Lovansay, and Khamtay Siphandone. The Central Committee met on a regular basis, and it was at those meetings, that plans were made to conduct the war against the Royal Lao

Government and to provide for those who were engaged in the struggle.

The PL developed an underground city, and at the height of the war, more than 23,000 lived and worked in the Vieng Xai cave complex. It was home to the Communist army, a sanctuary where troops could recover from injuries and illness and enjoy brief periods of rest and recuperation between combat operations. The caves were equipped with electricity, powered by huge Russian-made generators. Communication between the leadership was facilitated by a primitive telephone system. Housed in the caves were a hospital, army barracks, print shop, factories, government meeting rooms, residences, schools, bakeries, shops, and a large theater. Initially, kitchens were located outside cave entrances, but the incessant air strikes against the complex moved food preparation inside the caves. Generally, people did not leave the caves during daylight hours, and farmers tended to their crops at night. Concrete barriers were built at cave entrances, and a series of anti-aircraft sites were built into the sides of the mountains. I saw numerous bomb craters and the remains of Russian made armored vehicles in the narrow valley floor below the cave entrances.

With child-like fascination and excitement, I explored different areas of the complex and did my best to imagine what living one's life underground must have been like. I walked along the long and dark walkways, and climbed and descended the steep stairways that connected the caves. Others could only be accessed by leaving the safety of one cave and walking to the entrances of others.

I noted that when hostilities ended in 1975, each of the seven members of the Central Committee built homes in front of the caves in which they had lived. Perhaps they were fearful they might have to return to their caves in the event hostilities resumed. More than likely, however, it was a conscious decision on their part to demonstrate their solidarity in their dedication and commitment to their cause and a means of honoring the spiritual home of the Pathet Lao.

The largest and grandest of the homes had been built by the Red Prince, who had a large family. In what might have been his way of making a statement, Prince Souphanouvong built a swimming pool in a bomb crater in his front yard. The Red Prince also built a tennis court on his property, but by its condition, no one has played tennis there for many years.

The tour of the caves provided fascinating insight into a vitally important aspect of the war, about which I had little knowledge. We had grossly underestimated the multifaceted nature of the complex or its enormity. As I explored the complex, discovering its secrets, I began to understand and appreciate the steadfastness of the PL to its cause. The PL were totally committed to their goal of defeating the Royal Lao Government and its ally, America. They lived simple and disciplined lives and made enormous sacrifices to attain their goal of seizing control of Laos. In their struggle against RLG forces who, at times, refused to fight unless they got paid and were reluctant to fly night missions, there was no question that, ultimately, the PL would prevail. It was a fascinating few hours during which I had the privilege to explore the Caves of Vieng Xai. The ghosts of Vieng Xai were everywhere.

The utility of the Caves of Vieng Xai did not end with the climax of the Second Indochina War. The caves became one of several locations for the infamous Communist inspired re-education camps in Laos. Following the end of hostilities in 1975, hundreds of RLA and RLAF officers, provincial governors, and civil servants were invited to attend a meeting in the PDJ to discuss a transitional government. Once the group had assembled, they were stripped of their uniforms, taken prisoner, and shipped off to Vieng Xai. Eventually, thousands of others from the officer corps and civil servants were invited to attend similar "seminars," which, they were told, would last no more than several weeks. Instead, they were imprisoned into forced labor, and, for some, those "seminars" lasted as long as 13 years.

On our return to Sam Neau, traffic was stopped. We learned the Mines Advisory Group (MAG) was in the process of destroying UXO that had recently been unearthed. Several minutes later, we could hear the countdown over the official's handheld radios. In rapid succession, we heard four or five explosions and could clearly see flying debris. That was the second time we had witnessed the destruction of UXO.

MINES ADVISORY GROUP

Mines Advisory Group (MAG) is a non-governmental organization, based in England, that operates world-wide to help nations remove unexploded ordnance (UXO) from their villages and farms. Working with local communities and employing local citizens, MAG operates 11 UXO clearance teams and nine UXO community liaison teams.

Liaison teams conduct education programs with local communities and schools, explaining the dangers of UXO and the risks they pose to villagers. Clearance teams search for explosives, and once located and identified, decide upon the proper course of action to eliminate the potential threat.

—13—

NAM ET PHOU LOUEY

13 December 2014 - Day # 10

We left Sam Neua, heading south on Rt. 6. At the small village of Nam Neun, which sits astride the Nam Neun (River) at the intersection of Routes 6 and 1C, we turned westward. During the war years, Rt. 1C had been a dirt trail, largely controlled by the PL. For the next hour or so, we drove along a mountain-side road that twisted through remote areas of northern Laos. The journey ran, roughly, parallel to the Nam Neun in the valleys below. The area was remote and the few villages we passed through were tiny, consisting of only a few houses. We had entered an area of Laos that had been designated as National Biodiversity Conservation Areas (NCBA). There are 21 such designated areas in Laos, which serve to protect the areas' animal and plant life. Entry into the areas is strictly limited and controlled by the government. To the north of us was the very large Nam Et NCBA and ahead of us was the smaller Phou Louey NCBA. The two protected areas shared a common border, and many times the area is simply referred to as the Nam Et-Phou Louey NCBA, the largest of the protected areas.

By late-morning, we reached my objective for the day, the Nam Et. During the war, rivers were a major LOC for the NVA and PL, and I had great interest in visiting two rivers in particular, the Nam Et and Nam Ou. The remoteness of the area through which we had just passed made the rivers ideal for the transshipment of materiel. In fact, the PL and NVA had almost complete control of the area and unfettered access to the rivers. It was understood that any boat traffic on the rivers was the enemy, and the areas were, essentially, free fire zones. From time to time, River Watch Teams were inserted into the area to monitor and report on boat traffic. When targets were identified, air assets were assigned to the targets of opportunity and controlled by a FAG.

§

The use of mines was the primary weapon to combat the enemy's river operations. Due to its considerable width and depth, the Nam Ou was heavily mined, and the area was subjected to regular air strikes, much more so than the smaller Nam Et. Our weapon of choice for river mining was the MK 36 DST Destructor Mine. In the air war, the most frequently used munition was the 500-pound MK 82 bomb. It was a dumb bomb inasmuch as it did not have a guidance system, and its success in destroying an intended target was determined, solely, by the pilot's bombing skills. Destructor mines were MK 82 bombs that had been modified with the installation of the MK 75 Modification Kit (i.e. arming device, explosive booster, influence firing mechanism, and battery). The Destructor Mines were delivered by air, settled to the bottom of a waterway and could be detonated by a magnetic, acoustic, or pressure force.

Near the village of Son Khua, the Nam Neun merges into the Nam Et, which flows in a southerly direction toward the important city of Luang Prubang. It was at Son Khua where I would be taken, by boat, upstream to spend the night in the jungle in the Phou Louey NCBA. I would rejoin my guide the next day for another boat trip.

While waiting for the long boat to get loaded, I took advantage of the opportunity to walk around the village. I met an elderly man who was mending fishing nets. He invited me into his house and seemed pleased to meet an American. I sat with him for a while and asked lots of questions. He had lived in the area his entire life. During the war years, he had lived further upstream (in an area I would later learn to be the core zone of Phou Louey NCBA in which no one was permitted to live or access without permission). The area was in firm control of the PL, and during the war, this kind old man, like his friends and those in nearby villages, had been a sympathizer and aided the Hmong resistance fighters. He indicated that the villages along the banks of the river were frequent targets for American and RLG fighter-bombers, and whenever they heard the planes, the villagers fled into the surrounding jungle. However, in light of the remoteness of the area, the attacks from the air were infrequent, and I got the impression they were considered more of a nuisance than a threat. When I told the fisherman my story, he got up, embraced me, and started talking very fast. He was honored that I had come all the way from America to visit his village and to take the time to visit and talk with him. I was gratified to hear him say that since the war years were so far in the past, he rarely thinks about those times. Like others I had met, this humble man held no ill will against America and was pleased he had a new American friend. I was happy to leave my new friend with a coin and my usual gift of Kip. I remained in his village for another half hour or so, and each time I looked back at his house, he stood in the doorway, watching me. When our eyes met, he waved. When I returned to the village the next morning, I made sure to stop by to greet my new friend.

§

As I walked along the village street, I noticed several young children who were having a catch, using a bunch of plastic bags as a ball, being held together with tape. I made a motion for one of the girls to throw the ball to me, which she did. Other children joined in, and the laughter was wonderful "music" to my ears. They were surprised when I threw pop-ups to them, evidently, a skill they had never attempted before. I bought the boys and girls some cookies, and we had our picture taken. I now had some fans, and they followed me around until the boat was loaded and we left the dock. When I returned the next day, the children greeted me, still displaying their beautiful smiles.

Khamkeo, an English-speaking guide, was waiting for me. He and two others had prepared the long boat for our trip upriver. Soung and Mailum were both 19 and learning to become guides. Neither of them spoke English, but they were very knowledgeable and helpful. In addition to guiding the boat upstream, they gathered firewood, started the fires, prepared out meals, and led a night safari. With permission from the government, we entered and stayed the night in the Nam Et-Phou Louey NBCA. Each of the protected areas has a core zone in which human activity is prohibited and a buffer zone in which pre-existing villages are allocated land for subsistence living, with the major crops being rice and corn. Villages that had been located within the core zone were abandoned, and all villagers were moved elsewhere.

§

Nam Et-Phou Louey is named for its two main features, the Nam Et (River) and Phou Louey Mountain (Forever Mountain). The area is composed of primary forest that supports a wide range of animal species including some of which are endangered such as the tiger, Sambar deer, leopard, clouded leopard, civet, Asian elephant, sun bear, and white-faced gibbon. The area is quite mountainous. It is also the source of several major rivers and many other tributaries, which significantly contribute to the livelihoods of the local villagers. The river is used as a water source, transportation, fishing, and to irrigate crops.

With the longboat loaded, we headed upriver. It would take us more than an hour to reach the lodge. It was a sunny day, and the ride was pleasant. Since it was the dry season, the river was low and there were several rocky areas that produced white water, necessitating one of the guides to assist by poling us through the shallow areas. The further we motored upstream, away from Son Khua, the river became almost totally obscured by tree canopy. No doubt, the PL and NVA used this well-camouflaged portion of the Nam Et to rest during daylight hours as evidenced by the bomb craters on the riverbanks.

While still in the buffer zone, we passed several villages and observed people involved in various activities. While water buffalo foraged along the riverbanks, young men were waist-deep in the river, hurling out their fishing nets. As we progressed further upriver and deeper into the NBCA, the villages disappeared, and we were left to enjoy the spectacular splendor of the dense jungle.

We arrived at the lodge, which consisted of five hooches for guests and two other structures, one serving as a kitchen and the other a dining area where the guides slept. I was the only guest on this overnight trip. The structures were elevated, open on one end, had a slightly raised sleeping area, and a sitting area. There were bamboo screens covering three walls. While Khamkeo and I enjoyed lunch, Soung prepared my hooch. He placed a thick mattress on the bamboo platform, laid out a sleeping bag and pillow, and set up a mosquito net.

§

About 100 yards from the lodge was the park ranger's compound, and Khamkeo took me there to meet the rangers. Poaching is a major problem in the NBCA areas in Laos. While the country is attempting to control this on-going problem, its resources are woefully inadequate. In the Nam Et-Phou Louey NBCA, which covers almost 4,000 square miles, there are only six teams of rangers to patrol the area, a daunting task.

After lunch, we got back in the boat and headed further upriver. In the hopes of seeing some deer and jungle cats, our destination was a salt lick. It was a riverbank composed of sandy soil the composition of which had a high salt concentration. Animals came to the location to lick the dirt, adding important nutrients to its diet. While there were no animals to be seen, the sandy shore was loaded with foot and paw prints.

As the afternoon wore on, we headed down stream, and the boat was beached. The young guides got busy making a fire and preparing our dinner. A large kettle was dipped into the river, and the water would be used to make tea. One of the items on the menu was fish, and using banana leaves as their counter, the young men gutted and cleaned the fish, concocted a sauce, and prepared several other dishes. In addition to fish, which was grilled, the menu included grilled chicken, fried banana chips, salad, and, of course, sticky rice. We sat around the fire, enjoying the heat it generated, and enjoyed a delicious meal. As I sipped hot tea, the guides drank some local whiskey. We talked about our different cultures, backgrounds, and families. My new friends were pleased to be able to meet an American who had fought in a war they had only heard about. We packed up, boarded the boat, and floated downstream, to the lodge. Since we were in such a remote area, the star lit sky was stunning. Except for the gurgling sound of the water, we moved in total silence. From time to time, the guide's headlamps illuminated the eyes of nocturnal forest animals moving in the tree canopy. It was a pleasant and memorable evening on the water of a river that had once been a safe haven for the PL.

As soon as we returned to the lodge, a fire was started, and soon, we were enjoying the heat to ward off the chilly night. While drinking ginger tea, we talked more about life in America and my involvement in the war. The guides had only heard their country's version of events in which America was depicted as an aggressor that heaped untold suffering and destruction on the Lao. I did my best to describe our motivation to assist an ally in its struggle for freedom from an oppressive force. After an hour of warming up by the fire, drinking hot tea, and getting to know each other, the fire was doused, and we went to bed. I went to sleep listening to the comforting, gurgling sounds of the nearby river, but was awakened during the night to strange sounds coming from the jungle and creatures scampering across the roof of the hooch.

—14—

PHATOK CAVES

14 December 2014 - Day # 11

While Soung was preparing breakfast, Mailum led me on hike. Almost immediately, we started a gentle uphill climb. With Khamkeo translating, I received a lesson in the medicinal value of a variety of native plants. Mailum was Hmong and grew up using the home brewed medicines and had extensive knowledge on the subject. He explained that the site of the lodge and the surrounding hill we were climbing had once been a Hmong village. In fact, the village had been over 100 years old until the villagers were made to relocate when the government began to establish an NBCA in the 1990's. Today, the old village is being reclaimed by the jungle.

We continued to climb upwards, and at the very top of the hill were the crumbling remains of a stupa. While religious in nature, a stupa is not a temple. They are structures that are built at the very top of hills and mountains near villages. Stupas honor Buddha. They are built at those locations to cover "holes" at the mountain tops from which dragons might emerge. By building stupas over the holes, dragons are prevented from escaping and causing harm and destruction to the villages below. With the crumbling stones in the midst of encroaching vegetation, I was treated to a beautiful site. The stupa was nearly 40 feet tall and majestic looking. On one side of the base, looters had opened up a section in hopes of retrieving valuable objects that might have been buried beneath the religious symbol.

By the time we returned to the lodge, Soung had breakfast waiting for us. The hot tea helped take the chill out of the cool morning air. We packed up and got into the boats for our return to Son Khua. Boun Lieng and Nou were waiting for me as well as a few of my little friends. As I was saying goodbye to the wildlife guides who had taken such good care of me, a villager approached me. I was humbled when she presented me with a traditional Lao scarf. She indicated it was a gift from the village as an expression of thanks and appreciation for having visited their village and helping to support its efforts to protect the wildlife area. She also thanked me for playing with their children. I was overwhelmed with the kind gesture and sentiment and will always treasure the wonderful gift.

§

We resumed our journey along Rt. 1C. Our destination was the picturesque town of Nong Khiaw which straddles the Nam Ou and lies in the northern province of Luang Prubang. Except for the city of Luang Prubang, most of the province remained under control of the PL for much of the Second Indochina War, and because of that, many air strikes were fragged against PL strongholds in the region. Along the way, we made several stops to visit several small villages and meet some of the locals. Just a mile from Nong Khiaw, we stopped at the Pathok Caves. It was in this cave system that the PL had its district headquarters, and in which civilians sought refuge during the intense and repeated bombing attacks. Nong Khiaw and its surrounding areas had been one of our targeting priorities during the Laotian air war, second only to the PDJ.

After paying a small fee, we crossed a bamboo bridge, walked through a rice field and arrived at the foot of yet another of Laos' karst mountains. The numerous bomb craters at the base of the mountain gave mute testimony to the importance of the caves and the destructive forces that fell from the sky during the war. Steep stone steps led to the cave complex. We explored the two largest of the caves. Legend has it that King Setthathirat discovered the caves sometime in the 16th century. Since then, the caves have been revered. As we entered the caves, the blackened rock surfaces provided evidence of previous attempts to dislodge those using the caves as sanctuary with rocket and napalm attacks. Also at the cave entrances were the bamboo and sandbag remains of AAA gun emplacements that defended the Pathok Caves.

Different sections of the caves are marked with signage indicating usage during the war; military headquarters, government headquarters, kitchen, sleeping quarters, hospital, arts and crafts, bank, and civilian living area. Several earthen and bamboo bunkers were identified as safe "homes" for the Governor and Assistant Governor and other high ranking PL officials. Thankfully, I had a small flashlight, which helped as we moved further and further into the caves, exploring what had been home to hundreds and perhaps thousands of Laotians, combatants and civilians alike, seeking refuge from the air war. Today, residents of the caves are limited to spiders, rats, and bats. Once again, I was reminded of the resolve of the PL and their willingness to endure hardship for a cause in which they believed. I knew I was privileged to walk in what had been home for so many.

After leaving the cave complex, we stopped for lunch, and it was at a small roadside restaurant where I met Khamta. He was a guide for a tour company, and like us, his group had stopped for lunch. We started talking, and in the course of our conversation, he shared with me the fact he had been born in a cave. His mother had sought refuge from the American bombing raids. Incredibly, he had been born in the caves at Tham Piu in 1970. While I was overhead, flying missions with Alleycat, and destruction was reigning down on his homeland, Khamta's life had begun. His eyes lit up when I told him I had visited his birthplace. We were both amazed at the connection and how destiny had brought us together. I had come face to face with another "victim" of the Second Indochina War. When asked, he told me he harbored no hatred or anger towards the United States and the forces that motivated so many Laotians to seek refuge from the bombings. Of course, Khamta had no memory of the war. He told me that his mother had never said much about the war years, only that there had been great hardship. To him, the war was far removed from the world in which he lived. As we parted, I marveled at how the paths of our lives had crossed so many years before and by the grace of God, we had been reconnected.

For the night, we stayed in Nong Khiaw, a large town that spans both sides of the Nam Ou. During the war, the river, which has its head waters in North Vietnam, was a major infiltration route of soldiers and materiel. I stayed on the east side of the river, at the Nong Khiaw

Riverside Resort. As the name suggests, the hotel is located high above the fast-flowing waters of the Nam Ou, and the view is stunningly beautiful. The largest portion of the city of Nong Khiaw is located on the west side of the Nam Ou. Modest homes are mingled within the numerous store fronts, and it is on the west side where access to the river is located. By far, the most prominent structure in town is the bridge that spans the river and connects the two parts of town. The bridge rises close to two hundred feet above the river and is supported by concrete pillars.

Incredibly, the bridge was built during the early 1970's, at the time the Second Indochina War was winding down. Nevertheless, the construction project and surrounding area were subjected to regular aerial assaults. The construction project reflects the single-minded determination of the PL. It has only been within the past decade or so that the name of this town has appeared on tourist maps; however, during the war years, Nong Khiaw appeared on all of our charts and was among the most frequently targeted locations.

§

The area surrounding Nong Khiaw introduced me to my duties and responsibilities as an Intelligence Officer with ABCCC. The area was in firm control of the PL. During my first few inaugural flights, air assets were diverted to Kneecap, a FAG who was operating just south of LS-01 at Muong Ngai and just several kilometers north of Nong Khiaw. For several evenings, C-123 flare ships (Candlestick) and Laotian piloted C-47 gunships (Spooky) provided support to our forces who were experiencing troops in contact (TIC). Finally, Kneecap and the members of his team were exfiltrated. During my year in SEA, operations by Vang Pao's SGU's against the PL and NVA in Nong Khiaw and along the Nam Ou occurred on a regular basis.

With daylight remaining, I walked across the bridge, admiring the incredibly picturesque views of Nong Khiaw. I wanted to walk in the village that had been under PL control and influence for almost the entirety of the war. The peaceful beauty and tranquility was in stark contrast to the repeated air strikes that had once been the way of life in Nong Khiaw. The village lies in a deep valley with steep karst slopes ascending from both sides of the river. At the village, the Nam Ou takes an almost 180 degree turn to the west before returning to a, generally, southern direction. It seemed that everywhere I went, I came across evidence of the war. Bomb shells, fuel tanks, and CBU canisters were used for decorative purposes as well as planters and water troughs for livestock. The vast amount of debris from American weapons that I saw in Nong Khiaw, as well as throughout Laos, was indicative of the unprecedented amount of munitions that was dropped on the people of Laos. Sadly, the removal of unexploded ordnance will be a challenge for the Laotians for decades to come.

—15—

THE NAM OU
AND THE ROYAL CAPITAL

15 December 2014 - Day # 12

Nou loaded my bag into the van, and Boun Lieng and I walked across the bridge and down a flight of stairs to the docks below. We were headed to Luang Prabang, and the first part of our trip would be by long boat. Nou would meet us two hours later when we would be forced back on the roads because of the construction of a new dam across the Nam Ou. The captain of the long boat was Som Chan, and Boun Lieng and I were his only passengers. It was an overcast morning and cool. I was happy to have a knit cap and gloves to wear. The Nam Ou is the largest tributary to the Mekong, and second to the Mekong, it is the widest and most navigable river in Laos. While I was aware of the significance and importance of the river, I was still surprised at its width. During the war, the NVA and PL used this major LOC to move men and materiel in both directions. Consequently, the river appeared on our targets list on a regular basis; operations included the aerial seeding of the river, air strikes against supporting structures along the river's banks, and the targeting of anything that moved on the river. The Nam Ou was patrolled almost continuously by Raven FACs and RWTs. During spring 1970, sources indicated that mining operations were so extensive that NVA and PL soldiers and civilian workers refused to work on the boats in the section of the river south of Nong Khiaw. As we motored down the Nam Ou, I wondered just how many unexploded Destructor mines were still lying at the bottom of the river amidst the scattered debris of destroyed boats, cargo, and men.

There was much activity on the river as well as along its banks. At the river's edge, we saw numerous herds of water buffalo, cattle and pigs. Villagers were loading, unloading and making repairs to boats, while others were wading into the water and casting their fishing nets. Women were washing clothes, and naked children were splashing and chasing one another. On the river, men were fishing, while other boats were hauling firewood, transporting huge rafts of bamboo, and taxiing people across the river. Small islands are located in the middle of the river. One ingenious resident had constructed a homemade generator. Using an assortment of materials, he had created a channel through which water quickly flowed. The propeller of an old boat motor was positioned in the water flow, which turned the prop to create electricity. Wires ran from the "Rube Goldberg" contraption to the stilt houses and other structures on the island.

After an hour of traveling south on the Nam Ou, our boat ride was over once we arrived at the construction site of a hydroelectric dam. On the west side of the river were row upon row of identical small homes, which housed Chinese construction workers. The completion of our journey to Luang Prabang would be completed by driving along Route 13, the only road that connects Vientiane and Luang Prabang, which made it a vital communications link. Route 13 parallels the river and for most of our journey, the Nam Ou was in full view.

The city of Luang Prabang was of crucial importance. It was the Royal Capital of Laos, and until the very end of the war, the city remained under the control of forces loyal to the RLG. The enemy conducted probing operations on a regular basis, testing the strength of the city's defenses. Gradually, the number of enemy combatants in the areas north and east of Royal Capital reached a strength of almost 10,000 troops. When I left SEA in March 1970, it was thought it was just a matter of time before Luang Prabang would fall to the enemy. To counter the increasing pressure placed on Luang Prabang by the NVA and PL forces, we responded by assigning a dramatic increase in air assets to the area surrounding the ancient city.

About ten miles north of Luang Prabang, we stopped at the confluence of the green waters of the Nam Ou and the brown waters of the Mekong.

It was there where I visited the last of the Lao caves. Pak Ou translates to "mouth of the Ou," and the two caves lie on the west bank of the Mekong. As we approached the caves by boat, we were treated to a spectacular view of the jagged holes into the cliff face that revealed the caves. I looked up in amazement as the boatman guided the boat to the bamboo dock. Tham Ting is the lower cave, and the upper cave is named Tham Theung.

The Pak Ou cave site is the most highly regarded of the holy sites in Laos. Legend has it that the caves were discovered by King Setthathirat in the 16th century. The caves are filled with over 4000 wooden, stone, and golden images of Buddha, some of which are thought to be over 300 years old. For the past 500 years, kings have worshipped at Pak Ou, a shrine to Buddha and the river spirit. Over the centuries, the site has also been the destination for millions of pilgrims who left behind images of Buddha. The images assume a variety of positions; meditation, peace, and nirvana (reclining). Both caves provide spaces for Buddhists to worship, burn incense, and pray. A steep stairway leads to the upper cave, the much larger of the two. A very large Buddha greets visitors. Tham Theung contains many more Buddha images than the lower cave and is lit by candles.

§

It was a fitting end to my visit to Laos that my final stop was at the royal city of Luang Prabang. The beautiful city lies at the confluence of the Ou, Khan, Suong, and Mekong Rivers. The city successfully avoided the destructive forces of combat operations during the Second Indochina War, and there were several places of historic and religious significance I wanted to visit. I stayed at the Le Sen Boutique Hotel for two nights, and it was, by far, the nicest and most luxurious hotel accommodation I had during my journey. I had been upgraded to a private villa that was spacious, beautifully decorated, and had its very own Wi-Fi connection. The shower was outdoors but there was plenty of hot water.

Since both Boun Lieng and Nou lived in Luang Prabang with their families and had been on the road for almost two weeks, I suggested it was more important they go home, and I would be fine on my own. Arrangements were made to meet the following day.

After dropping my bag in the villa, I walked to the center of the city. My destination was Mount Phou Si, a distinctive feature in the

Luang Prabang skyline, a hill that rises about 400 feet above the city. It has always been an important religious site for the Lao. After paying a small fee, I began the trek up the 355 steps that zig zag through the forested slopes of the hill. Wat Tham Phou Si, a Buddhist temple, is situated on the hillside about halfway up the hill. The temple features a Buddha nestled in a grotto as well as a reclining Buddha.

Wat Chomsi, another Buddhist temple, is located at the summit of Mount Phou Se. It had been built in 1804. By far, the largest and most spectacular structure at the top is the Golden Stupa. Also located at the hill's summit is one of the few relics of the war that I saw during my time in Luang Prabang. It was the rusted remains of an anti-aircraft gun.

The summit provides a spectacular 360-degree view of the Luang Prabang peninsula bordered on one side by the Mekong River and on the other side by the Nam Khan. From the summit, I could see the impressive Royal Palace and the many Buddhist temples of Luang Prabang. I also enjoyed a view of the surrounding landscape and mountains in the distance. I rested on a stone bench at the summit, enjoying the warmth of the afternoon sun and the peaceful setting, and reflected on my Southeast Asia adventure. As daylight slipped away and day turned into night, I enjoyed a spectacular sunset from Mount Phou Si. Below me, I could see the glow of the bare light bulbs of the Night Market. I chose an alternate route to exit Mount Phou Si by descending steps at the rear of the summit.

§

By the time I left the hill, the night market vendors had their stalls set up and were open for business. The main street was closed to vehicular traffic. The night market was well lit, and I found myself among hundreds of people who passed up and down the rows of street vendors. For sale were items such as clothing, jewelry, hand woven products, Hmong traditional garb, children's clothing, coffee and tea, hand crafted goods, artwork, and souvenirs of all kinds. I quickly learned that the art of negotiating prices was both practiced and expected. After appearing not to be interested in a quoted price, the vendors quickly took out their hand calculators and punched in a lower price to which they referred to as your "lucky number". After countering with a lower number, the negotiations continued until a price was agreed upon. The night market is open every night from 5:00 until 10:00 PM, and it draws huge crowds. Along a couple of alleys that ran off the main street, dozens of food vendors were feeding the throng. Meat and fish were being grilled, and huge buffet tables were set up as well. Just like buffet restaurants in the states, for one price customers have a large number of dishes from which to choose and can fill their plates to overflowing. After a dinner of noodles and vegetables, I walked back to the Villa for a good night's sleep. My incredible journey to the Land of a Million Elephants was drawing to a close.

—16—
TAKING MY LEAVE

16 December 2014

Today was my last full day in Laos. Before leaving the Royal Capital and flying off to Cambodia, there were two sites I wanted to visit; the Royal Palace, Saw Nam, and one of Laos' most revered temples, Wat Visoun. Even though I was leaving Laos and the Second Indochina War behind, the memories would remain with me forever.

17 December 2014

Boun Lieng and Nou met me at the hotel at 10:00 AM for our drive to the airport. My flight to Siem Reap departed Luang Prabang at Noon.

After dropping me at the curb and helping with my bag, I thanked Nou for his friendship and driving me safely throughout Barrel Roll. We embraced, shook hands, and said goodbye.

Boun Lieng and I entered the airport together, and he helped me to check-in for my flight to Siem Reap. We sat down for a few minutes and discussed the wonderful experience we had shared. I expressed my heartfelt thanks for the wonderful learning experience he had provided regarding the history and culture of Laos. Thanks to his extensive knowledge and love of his country, he "guided" me into the hearts and minds of the gentle Lao. It was a gift for which I will be forever grateful and one that, without which, I would never have been able to achieve the goals I had established for my journey.

Another aspect of the journey for which I was grateful and one I had not anticipated, was the opportunity to share with Boun and Nou my knowledge of the war in Barrel Roll. For the most part, Boun Lieng and Nou were not aware of many of the essential details regarding the Second Indochina War as they impacted their country. As in all nations controlled by Communist regimes, the information flow to its citizens was limited to propaganda. Information that might reflect negatively on the government and its "leaders" is highly censored. In our discussions, they acknowledged that fact, and, also, seemed genuinely pleased to not only learn new information regarding the conduct of the war but to "hear" it from an American perspective. During our time together, Boun Lieng, Nou, and I had developed a bond and become friends as we searched for an understanding of how the events of the Second Indochina War had impacted the lives of the Lao. We shared a wonderful journey.

My long trek home was about to begin. My return to Southeast Asia and Barrell Roll had exceeded, by far, my expectations. The reflection process regarding my incredible journey had immediately begun. I was moved by the experience and at times, overwhelmed with emotion.

Over the ensuing weeks and months, not a day passed when I didn't think about Laos, its wonderful people, and the beloved Hmong. I was on another journey, searching for the meaning of it all. In time, I came to realize just how life-changing my return to the Battlefield of the Plaine des Jarres had been.

I had left Laos, but Laos never left me.

EPILOGUE

THE MEANING OF IT ALL

Several years have passed since I returned from my trip to Laos, and rarely a day goes by that I don't pause and reflect on my remarkable journey across the war-torn land of Southeast Asia. The trip had unleashed a torrent of memories, feelings, emotions, and sentiments, some of which had been buried in my psyche since 1970. I knew my heartfelt interactions with the incredible people I met there would stay in my memory forever. Slowly, I began to understand that my first journey to Southeast Asia had impacted me far greater than I had realized or even thought possible. Not knowing why or what it was, I had gone in search of "something." It took time, but gradually, I began to realize what had been eluding me for so many years.

Whenever I would meet a fellow combat veteran there was a mutual curiosity of the various roles the other person had assumed during the war years; we were eager to learn where and when the other person had served. Perhaps, I ascribed my feelings onto the others, but I believe we celebrated the fact we had worn the uniform, served our respective nations, engaged in combat, and survived the war. With a profound sense of pride, we embraced, both literally and figuratively, our Brotherhood and one another. We were genuinely happy to have met and grateful for the opportunity to share precious time together with our brothers. But in my return to Hanoi and Laos all those year later, I had learned that Brotherhood extended much further than I thought.

During my return to Southeast Asia, I instantly bonded with those I met, regardless of whether we had been ally or enemy during the war.

Spontaneously, smiles crossed our faces, and we embraced. Based on how we reacted to one another, I was confident we were experiencing similar emotions. We held hands and stood looking at one another, each of us lost in our own thoughts. It was enlivening, and we each seemed thrilled with the providence that had brought us together. It was as if we had known each other and been friends for many years, and we were excited at being reunited. Because of our shared combat experience, there was a feeling of mutual respect and admiration for one another, a true brotherhood. Unlike some American veterans of the Second Indochina War, the Lao had left the war behind, years ago.

While those I met expressed sadness regarding the loss of loved ones during the war, they neither faulted or blamed America, nor expressed any anger or resentment toward me. They were at peace, and I am quite certain the expressions of forgiveness I received were tenets of their Buddhist religion. In their own way and in their own words, the Lao I met, were "quoting" the words of Philippians 3:13, the very same scripture that had had such a positive and profound impact on me prior to the journey. Their munificence was humbling and shall always be remembered, with love in my heart, for the gentle and forgiving Lao.

During my return to Southeast Asia, I was stunned by what I was repeatedly told. I was certain there would be some level of resentment and hostility toward America. It took some time, but I finally came to the realization that the gentle people of Laos were expressing and offering their Forgiveness.

Thanks to my Mom, I had become familiar with the Serenity Prayer early in my religious education.

God grant me the serenity to accept the things I cannot change, courage to change the things I can, and the wisdom to know the difference, living one day at a time; enjoying one moment at a time; taking this world as it is and not as I would have it; trusting that You will make all things right if I surrender to Your will; so that I may be reasonably happy in this life and supremely happy with You forever in the next. Amen.

Its simple message placed my Second Indochina War journey in its proper perspective. It permitted me to realize that the strategies and tactics used to conduct and manage the war were beyond my sphere of influence and responsibility.

Nor was I accountable for the collateral damage inflicted upon the civilian population. Under my control, however, was the manner in which I fulfilled the duties and responsibilities to which I had been assigned. I was proud of the passion, commitment, professionalism, and leadership skills I brought to ABCCC to fulfill its mission. That was my mission, and I performed it to the best of my ability. The journey to Laos delivered and relieved me from those doubts and feelings of guilt I had harbored for so long. It was liberating. It was Redemption, another wonderful gift of the Lao.

For those of us who proudly wear the Vietnam Service and Vietnam Campaign Medals, our shared experience has allowed us to hold our heads a little higher, proud to have worn the uniform. We are proud of our service to the nation and that we remained faithful to its heritage, traditions, and legacy of freedom. We are proud of our loyalty and faithful commitment to one another. We are proud that we sacrificed so much to achieve freedom for those who deserved to be free. We are proud that we were faithful to the oath of office to which we had all sworn allegiance. We are proud that, despite the rectitude of the cause, while many others chose "not to go," we served. It was to their detriment they left the heavy lifting to others. In a strange way, I feel sorry for them.

Yet, a little bit of each of us who survived "that world" remains in "that world." As every combat veteran has learned, "that world" never leaves. Nevertheless, I am forever grateful for having had the opportunity to have served. The year in Southeast Asia opportunity provided me with an abiding gift, one that I will cherish for the remaining years of my life. I was given the opportunity to serve my country and test my mettle while engaging in combat. Danger awaited every time we flew. In spite of those perils, I am grateful I was given a strength of mind and spirit to focus only on the tasks at hand, my mission.

That gift from Him, a strength of purpose, enabled me to think and act decisively to contribute to mission success and still focus on my personal mission to support our beloved Hmong fighters. The gift is an attribute that is unique and very personal to each individual. It is recognizable but never discussed; to do so would be arrogant and a display of self-aggrandizement. It is called Valor.

I will be forever grateful that my childhood dreams of becoming a member of our Nation's Armed Forces became a reality. I have taken great personal pride in my service to the nation, but I am most proud and grateful for the gift of strength of mind and spirit I had been given.

And, Finally…

Thanks to a friend with whom I had served with ABCCC, I reconnected with one of our Barrel Roll FAGs, Counter. We were both thrilled with the opportunity and began a correspondence that lasted for 14 years. His name was Samarn Charoenjai, and like Hilltop was a Thai. He lived in Bangkok, and over the years, we exchanged e-mails, cards, and gifts. In each of his messages, he expressed his appreciation for the support Alleycat provided to his team throughout the war. He was effusive with praise, and it was gratifying and humbling to know our efforts helped to save lives, contributed to the completion of their mission, and were greatly appreciated.

My first question for Counter was if he knew anything about the fate of our mutual friend, Hilltop. Counter knew Hilltop very well. They had shared a room at Long Tieng, participated in numerous operations together, and spent several restless nights together in the shelter of bomb craters. Hilltop was the senior FAG in all of Laos and well respected by the Hmong leaders and warriors. A friend of Counter's, Supot Mour, a Hmong radio operator, informed Counter that Hilltop was among the first element of Hmong who were evacuated to the United States in 1975. According to Mr. Mour, Hilltop settled in Wyoming and, two years after arriving in the United States, tragically, he was killed in a car accident on a Wyoming highway. It was disheartening to learn about Hilltop's death. How ironic that he survived almost ten years of combat during the Second Indochina War, and after securing a safe and peaceful life in America, his life was taken on a highway in Wyoming. Sadly, I have lost contact with Counter. The last I heard from him was Christmas 2020 when we exchanged cards and gifts. He sent me a beautiful Thai silk scarf. During 2021, my e-mails and letters went unanswered, and I never heard from him again nor have I learned anything about the fate of my friend and brave warrior, Counter.

Senior Lieutenant Ngo Thoi Binh was a highly decorated officer in the Peoples' Army of Vietnam (North Vietnam). He engaged in combat for more than ten years in South Vietnam and Laos. He traversed the Ho Chi Minh Trail on multiple occasions and recovered from his wounds in the caves of Laos.

NGÔ THỜI BÌNH

It was pure happenstance that had brought us together on a street in Hanoi. It was as if we were long lost friends. We shook hands, embraced, and felt an instant bonding. I was humbled by his extraordinary gift; his metal name tag that I will always cherish. As we parted, we embraced one final time, and he kissed me.

Long Bien Bridge, Hanoi

Hoa Lo Prison – "Hanoi Hilton"

Ho Chi Minh's Stilt House

Ho Chi Minh Mausoleum – Ba Dinh Square, Hanoi

Phayvanh Asang was a three-year-old child in 1970, living near the hotly contested Lima Site of Muong Soui. She has vivid memories of the continual fighting that took place in her village and frequent air strikes by American planes. During the fighting, she and her family sought sanctuary in the nearby Buddha Caves.

Buddha Cave – Muong Soui

Grave sites of North Vietnamese soldiers who died while being treated at the
Buddha Caves field hospital at Moung Soui

LS-108 Muong Soui – Original airstrip on the left

Visiting Lower Level School in Phou Kouk.

Visiting Secondary School in Moung Soui

Our hosts, two life-long friends with their wives.

In March of 1970, during an intense bombing campaign on their village of Khong Khai, the 12-year-old childhood friends, were walking to school when American fighter-bombers appeared. While attempting to seek shelter in the nearby forest, each of them sustained serious injuries during the attack and lost a leg.

Thong Hai Hin (PDJ Funeral Jars Site #1).

Bomb crater among the Funeral Jars of the PDJ.

Funeral jars of the PDJ.

One of the few funeral jars with its lid intact.

Seng Keu was born and raised in General Vang Pao's hometown of Nong Het. He volunteered to serve in *L'Armee Clandestine*, becoming a member of a Special Guerilla Unit in the mid-60's. He and his wife lost two sons in the war, and he was wounded several times.

Seng Keu with two of his more than thirty grandchildren.

Somdy Khantavoung was only 14 years of age when he was forced to join the Pathet Lao Army. For five years, he endured the hardships of combat as an anti-aircraft gunner. He was disabled by multiple wounds and forced to "retire" at the age of 19.

Living in an area allied with the Royal Laotian Government, Kong volunteered to be a truck driver for General Vang Pao and the *L'Armee Clandestine*. During the six years of service, he was wounded several times. Once hostilities ended, he had been a prisoner for over a year by the Communist government before being permitted to return home.

Celebrating after interrogation by Communist Army and Political officials at Xieng Gna.

Hilltop at Long Tieng

Counter (center)

Hilltop (R) Atop Captured NVA PT-76 Tank in Ban Ban Valley

Abandoned NVA PT-76 Tank in Ban Ban Valley
I'd like to think this is the same tank captured by Hilltop and his team

LS-22 Xieng Khouang or Lima Lima – One of the few hard surface runways of the Lima Sites

Abandoned Soviet made armored vehicles on the PDJ

Nang Boua was a 13-year-old child living in the Caves of Tham Pieu with her mother, grandmother, and five siblings. She had left the caves in early morning to visit her aunt on the day the American planes arrived. During the bombing of the caves, a direct hit killed all the members of her family.

In 1969-1970, Khamta's mother sought refuge from American bombing raids by living in the caves at Tham Piu. Khamta was born while his mother lived in the caves.

Caves of Tham Piu

Victory Statue at Vieng Xai

Caves at Vieng Xai

Nam (River) Ou

Nam (River) Et

Central Committee meeting room.

Central Committee member's bedroom

Emergency room to which fresh
air could be pumped

ACKNOWLEDGMENTS

It all started with a college creative writing course. My early attempts were rudimentary, and my grades were just barely average. However, that didn't stop me. I found joy in expressing myself in the written word and made use of the skill during my professional life. Soon, my journal writing became an obsession, and I kept written records of all my journeys and adventures, with no thought as to who might read my words. I kind of hope that one day, one of my grandkids might browse through the journals and be inspired to travel to some of the destinations I had visited and walk in my steps.

That all began to change, ever so slowly, two years ago when I shared some writing with my good friend Carol Anderman Harkavy. Carol and I had been high school classmates and because of the alphabetical proximity of our last names, we often found ourselves seated next to one another. In fact, we marched into our graduation ceremony together. Carol, who is a published author herself, always had positive comments to make about my writing. In time, such affirmation turned into words of encouragement for me to consider publishing some of what I had written.

The thought of publishing had never occurred to me. Carol was persistent, however. She gently offered words of encouragement and was steadfast in her resolve. Finally, after one of our many e-mail exchanges, I thought, "Why not?" With Carol's inspiration and encouragement, this writing project has become a reality for which I will be eternally grateful to my dear friend, Carol Anderman Harkavy.

In addition to nudging me to the decision to publish my manuscript, Carol also introduced me to her publisher, Stefani Milan. Stefani graciously offered to review my "work in progress," and as a courtesy to her friend, agreed to work with me. Stefani's kind words, guidance, and counsel were nothing short of spectacular. She demonstrated a remarkable ability to lead me through the editing process all the while making me believe the revisions were my ideas.

I learned to rely on her vision and good judgment, and very much appreciated the enormous patience she demonstrated as she led me through the book publishing process. This book would never have become a reality without Stefani's expert and enthusiastic direction and guidance.Aspiring writers can contact Stefani at **milanbookpublishing.com.**

I am deeply grateful to Carol and Stefani for believing in me and for caring. Bountiful blessings to you both, always.

ENDNOTES

Part 1

1. Victor Anthony and Richard Sexton, The War in Northern Laos 1954-1973, (Washington, D.C., Center for Air Force History, 1998, 277.

2. Thomas R. Yarborough, Truck Hunting on the Ho Chi Minh Trail, 2017, (Tysons, VA, History Net Web Site, www.historynet.com)

Part 2
Chapter Six The Last Domino Falls

1. Kenneth Conboy and James Morrison, Shadow War, (Boulder: Paladin Press, 1995), 345-348.

2. CIA, National Intelligence Bulletin (Declassified), (Washington, D.C.: CIA), 7.

3. Gayle Morrison, The Sky is Falling, (Jefferson, N.C.: McFarland Press, 2008).

4. Kenneth Conboy and James Morrison, Shadow War, 415.

Chapter Eight The Chao Fa

5. Ian G. Baird, Chao Fa Movies: The Transnational Production of Hmong History and Identity, (St. Paul, MN: Hmong Studies Journal), 1-4.

6. Roger Arnold, Laos: Still a Secret War, (Plano, TX: WorldPress.org), 1-2.

7. Hmong: Alarming Crackdown on the Chao Fa in LPDR, (Hague, Netherlands: Unrepresented Nations & Peoples Organization, Online newsletter), 1-3

Chapter Nine The Legacy of General Vang Pao

8. Tim Wiener, Gen. Vang Pao's Last War, (New York: New York Times), 1-12

9. Tim Wiener, Gen. Vang Pao's Last War (New York: New York Times), 1-12

10. Wameng Moua, General Vang Pao Legacy, (Minneapolis: Twin Cities Daily Planet, 2011).

11. Wameng Moua, General Vang Pao Legacy.

12. James E. Sullivan, Vang Pao and the Hmong Diaspora: The Secret War in Laos and Into the 21st Century, (Original Manuscript, San Rafael: Dominican University, 2019) 14, 17-18.

Part 3
Chapter Six Vientiane

13. "Secret War In Laos", Legacies of War.Org Newsletter, New York, NY.

14. Melvin Laird "US Military Operations in Laos", Memorandum for the President (Declassified), 6 October 1968.

APPENDICES

Appendix A: Southeast Asian Geo-Politics: A History
The First Indochina War

Throughout most of its history, the people of Laos have been subjected to conflict and had fallen under control of its neighbors, Thailand, China, Burma, Cambodia and Vietnam. Its earliest inhabitants were migrants from China. The first kingdom of Laos emerged in 1345 under the leadership of Fa Ngum, a Laotian prince. For the next 500 years, Laos remained a kingdom; however, for varying lengths of time, neighboring countries controlled portions of the kingdom and the nation was divided under varying spheres of influence. Present day Laos, which means the Land of a Million Elephants, had its origin in the early 1860's when the French colonial empire expanded into Southeast Asia, and France assumed control of Laos and Cambodia. As a result of its defeat of China in the 1884 Franco-Chinese War, France also gained control of Vietnam, and the entire region became known as French Indochina. Except for the brief occupation of French Indochina and portions of Thailand by the Japanese during World War II, France controlled the area until its defeat at Dien Bien Phu in 1954.

When the French colonial empire expanded into Southeast Asia, the three rival kingdoms of Vientiane, Luang Prabang, and Champasak came to be known as Laos. The French left the monarchies in place, however, real power and decision-making for French Indochina was in the hands of the Governor-General, who resided in the Presidential Palace in Hanoi.

During the 1930's, an anti-colonial sentiment emerged, first in Vietnam and later, in Laos. In 1941, the Viet Minh (League for Independence in Vietnam), a coalition, seeking national independence for Vietnam emerged. Among the leaders of this movement was Ho Chi Minh. Initially, the Viet Minh sought independence from France, but once Japan occupied French Indochina during WWII, its focus shifted to opposing Japan's occupation. When hostilities ended and Japan surrendered, the Viet Minh, once again, found themselves subservient to the French and resumed its opposition to France's re-occupation of Indochina.

At the same time the Viet Minh resumed its opposition to France (1945), a nationalist movement emerged in Laos. The Lao Issara (Free Lao) was a non-communist group that sought to prevent the return of the French. The movement was led by the nation's three princes. Phetsarath Rattanavongsa became leader of the movement, and his brother, Souvanna Phouma became Minister of Public Works. Their half-brother, Souphanouvong, who would later become known as the Red Prince, was named Commander in Chief as well as Minister of Foreign Affairs. With weapons stolen from a local militia, Prince Souphanouvong led a small band of nationalists who, eventually, succeeded in seizing control of the capital city, Vientiane. However, the initial success of the Lao Issara occurred in a power vacuum created by the departing Japanese while the French had not yet returned, in full force, to Laos.

For a period that lasted less than a year, the Lao Issara attempted to govern the country and exert its control and authority. Initially, the fledgling nation had military support from Viet Minh and the Chinese; however, in agreements with the French, both agreed to withdraw its forces from Laos. Negotiations between the French and Viet Minh quickly broke down and were followed by ten years of war, The First Indochina War, followed. The war between the French and Viet Minh spilled over into

Laos and significantly impacted the struggle for control of Laos that was emerging.

Militarily, the Lao Issara were woefully inferior to the French, and due to the high cost of supporting and maintaining its army, the new government quickly ran out of money. The Lao Issara's control of the country, tenuous at best, was short-lived. The party faced several major challenges:

• The three leaders of the movement had all been educated in Europe and never really connected with the less sophisticated and less educated Lao;
• The Viet Minh controlled much of the northeastern region of the country and denied support to the fledgling government;
• French supported guerillas controlled the southern-most provinces;
• France began the re-conquest of Laos by deploying troops and conducting military operations, first in the panhandle and then throughout the country; and
• Perhaps the biggest reason for the ultimate collapse of Lao Issara was that the three leaders' father, King Sisavang Vong, supported the reinstatement of French rule.

It wouldn't take long for the King's support of the French to be the critical factor in deciding the eventual fate of Laos. In the fall of 1946, one year after claiming control of the nation and after suffering major defeats at the hands of regular French army units, the leaders of Lao Issara were forced into exile. Phetsarath Rattanavongsa had chosen exile in Thailand as did Souvanna Phouma. Souphanouvong and his followers eventually settled in Vietnam, seeking counsel and support from the Viet Minh. France, which faced serious opposition from the fast-growing Viet Minh movement in Vietnam, sought a means to pacify the Lao and transformed the country into a constitutional monarchy, and established a national assembly.

In July of 1949, France permitted the Royal Lao Government (RLG) to establish an Armee Nationale Laotienne (ANL), a national army. (To avoid confusion, the term Royal Lao Army or RLA will be used to refer to the state supported, anti-Communist army.) On the threshold of establishing a free and independent Lao, the RLG offered amnesty to former members of Lao Issara. Of the three brothers, only Souvanna Phouma accepted the offer of amnesty and returned to Laos to help in the formation of the newly established government. Phetsarath Rattanavongsa remained in Thailand. The Red Prince returned to his homeland, however he did so as one of the leaders of a Communist guerrilla movement, patterned after Ho Chi Minh's Viet Minh, and opposed the RLG. With a goal of seizing control of Laos by defeating the French and the newly established RLG, the newly created Resistance Committee established its headquarters in the northeastern province of Sam Neua. This new communist guerilla movement and political front called itself the Pathet Lao (PL).

In April of 1953, a force of more than 40,000 soldiers of North Vietnam's Peoples' Army of Vietnam (PAVN), led by General Vo Nguyen Giap, invaded northern Laos to provide "assistance" to the Red Prince and his PL army of approximately 2,000 soldiers. While the "invasion" failed to capture the Royal Capital of Luang Prabang or the strategically important region in Norther Laos known as the Plaines des Jarres (PDJ), the NVA solidified PL control of Laos' two northern provinces. Souphanouvong, the Red Prince, moved the PL headquarters to

Sam Neua where he remained for the duration of the Second Indochina War.

In December of 1953, the French, in an ill-advised campaign, sought to protect Laos from the North Vietnamese invasion by seizing control of the Dien Bien Phu Valley and severing the Viet Minh supply lines into Laos. The Dien Bien Phu valley is located only 15 kilometers inside North Vietnam's border with Laos. Within five months, by May 1954, despite suffering staggering losses, the Viet Minh had overrun all French positions at Dien Bien Phu. While it would take two years for the French to totally withdraw from Southeast Asia, the First Indochina War was over.

The stage was set for the continuation of armed struggle in what had once been French Indochina. Clearly, the ultimate goal of the Communists was to establish Communist governments in Vietnam, Laos, and Cambodia. President Eisenhower foresaw this possibility when he referenced the Domino Theory.

Appendix B: The Second Indochina War: Laos

Even before the First Indochina War had ended, the Second Indochina War had already begun. By 1950, the CIA had a presence in Vietnam, with official United States "legations" in both Saigon and Hanoi. A China-based airline that had been founded by Gen. Claire Chennault following WW II was used to transport heavy equipment, tanks, and war materiel for the French during the First Indochina War. Civil Air Transport (CAT), the "civilian" airline, was secretly owned by the Central Intelligence Agency (CIA). CAT continued to fly covert missions in Southeast Asia during the Second Indochina War. In 1959, the name of the airline was changed to Air America, but it was still owned and funded by the CIA.

The Geneva Accords of 1954, which, purportedly, were established to bring peace to the region following the First Indochina War, provided for independent nation status for Vietnam, Laos, and Cambodia. After a two-year transitional period, the Accords called for free elections in each nation. Peace and free elections were not to be, and civil wars (Second Indochina War) in Vietnam, Lao, and Cambodia would rage for the next 21 years.

Continued attempts to establish coalition governments in Laos and bring Royalists and Communists together, failed. From the outset, the provisions of the Geneva Accords were routinely ignored and violated. Fearful that Laos would become one of the dominoes in the Domino Theory espoused by the Eisenhower administration, the United States expanded its role in support of the RLG. Our involvement in Laos during the Second Indochina War was characterized by the gradual and continual escalation of combat operations in response to continual Communist (NVA and PL) violations of the Geneva Accords of 1954. The American presence in Laos increased dramatically:

- In early 1955, the United States created Operation Mission, which resulted in America funding 100% of the RLA military budget;
- Later that year, the Programs Evaluation Office (PEO) was established. While the PEO was "officially" given State Department status, in reality the office was responsible for coordinating military and paramilitary activities in Laos;
- The PEO increased aid to the training of the RLA by the French Military Mission and paid 100% of RLA salaries;
- In November of 1958, the PEO assumed the training of all RLA forces and created a front company called Eastern Construction Company. In fact, the newly founded company was comprised of 149 American Special Forces soldiers and 103 Filipinos;
- Working under the code name Hotfoot, US Special Forces training teams arrived in Laos in 1959 to assist in the training of RLA forces. Hotfoot was in response to the establishment of Group 559, an NVA force responsible for building, maintaining, and defending the Ho Chi Minh trail complex along the eastern border of the Lao panhandle (within a decade, the trail complex would become a network of over 12,000 miles of roads, rivers, and trails operating throughout Lao, the so-called Ho Chi Minh Trail);
- Operation Hardnose was launched, which inserted road watch teams (RWT) to monitor NVA infiltration and gather intelligence. RWTs would be used in Laos, continually, throughout the Second Indochina War;
- Disposing of any pretense of being a civilian program, the PEO

became the Military Advisory Assistance Group, and the Hotfoot teams donned their military uniforms and became White Star Mobile Training teams;

• Civil Air Transport (CAT) morphed into Air America and continued to fly missions in support of RLG ground forces;

• The CIA began to secretly recruit Lao indigenous hill people, the Hmong After training and service in local militias, the recruits were organized into battalions of irregular troops called Special Guerilla Units (SGU). These battalions were composed, almost exclusively, of Hmong. By the summer of 1961 the so-called CIA secret army consisted of approximately 9,000 Hmong fighters. Eventually, the L'Armee Clandestine numbered over 40,000;

• General Vang Pao, emerged as the undisputed leader of the Hmong forces;

• The Geneva Accords of 1962 mandated that all foreign technicians and soldiers were to leave Laos. The United States disbanded its Military Advisory Assistance Group and withdrew its military missions; however, the Communist Vietnamese withdrew less that 50 of its force of over 2,000 soldiers;

• With repeated violations of the 1962 Accords by the North Vietnamese, the United States embarked on its "secret war"; and

• In 1964, the United States Air Force established Water Pump, a pilot training program to train pilots for the Royal Laotian Air Force. Udorn Royal Thai Air Base was used to train pilots to fly United States supplied T-28's. In time, pilot training would be expanded to include AC-47 gunships. Thai volunteers were also recruited to augment the Royal Laotian Air Force.

The Second Indochina War: Vietnam

As the United States' involvement and presence in Laos was unfolding, even prior to the end of the First Indochina War, a similar pattern of clandestine engagement was taking place in South Vietnam. The Geneva Accords of 1954 established a "provisional cease fire line", which ran, approximately along the 17th Parallel, the dividing line between North Vietnam and South Vietnam. A three-mile demilitarized zone was established on each side of the demarcation line. The Accords called for a free general election, to be conducted in 1956, in which the people of Vietnam would determine their choice of government for a unified state. The President of South Vietnam, Ngo Kinh Diem, refused to allow the election to be held, due to growing discontent among the Buddhist population regarding Diem's Catholic supporters.

In retaliation for Diem's oppression of Viet Minh cadres in South Vietnam North Vietnamese leadership approved measures to revive its insurgency in the South. Communist-led uprisings began several months later. As those events were unfolding, the American footprint in South Vietnam expanded significantly, just as it had in Laos.

Following the signing of the Geneva Accords of 1954, CIA Director, Allen Dulles, sent Air Force Colonel Edward Lansdale to Vietnam to initiate a series of clandestine operations against North Vietnam. Lansdale's cover title was that of Assistant Air Attache. Ultimately, those clandestine operations, under the codename, Nautilus, led to America's "official" entry into the Second Indochina War and continued well beyond:

- In the early 1950's, in addition to Laos, CIA stations were established in Saigon, Hanoi, and in other regions in South Vietnam;
- In 1954, South Vietnamese soldiers were trained in psychological warfare and a campaign was conducted throughout South Vietnam;
- Paramilitary teams were sent to South Vietnam to train the South Vietnamese;
- In one of America's first attempts to establish pacification programs, Operation Brotherhood was launched in 1954, which, by 1955, brought medical teams to South Vietnam and trained Vietnamese personnel;
- In retaliation to the more than 40,000 North Vietnamese soldiers that infiltrated into South Vietnam via the Ho Chi Minh Trail complex, in 1961, President Kennedy authorized a program of covert operations to be conducted by the CIA;
- In 1961, the CIA was authorized to prepare for the eventual amphibious landing of United States troops;
- Indigenous hill people were recruited to serve as intelligence gathering resources;
- In April of 1962, the United States Navy launched its first DESOTO patrol off the coasts of China and North Vietnam. The signal intelligence gathering missions were a part of a larger Top-Secret operation, Operation 34-A or OPLAN 34Alpha. Utilizing swift boats the operation entailed the insertion of CIA teams (comprised of South Vietnamese soldiers), commando raids, and psychological operations;
- On 2 November 1963, a successful coup was launched, which led to the assassination of the President of South Vietnam, Ngo Kinh Diem. The coup was led by a group of dissatisfied South Vietnam Army generals with the approval of the United States;
- On 2 August 1964, on the 18th DESOTO mission, OPLAN 34A commandos conducted a raid on a North Vietnamese radio transmitter on an offshore island. One of the destroyer escorts, the USS Maddox, was reportedly fired upon by three North Vietnamese gunboats: and
- A second attack on a United States ship, the USS Turner Joy, was alleged to have taken place on 4 August 1964 while engaged in another OPLAN 34A mission. Despite the fact that no North Vietnamese gunboats were in the area, the Task Force Commander, Captain John Herrick, reported the ships were under attack. The two "attacks" on United States Navy ships became known as the Gulf of Tonkin Incident. Years later, it was conclusively determined that no such second attack ever took place.

Essentially, the United States was fully engaged in the Second Indochina War but was in search of a "reason" to become fully engaged in the war. The Gulf of Tonkin Incident provided President Johnson with that justification.

Johnson and his advisors chose not to seek a public declaration of war, which would have provided the American people with a clear statement of intent and necessitated a degree of public support. Instead of sharing the responsibility for the Second Indochina War with the American people, Johnson asked Congress for and received a resolution empowering him to "take all necessary measures to repel an armed attack against the forces of the United States to prevent further aggression". The Gulf of Tonkin Resolution provided the Johnson Administration the authority to wage war in such a manner that would, most assuredly, guarantee defeat, which it did.

ABOUT THE AUTHOR

Fred is the former District Director of Health, Physical Education, and Athletics for the Manhasset and East Williston Public School Districts on Long Island, New York. During his 36-year career in education, he held numerous leadership positions, made presentations at local and state conferences, and has had several articles published in professional journals. Fred has been the recipient of numerous awards and honors, and in 2003, he was named New York State Professional of the Year.

Community service has always been an important part of his life. While living on Long Island, Fred volunteered his time to serve on the local Selective Service Board, coach youth soccer, teach classes for the American Cancer Society, and serve, for many years, on a community substance abuse task force. During the ten years he resided in Mill Creek, Washington, Fred proudly served in a variety of roles for VFW Post #8870 and is Past Commander of the Post. Fred also served as Operations Officer for Freedom Fighters Honor Flight.

Fred is most proud of his service to our nation. He joined the United State Air Force in 1967 and following completion of Officer Training School, he attended the Armed Forces Air Intelligence Training Center at Lowry AFB in Denver, Colorado. He volunteered for combat duty in Vietnam and was assigned to the 7 th Airborne Command and Control Squadron (7ACCS) at Udorn Royal Thai Air Force Base. During his yearlong deployment as an Air Intelligence Officer, he flew 116 combat missions in the skies of Northern Laos.

Fred lives in Savannah, Georgia and is on what is, seemingly, an endless road trip visiting American historic sites.

You can contact the author at 1ltintel@gmail.com.

www.ingramcontent.com/pod-product-compliance
Lightning Source LLC
Chambersburg PA
CBHW011213120626
46545CB00008B/2977